a player's guide to
TABLE GAMES

a player's guide to guide to TABLE GAMES

by *John Jackson*

STACKPOLE BOOKS

A PLAYER'S GUIDE TO TABLE GAMES

Copyright © 1975 by
John Jackson

Published by
STACKPOLE BOOKS
Cameron and Kelker Streets
Harrisburg, Pa. 17105

Printed in the U.S.A.

Library of Congress Cataloging in Publication Data
Jackson, John, 1945–
    A player's guide to table games.

    Bibliography: p.
    1. Board games. I. Title.
GV1312.J32   790   74–32171
ISBN 0–8117–1902–2

To the members and associates—past and present—
of the Pryall Club of San Rafael, California

Preface

When you play hearts, do you frequently score more than twenty points in a single hand? Conversely, do you consider yourself lucky to score twenty points on a Scrabble play? In Monopoly, have you ever sunk hundreds—or thousands—of dollars into the greens, only to go bankrupt after landing on Boardwalk? Do your horses, race cars, or tokens finish last? Or even second? If you are a football fan, are you having trouble deciding which board game version of your favorite sport to buy? Are you wondering whether all those war games on the market are worth your time? Do you wish you could take a peek inside the often deceptive wrapping *before* you plunked down ten dollars for a new game?

If the answer to one or more of the above questions is "yes," then this book is for you. Read on.

You may think of this book as a private compendium of Everything You Always Wanted to Know About Table Games . . . But Couldn't Find Anyone to Ask. If half of it consists of the sort of information you would like to know before you buy a game, the other half consists of suggestions, rules changes, variations, tactical tips, and advice designed to improve your play and enhance your enjoyment of the game after you get it.

You may have a perfectly legitimate desire to be a good game player without wishing to expend ten to twenty years or more becoming a chess grand master or a life master in bridge, and if I can't tell you how to beat Bobby Fischer or the Italian "Blue Team,"* I *can* make you a real expert at Monopoly and a terror at Risk or Diplomacy, and I can give you a good start at a variety of games as challenging as chess or bridge—and possibly more interesting.

The present work is not devoted solely to complex or difficult games requiring vast amounts of time, concentration, or intelligence. Every game has its own biases, its hidden pitfalls, and its paths to victory; a piece, token, property, route, strategy, or method of attack that is good or workable under some circumstances is undesirable in others. A game that is fun for four people may be seriously unbalanced for three and just plain dull for two. The kind of information hitherto acquired only by experienced players is now available to anyone at the flip of a page.

Furthermore, most popular games like Monopoly or Clue offer greater opportunities for thoughtful analysis and skillful play than even veteran players realize. Even in games in which luck plays a large part, you can significantly enhance your chances for victory by utilizing the advice in the book. If, for example, you believe that good Monopoly play is limited to making the best of the properties brought you by the luck of the dice, you are probably not making a dent in even that meager target, and you are certainly not playing the game to *win*; see Chapter 4 for proof. If an opponent has deduced that it was Miss Scarlet with the knife in the ballroom before you have begun to narrow your list of suspects, don't blame the cards you were dealt; instead, consider revising your use of the "Detective Notes" as suggested in the section on Clue in Chapter 7. If you keep getting stuck with the queen of spades, read the section on hearts in Chapter 1 (and by all means stop passing low spades).

Are some success formulas more successful than others? How

---

* And since there are hundreds of other books on the subject, I won't even try.

much Shakespeare do you need to know to play Shakespeare? What's wrong with France, 1940? What's the best way to play Feudal? How can you improve D-Day or Le Mans? What's the best stock market game? Can Diplomacy or go or Panzerblitz or Bottoms Up really be played in an evening? The answers to these questions and hundreds of others are to be found in the ensuing pages, if you look.

A word of warning: you *may* have to *look*. A point that is relevant to fifteen games is not repeated fifteen times. If it were, this book would be the size of a dictionary and would be as tedious to read as it would have been to write. Instead, it can be (and is, in fact, designed to be) read from cover to cover. If you are trying to find a particular bit of information immediately, try, first, the section on the game in question and then the rest of the chapter, which covers games that are somewhat similar in form and/or content. Failing that, you'll just have to start from page one and keep going. If, after reading the whole book, your question is still unanswered, chalk it up to Murphy's Law; write me a letter (c/o the publisher), and I'll send you a reply or put it in the next edition.

Although this book focuses on board games, several familiar card games (like hearts) are included, in part because I had something to say about them, and in part because, under various facades, they appear as basic structural elements in many games throughout the book. Also, even though traditional board games like backgammon, parcheesi, and go are included, the real focus of the book is on the kinds of board and other modern games found in game, hobby, and book stores.

Book and magazine titles will appear throughout the book in italic type, and the titles of games which are protected by patents, copyrights, and/or trademarks will be capitalized in the text. When the names of such games appear in headings, they will be followed by the symbol ®. If the title of a protected game does not appear in a heading, it will be followed by this symbol the first time it is discussed in the text. When the game is discussed, credit will be given at least once to the publisher, and a complete list of game publishers and their addresses will be found at the end of the book. This seemed to me the simplest way of acknowledging the copyrights involved without slowing the book unduly; it is not intended to detract from or misrepresent the copyrighted nature of much of the material herein discussed.

This book has benefited from the advice and cooperation of so many game publishers and their representatives that it would be tedious to list them all and tactless to mention the few uncooperative exceptions, but let me acknowledge, however briefly, my thanks to all of them. I would also like to thank the very nice people at Chess and Games Unlimited, in Los Angeles, who generously furnished me with aid and assistance above and beyond the call of duty; Bob Eckert, for his suggestions regarding Speed Circuit; and the multitude of people upon whom I imposed shamelessly for gaming sessions, especially Dave Brown and the other enthusiasts in the UCLA Chemistry Department, Jerry Solomon and Sandy Hill, Terry Adamski, Irene Whitcome, the Pryall gang, and, most of all, Sherry Jackson (my wife), for her patience and unfailing support in all stages of this project.

Contents

CHAPTER 1

Card Games

HEARTS

The discussion of hearts in several books is marred by the fact that it involves rules you simply don't encounter in everyday play. Perhaps there are certain members of the geriatric generation who allow hearts to be led on the first trick, but I have never seen or heard of anyone who did. As I have encountered it from one end of the United States to the other, the game is for three or more but is best for four or five. When more than six people play, a double deck should be used (in which case, the first card played of a given rank has precedence). When three or five play, the deuce of clubs and/or diamonds is discarded, to make the deal even; when several extra cards are involved (as when six play with a single deck), it is better to collect them in a kitty, which is taken along with the first trick.

After the deal but before play begins, each person passes three cards to his left. (A variation is to pass left on the first round; second round, pass right, and third round, hold, the idea being to minimize the influence of a particular person's good or bad passes.) Generally, the person to the left of the dealer leads; some people play the game so that the holder of the deuce of clubs leads it, but that procedure puts too much emphasis on the club suit and limits play unnecessarily. From then on the game proceeds like bridge or whist or (almost) any other trick-taking game: the highest card played of the suit led takes the trick; the winner of one trick leads to the next. However, hearts may not be led until they are "broken"—that is, until someone discards a heart (or the queen of spades) on a trick of another suit.

Each heart taken in a trick counts as one point; the queen of spades counts thirteen. However, a player who takes all twenty-six points (called "shooting the moon" or "making a run") *subtracts* twenty-six points from his score, instead. The object is to score as few points as possible.

The first problem you face in a round of hearts is what to pass. Your most immediate concern—always—is spades. Never pass any spade lower than the queen. With adequate protection, I believe you are better off with the queen in your hand; you run the risk of being stuck with it, but at least you have the element of surprise on your side. What constitutes "adequate protection" depends on the number of players in the game; the easiest way to determine it is to take the number of cards in your hand at the beginning of the game and divide by four. The result (which will range from 2+ to 4+) is the average suit length. If your spade holdings are one more than this number (i.e., three to five), you should probably hold your high (A-K-Q) spades; if you have *more* spades, you should definitely keep all of them.

If you are holding the queen of spades, your first goal is to void yourself in one of the side suits; even without the queen, this is often a good idea, partly as protection against your being passed the queen, and partly because it is the easiest way to get rid of your least desirable cards. For this purpose, diamonds and clubs are better than hearts,* but voiding yourself of hearts obviously has certain other advantages. Still, hearts may not be led for some time, and you may get passed the A-K-Q of hearts; so a heart void has its problems. If you have a choice, get rid of the suit with the highest cards in it: first, because it helps disguise your intentions,

---

* If you play that the deuce of clubs always leads, clubs is obviously the first choice of suits for a void.

and second, because a middle-card pass into your void is obviously less annoying than a high-card pass. With few cards in your hand, it is sometimes possible to go void in two suits—an ideal situation (for which reason, some people use only a two-card pass with hands of eight to ten cards).

The third consideration in passing is high cards. High hearts are popular discards, for obvious reasons, but it is important to look at the entire holding in a suit before deciding what high cards to pitch; a suit with low cards (2-6) in it can tolerate the presence of high cards much better than a shorter suit lacking those low cards. As long as it has low cards, a long suit should probably be maintained, not weakened; such a suit is harmless unless you get stuck with the lead late in the game—and you should play so as to prevent such an occurrence. A seemingly conservative discard of a high spade, a high heart, and a high card in one of the other two suits is, in the long run, a guarantee of mediocrity (at best) and is probably riskier than a good many other alternatives.

Leading spades is the most popular method of going for the jugular vein, it being the easiest and most obvious way to flush out the queen in comparative safety. Those leading the suit generally don't care whether the queen itself takes the trick or whether the ace or king gets stuck with it. Once the queen is out of the way, everyone can get down to the somewhat anticlimactic business of distributing the hearts. Middle spades are preferable to small ones for this business; the jack is ideal, as it means that the leader will win the trick (and can lead again) unless someone plays one of the three high spades. Small spades are better saved for later in the game, when a player with a large spade holding without proper exits may be unable to lose the lead (and thus get stuck with everyone's remaining hearts).

This ploy will fail if the queen is protected, and if you are vulnerable in spades, another line of play is preferable, anyway. The most obvious alternative lead is in your shortest suit (if, for example, someone has passed a card into your void, or if you have pared a suit to a singleton); on the other hand, to disguise your intentions, it is subtler to lead, say, the ace of the other side suit and then (hopefully) exit with the singleton.

A suit gets more dangerous each time it is led; so it is best to play a high card first, rather than save it, unless you have reason to expect an immediate void in the suit. An elementary but important calculation is knowing how long a suit will hold; if the average suit length is three, sheer statistical variation will ensure the probability of a discard on the third round, and the suit cannot possibly hold for another. Nor does this take into account the fact that players are *trying* for voids and short suits.

It is desirable to keep track of the cards in all four suits, but most people have considerable difficulty doing so. At least keep track of the number of times each suit has been led, and pay close attention to the cards in your longest suit, which will often be either your salvation or your doom, depending on how you play it.

Often you will find yourself holding a hand that will either take most of the points or almost nothing, depending on who has the lead. This often comes from having a lengthy holding in one or two suits. In such circumstances you must be sure you don't end up with the lead. You may have to take some preliminary tricks—and some points—to do it, but it must be done. You must be able to nullify all potentially harmful leads, either by playing the suit until everyone is void in it, or by holding cards low enough to duck the suit every time someone leads it. When you have accomplished this, you must have left yourself a means of getting out of the lead—a card you can play that *must* be taken by someone else. Your exit card can be a very low card, or it can be any card in your long suit—as long as it is lower than the cards held by everyone else, and as long as they cannot return the suit.

The best hearts players I know "shoot the moon" at least occasionally. The easiest way is to gain control of the hearts, which means having enough of the top ones to run the suit until everyone else is void. The two problems are (1) the queen of spades and (2) breaking hearts. A holding of the A-K-Q of spades and the A-K-Q-J-10 of hearts solves both problems and is almost a rock-solid shot. However, a more likely holding of the top hearts and one of the top spades works nearly as well: all you do is lead the high spade; if someone takes the gambit (and the queen), you're in decent shape, even if you take most of the remaining hearts. If not (and few will care to prevent your "shooting the moon" at a cost of thirteen points), you've got it made.

I don't recommend planning to take them all before the pass;

it's too risky. On the other hand, some hands are so bad that even after discarding three cards, your prospects are still miserable. In that case, go for it, but try to discard something noncommittal; it will do your cause no good to be known by the player on your left even before the first lead. Similarly, if there is a problem area, try to resolve it first, before committing yourself. There is nothing more frustrating than taking twenty-*five* points; nor is there a quicker way to eliminate yourself from competition. Shooting the moon occurs often when everyone is too busy sticking some poor unfortunate with points to notice that no one else has taken anything. It is justifiably forbidden to warn other players of an attempt to shoot the moon (or to ask, "Has anyone else taken a heart?"); and violators of this rule should be drawn and quartered (at least). For this reason, it is always good policy to take a single heart (or even two or three): one point doesn't hurt, and it prevents a twenty-six-point debacle.

Some authorities mention a "club" rule, forcing the queen of spades to be discarded at the first opportunity. I don't think it's a good idea. Sticking a particular person with the queen is the highest demonstration of skill in hearts, and it is often the only way to get rid of the low scorer (and take that ranking for yourself). Dumping the queen on a consistently bad player makes for an unnecessarily dull game.

OH HELL

Oh hell (also called blackout and a dozen other things), long a popular card game, is now out in a packaged game format. This seems superfluous, since the only things required to play are an ordinary deck of cards, a pencil, and a piece of paper for scoring.

Oh hell is one of the simplest of the bidding games. At the first round, one card is dealt to each player; at the second round, two; and so on, up to a maximum which varies inversely with the number of players, and then, usually, back down to one again. The middle round (the one with the largest hands) is played with no trump; all others are played with a trump determined by turning up the top card of the unused portion of the deck. Each player in turn bids the number of tricks he thinks he will take in the hand; at the end of the round, whoever has made his bid *exactly* (no more and no less) scores ten points plus one point for each trick in his bid.

The most important fact about oh hell is that a bid of "zero" is the easiest to make (at least until the hands get quite large). It is always safer to underbid than overbid; it is rarely too difficult to sluff a potential winner, but it is all too often next to impossible to manufacture a trick when you need one.

The first (and last) round is the real killer. Success here is entirely a question of proper bidding (and, of course, the luck of the deal). If you are not leading and don't have trump, bid "zero." If you *are* leading (to the trick, that is; your status in the game is irrelevant) and don't have trump, bid "one" *only* if you have a high card (say, a 9 or higher) *and* there are only one or two others in the game; otherwise, stick with "zero." If only three are playing, any trump is good enough for a bid of "one"; the more players in the game, the better the trump has to be to justify such a bid (though an 8 of trump would be good enough even with six players). Keep in mind that these rules apply to everyone in the game; if people before you are bidding "one," they probably have trump; so adjust your own bid accordingly.

In higher rounds, the bidding, of course, is more complex (but actually less chancy). In all rounds, you should pay *some* attention to previous bidders. If the trend is bullish (i.e., everyone is bidding high), consider decreasing your intended bid; if the trend is bearish, consider bidding more optimistically. Many players try to adjust their bid to make the round come out even (so that the number of tricks bid is the same as the number available), in the mistaken belief that everyone will be, in effect, helping each other. This sometimes works, especially in the lower rounds, but more often it produces *two* losers (or more) rather than none. Which, after all, is only good strategy: you not only want to make your bid, but you want to keep everyone else from making his. It is, admittedly, more difficult to manage this when your bid is "zero" —but certainly not impossible.

Many of the comments regarding the play of hearts can apply here, too. A long suit may take several tricks or none, depending on whether you play the high ones first or the low ones (or, indeed, on whether the suit is ever led). Voids can be used to sluff dangerous and unwanted high cards, to create other voids by discarding, or to allow a low trump to take a trick.

If overbidding is the commonest error in that half of the game, the bugaboo of playing lies in mishandling trump. A common example: holding the ace-small of trump, a player bids "one." When trump is led, he takes the trick with his ace. Then he attempts to exit with his remaining small trump and is chagrined to discover no one else has any trump left. He takes both tricks and misses his bid. It is not important how many cards were in the hand (it might as easily have been half a dozen or more); what matters is that the fellow misplayed it. His bid was correct, but on the trump trick he should have played his small trump, to make sure it would not take a trick (unless it was a *very* low trump, he should not have been the one to lead the suit). The ace, a guaranteed winner, should more adroitly have been used to trump someone else's "sure" trick (thus, hopefully, making *him* miss *his* bid). The problem of holding more than one trump in a low round will crop up with astonishing frequency, but it can be threshed out consistently if you keep in mind the example above.

The chief virtue of oh hell is, perhaps, the wide range of players it can accommodate. Though not really intended for two, it can be played by any number of people without changing the essential nature of the game. While it is definitely a game of skill, novices and young people can join in without ruining the quality of play.

GIN RUMMY

Space precludes more than a cursory examination of three common melding and discarding games: gin rummy, fan tan, and crazy eights.

Besides being a popular card game in itself, gin rummy forms the basis not only for other familiar card games (canasta, samba) but also for many of the games in the next chapter. The object—if you are by chance unfamiliar with the game—is to meld your hand into sequences (e.g., 10-9-8 of the same suit) and/or groups (cards of the same rank of three or more cards each).

The secret of good gin rummy play (as in many of its relatives) is discarding. With the first couple of discards you can afford to concentrate on improving your hand; thereafter, you must become increasingly defensive. In the early rounds, it pays to advertise: given a choice of potential discards, get rid of an unwanted high card if you are collecting high cards, and vice versa. You are thus encouraging your opponent to discard a similar card, which you may want. More specifically, with two 10s, say, discard a 9 or jack of either of the missing suits. With a 7-8 of one suit, discard a 6 or 9 of one of the others. If you hold a three-card combination, as, the 10 of spades-10-9 of hearts, the ideal "bait" would be a jack of one of the other two suits. Since your opponent may be doing the same thing to you, the safest discard in the early rounds is a card of a different suit and different—but adjacent—rank from the opponent's discard. In later rounds you must give considerable thought to discarding only cards that your opponent probably cannot use, even at the expense of reducing your own chances for "gin." Only if you have nine cards melded can you afford to throw away a completely "open" card (that is, one for which you have no evidence—either from your own holdings or from your opponent's discards—that your opponent might not want it) in the later stages of the game.

In general, avoid taking the upcard unless it gives you a completed set; otherwise, not only are you foregoing the chance at a potentially good draw, but you are also giving valuable information to your opponent. If you have a poor hand and are in desperate need of any sort of meldable material, you can consider taking the upcard if it gives you a three-card combination (like the 10-10-9 in the earlier example).

Sequences are somewhat preferable to groups, but trying for an inside straight (i.e., holding the 8-10 and hoping to draw the 9) is as much a mistake in rummy as it is in poker. On the other hand, there is no need to throw away such a combination gratuitously; there's nothing wrong with holding on to it as long as you have plenty of other fodder to eliminate.

The rule regarding "knocking" (going out with a partial meld and one or more odd cards totaling ten points or less) is simple: when in doubt, knock. One could almost say, knock, period. Go for "gin" only when any *one* of three or four (or more) cards would give it to you, or when you fear being undercut if you knocked.

FAN TAN

Fan tan is a layout game. All cards are dealt out, and then each player in turn attempts to play one card to the layout; if he cannot, he passes. Sevens can be played at any time; from there cards are played in sequence up and down according to suit. The first one out of cards wins.

The traditional strategy is to minimize openings for opponents; so the best play is a card in a sequence you control (playing the 6 when you have the 5-4 also). The second choice is a card in a suit (and direction) in which you have other, nonadjacent cards. Third choice is a card as near either end of a suit as possible (a 3 in preference to a 5 or a 9).

I would quibble with this strategy in one regard. If there is a suit in which you have, say, a middle card and a card on each end, I think it is often more important to play that middle card early—to get the opponents building up that suit—than it is to play a card in the middle of a controlled sequence. The latter, traditional play may well stymie your opponents for a time, allowing you several successive plays, but at the end of that, what then? Having shot your wad, you can only sit back and watch helplessly as they run the rest of their cards without getting to the key suit until it is too late. Control in the late stage of the game is, I think, more important than control in the early going.

CRAZY EIGHTS

Crazy eights is an elementary discarding game, more suited to young people than adults. From a hand of five to seven cards (depending on the number of players), each player in turn plays a card to the discard pile; it must match the top card thereof in either suit or rank. Eights are wild, can match anything, and can be used to name a suit of the player's choice. Anyone unable to play must draw from the stock until he can play. The first one out of cards wins.

The strategy is fairly simple: given a choice of discards, you want to direct the play toward the suit in which you have the most cards. Eights are often not played immediately but are kept for the later stages of the game; they are, of course, ideal to keep for last, since they can be played on anything. When players are down to one or two cards, play becomes largely a matter of trying to guess which suit an opponent does *not* have.

The remaining card games in this chapter have two things in common: they have been copyrighted and are sold in packaged form, and they are, in their different ways, "combination" games. More specifically, Rook (Parker Brothers) is a collection of games, Coup d'Etat (Parker Brothers) is a series of games, and Tripoley (Cadaco) is a combination of games.

ROOK®

Rook consists of a not-quite-ordinary deck of cards and a rule book. The difference between a Rook deck and a standard pack of fifty-two is slight: the suits are colors, there are fourteen cards in a suit, and all the cards are numbered (there are no "face" cards). There is a joker, called the Rook Bird Card. Since most games are played with an incomplete deck, the practical difference is minimal.

Parker Brothers has been publishing Rook for more than sixty years, and it has become, curiously enough, their all-time second-best-selling game.* The only difference between the most recent edition and the one I played as a child is that the rule book is longer and includes more games.

There are far too many to discuss each game, but most of the main ones have a great deal in common, regardless of whether they are for two or for four, playing in partnerships. They perhaps most closely resemble pinochle without the melding feature: players bid for the privilege of naming trump—a bid measured solely in points. Points are scored by taking "count cards" (the 5, 10, 14, and, when used, the Rook Bird Card) in a trick, although some games also grant points for the mere taking of tricks. There is a widow, or "nest," which the high bidder can use to augment his hand. When the high bidder makes his bid, everyone scores ac-

---

* Need I say Monopoly is first?

cording to the points he has taken; if the high bidder fails, he is set back the amount of his bid, and the other side scores double.

The strategy of bidding and play is a mixture of bridge and pinochle. Because of the scoring, it is, compared to bridge, less essential to get the bid; sacrifice bids are almost invariably unmitigated disasters. On the other hand, the bid can be more important to the play of the hand, because short suits can be voided, trump strengthened, and high cards added, through the office of the "nest." Since the widow in pinochle can't be relied on to help the melding, anyway, the larger nest in Rook becomes relatively more valuable than the widow in pinochle.

The bridge principle of leading *through* strength and *to* weakness holds in Rook, but standard bridge play must be tempered with the pinochle habit of "feeding" a partner count cards: e.g., to a partner's trick, play the 10 rather than the 4; to an opponent's, play the 9 instead of the 5 (a count card).

There are several decent games for two: Tennessee for Two bears some resemblance to German whist, as Over the Top does to honeymoon bridge. Of the four-player games, euchre fans will like The Red 1, but most people seem to prefer the less wild-card-oriented Official Tournament Rules.

COUP D'ETAT®

Coup d'Etat is a round-robin series of six games for three or four players. Each round of six games is begun by a new dealer; barring an attempted Coup, the dealer determines what game will be played (each may be played only once in a round). Although the so-called Spanish pack of thirty-two cards is used, five of the six games resemble hearts, and differ only in the cards which penalize players when taken. The penalties are monetary and are paid to the dealer. Any player can attempt a Coup (with or without the aid of the Coup Card, this game's Rook Bird Card), which amounts to "shooting the moon." If he succeeds, he becomes dealer until the end of the round (or until someone unseats him); if he fails, he pays a penalty to the treasury, from which it is eventually paid to the Director/dealer at the end of the round. Tactics, in general (unsurprisingly), follow that of hearts fairly closely; the other players (quite properly) try to stick the dealer with all the penalty cards.

The sixth game, Dominos, is like fan tan, with one exception: *any* card can be used to start the layout. The first player should, therefore, choose the rank of this card carefully; with a preponderance of high cards, for example, he could consider starting even with an ace (in this game, high) or king.

There are two major strategic decisions in the game. The first is deciding whether to try for the Coup; this is fairly obvious, most of the time. It is worth noting, however, that it is often to the advantage of the Director, if he gets dealt the Coup card, to go for the Coup himself if he has a wretched hand (that is, one filled with high cards), especially in the late stages of his Directorate, when the odds are good that he will get his money back if he fails. The second decision—which game to play—depends on the makeup of the hand of the Director, who wants to pick a game in which he will take the least points. The most common error of greedy Directors is to choose Guillotine (potentially the richest game, in which almost everything is penalized) prematurely; it should be saved for an occasion when the Director has a solid, low hand. It can be the big money-maker, but it must be treated accordingly.

It is easy to inveigle people into a game, since everyone plays cards. There is enough variety to keep everyone interested; however, the game can be played properly only for the full three (or four) rounds, so it can last awhile. The packaging is decent, but the knives used to keep track of games on the Director's Board, while visually in keeping with the somewhat artificial image of the game, in practice don't work very well. But that's a minor quibble over an otherwise very pleasant game.

TRIPOLEY®

Tripoley is typical of several packaged combination games, all of which are "souped up" versions of a game of the stops family variously called Michigan or Michigan rummy. It claims to combine hearts, poker, and Michigan rummy, but in fact the hearts portion bears no relation to the game discussed at the beginning of the chapter (*au contraire:* the possession of certain high hearts gains the player bonuses).

The box also boasts (if that is the word) that Tripoley is "so uncomplicated you can keep right on talking," which should tell you something about the kind of player at which the game is aimed. As played by a large number of people (up to nine can participate), the basic game demands little thought and less skill, and should appeal to bingo lovers everywhere. If you have a number of small children, they will probably enjoy the mindless gambling involved, and your greater maturity will not put them at a grave disadvantage.

Skill can be injected into the game, however, by limiting it to no more than six players and by using the variations. Bidding for the extra, "dead" hand gives everyone a chance to escape the (bad) luck of the deal. Having players collect on the pay cards (hearts) in the course of play at Michigan rummy (something of a cross between fan tan and crazy eights) adds an element of suspense and skill to what is otherwise purely a function of chance. A final variation, not mentioned in the rules, is to make everyone play the Michigan rummy portion (and collect on the hearts) with the same five cards he selects for his poker hand; since a good hand in one game is not necessarily a good hand in another, considerable judgment is required, and a player has a good chance to make the best of his cards.

Even with these changes, Tripoley won't be the most exciting or challenging game you've ever played, but if you're fond of social gambling, it may suit you well enough. Otherwise, save it for the children.

CHAPTER 2

Quasi-Card Games

DOMINOES

Dominoes is less the name of a game than a generic term for any of a number of games akin to fan tan or crazy eights but played with tiles. These tiles are rectangular in shape and represent the faces of a pair of dice, one tile for each of the twenty-one possible combinations (i.e., a 6-1 and a 1-6 are represented by the same tile). The sets most commonly used have blank combinations as well (as, the 6-0 or the 0-0), making twenty-eight tiles in all.

All (or nearly all) domino games are fairly similar in play; the differences lie mainly in the presence (or absence) of a draw, and in the scoring. Tiles are played end-to-end in the layout, so that each end matches the end of the adjacent tile, as: 6-0, 0-3, 3-5, 5-4. Doubles are played crosswise, and in some versions are playable on all four sides.

There are, basically, two large classes of domino games. The block game is most often played by four, in partnerships. Each person, in turn, plays one tile to the layout; if he cannot play, he passes (à la fan tan). The first person to go out scores for his side the number of pips on the tiles of his opponents, minus the number held by his partner. The tactics involved are simple: if everyone plays a tile in turn, the first player will be the first one out of tiles. Therefore, he and his partner try to keep the layout as open as possible; his partner in particular will try to play a tile that will enable that first player to play. On the other hand, the opponents, in general, will be trying to close off the layout and, specifically, will attempt to prevent the player who went first from playing a tile at some point.

At the other extreme are some of the draw games, which tend to stress scoring—and offense—instead of being first to go out—and defense. A person who cannot play draws a tile from the stock (the "boneyard") until he *can* play (like crazy eights). Further, if the pips on the ends of the layout total five or a multiple of five (or three, or either, in other versions), the player scores a point for each multiple of five. In the extreme case, doubles can be played on either sides or ends, and a scoring play gives the player an additional turn. Most of these games can be played by any (small) number, but they are less naturally partnership games than the block games. In all of them, the emphasis is on high-scoring combinations, rather than on being the first one out in a round. Given a choice of locations, a scoring tile should be played where it will score the most points; a nonscoring tile should be played, in general, so as to reduce the number of pips on the ends (thus reducing the potential score of the next player).

MAH JONG

Some years ago, mah jong enjoyed a considerable vogue in certain parts of the country, particularly among housewives. Despite the intricate scoring and initial procedure, mah jong is nothing more than an elaborate, four-person rummy played with tiles. There are only three suits and nine different ranks, but each of the tiles is duplicated four times, so that a group of tiles (a pung) must be not only of the same rank but also of the same suit. There are, additionally, other meldable tiles (dragons and winds) and some bonus tiles. Each hand is of fourteen tiles; to "mah jong" (i.e., to go out) a player must have four sets of three and a pair. A group of four (a kong) scores higher than a pung but acts otherwise as a three (you just get one extra tile).

Strategy is fairly similar to rummy, although groups (pungs) are relatively better: a player can "pung" on *any* player's discard, but he can pick up the third in a sequence ("chow") only when the player on his left discards. An ideal discard is the fourth tile to a player's visible (played) pung, since such a tile cannot be picked up. Because of the scoring peculiarities, some sets of tiles are worth more than others; which ones depend on what version of the game you're playing. However, since the dealer wins or loses double, he must be concerned more with going "mah jong" than with how high his hand will score; he cannot afford to be picky.

Because of the multiplicity of bonus or special tiles (which usually double the score), special hands, and luck involved, I can't regard mah jong as a very serious game, and anyone who would gamble real money on it has to be demented. However, if the dealing and scoring are complicated, the actual play of the game, like most other rummy variants, is simple enough, and it's a lot of fun. The novelty of the terms, characters, and playing medium allows you to enjoy mah jong even if you don't much care for other rummy games.

Mah jong sets are generally made of hardwood, plastic, or ivory, and cost anywhere from about $20 to $100 or more, depending on the size of the tiles, the material, workmanship, and similar factors.

Though they may not look it at first glance, Mille Bornes and Waterworks (both from Parker Brothers) are rummy variants, too—with a bit of fan tan thrown in for good measure.

WATERWORKS®

The simpler one, Waterworks, is also more recent. It is played with a deck of cards, each of which represents a section of pipe; the object is to be the first to complete a pipeline of required length (which varies inversely with the number of players, of whom there can be two to five) from valve to spout. You draw and play a card each turn; if you can't play, you must discard. Unlike rummy, however, you cannot pick up another player's discard. The complications arise due to the presence of leaky pipe sections, which can be played on an opponent's pipeline. A leaky section must be fixed, either with an identically shaped good pipe card or with a wrench (a joker, in effect, of which each player has two), before the player can add to his pipeline. A leaky section can be played on top of a *lead* pipe card of identical shape, or it can be played adjacent to the end section, regardless of shape.

Of course, it pays to play the leaky pipe on top of a good pipe, since you don't want to add to an opponent's pipeline. Conversely, with a choice of a copper pipe section (which never leaks) and a lead pipe of the same shape, play the copper one first; an opponent will be forced to *add* a leaky pipe, which can then be covered by your good lead section. Played in the reverse order (assuming adverse action by your opponents), you end up with a pipeline shorter by one card.

The really dirty tricks involve T sections, which must, sooner or later, be capped. If a player rashly proceeds to add pipe without capping one branch of a T, you should play a leaky cap on the *long* (played on) branch; this forces him to play a good cap on your bad one and negates all the cards in the capped branch. Any T, therefore, is a dubious play, and sticking someone with a leaky T (which must be fixed *and* capped) is the worst you can do to him.

MILLE BORNES®

The procedure in Mille Bornes is similar, but the cards are a little more varied; most of the cards are "distance" cards of 25 to 200 miles (the object being to "complete a trip" of 700 or 1,000 miles, depending on whether 2, 3, or 4 are playing), but there are road hazard cards (like Flat Tire and Out of Gas) to play on the opponent's layout, remedy cards to fix the hazards (e.g., Spare Tire), and special cards which can *prevent* such hazards (e.g., Puncture Proof). The latter, called safety cards, are best played as a counter to an attempted play of a hazard; this is called a *"Coup Fourré"* and scores more than the simple play of the card would. If, of course, someone is close to finishing, any safety cards in the hand should be played at once.

The question of playing a card on your own layout *versus* playing a card against an opponent is more, I think, a question of taste than tactics. It is important to get on the board, as it were; so I would prefer an initial meld to an attack, but thereafter it depends on the luck of the draw, opportunities for hazards, and everyone's progress. Under most circumstances, I would rather play a 200-mile card on my own layout than a hazard on someone else's. There is a "safe trip" bonus for *not* playing any 200s, but it's not worth the trouble to pursue, unless, through a combination of luck and circumstance, you find yourself almost finished with your trip without having played one. My own preferences in discarding are low mileage cards and spare (duplicate or triplicate) remedy cards; remedy cards for which you have played the corresponding safety cards are obviously ideal, but you should be careful of discarding them *before* the safety card is played: other players will take the hint and spoil your chances for a *Coup Fourré*.

Neither Waterworks nor Mille Bornes is Monopoly, but neither is a bad game, either. Waterworks in particular can be played by people of varying ages without putting the younger ones at a great disadvantage. Mille Bornes requires a bit more skill in play and lasts a little longer, but even a long game should take less than an hour. Touring® (Parker Brothers), by the way, is no more than a somewhat simplified, Americanized version of Mille Bornes.

INFINITY®

Although it is played on a board, Infinity (Gamut of Games) is another rummy/fan tan relative. The board represents a four-armed spiral nebula, on each arm of which players place a series of tiles (made of thick cardboard) ranging from Creation, Stars, and Planets, through Birth and the development of life, to the ascent of man, his civilization, and finally Destiny. The game and its components are visually striking and would be more so if the tiles were not the size of postage stamps; the whole thing seems to cry out for a larger and more lavish (and, of course, more expensive) edition.

Infinity is ostensibly for two to four players; however, as is the case with a number of games in this and the following chapter, the game for two involves special rules (to simulate the effect of a third party) and is distinctly inferior to the game for more players. Four is best, if only for mechanical reasons.

Simply and briefly, each player has his own draw pile, from which he fills his hand (his "station") of six tiles every round;

each has limited access to the discards of the player on his left. Players get a Time-Piece for playing all six tiles in one turn and/or for playing more tiles in the turn than anyone else. The game ends when a player plays one of the Destiny tiles, at which point the player with the most Time-Pieces wins. You can play on any of the four arms; so you can inhibit another player's development by playing a Black Hole (which stops play on an arm until it is countered), a Disaster (which forces the victim to lose a turn), or simply the tiles he would have played on his next turn.

As always, the question of blocking an opponent versus advancing your own fortunes arises. The more players, the more important your *own* play becomes. However, if you have no other "special event" tiles demanding placement, you can sometimes lay a Black Hole without impairing your own development—but be careful; such tactics can backfire as quickly as the next draw. I confess to a fondness for a wide-open attacking game, but unplayable tiles can force you into a blocking game for a time.

Despite the basic simplicity of play, the directions may well seem bewildering at first and are sufficiently complicated that it will probably be a game or two before you are thoroughly comfortable with them. Infinity is not a long game, however, so this period of adjustment is not a severe problem. Like mah jong, the novelty and beauty of the components are likely to entice and enthrall even relative nongamers long enough to give Infinity a try.

A caution: Gamut of Games uses the same package for all their games; it is a modified "bookshelf" form designed for vertical storage, attractive and compact, slimmer than 3M's original setup and less sturdy. The boards or the box (or both) should be thicker or of different material, as the boards, which are made of cardboard, tend to warp, making them almost impossible to assemble and play on comfortably. There are usually twice as many components as seem likely to fit back into the box, so the games have to be repacked with some care, also.

IMAGE®

The subject of Image (3M) is people; a meld is a description of a person (real or imaginary, living or dead) built up by means of status (e.g., "male"), place ("North America"), time ("twentieth century"), and activity ("writer") cards. In his turn, a player can make a maximum of three plays; these can be from his hand or from the center of the board (the discard pile, in effect) and can be to any meld on the board, no more than four of which can be going at any one time. Melds can be from four to eight cards long, and can be ended at any time by playing an appropriate letter card and announcing the name of a character who will fit the "image" of the meld. The player ending an image scores points according to the number of cards in the image.

Not only can you add to another player's image (thus, often, sending it in a new direction), but you can even change it completely, by playing, for example, one activity card on top of another. When more than four persons play, such piracy must occur every round, because of the simple limitations of space. Partly because of this reason, the length of an image tends to vary inversely with the number of players; especially when five or six play, everyone tends to grab any available image and run, which makes for a less interesting game.

It pays, of course, to influence an image to fit the letter cards you hold, since many of the letters are not duplicated. It is largely a matter of luck whether your initial image lasts long enough for you to play on it again, but if it does, your best protection is to make it as peculiar as possible, thus forcing players to change several cards if they want to steal it. A broad background (especially in English and history) is helpful, of course, not only in disguising your image but also in identifying others and adapting them to your own purposes.

Image is good for those who do not often play board games, especially anyone of intellectual pretensions. The rules are simple, but adults would (presumably) have a considerable advantage over younger children, though it might be a good learning experience for the latter.

The problems of the game stem from ambiguity in the rules, particularly in regard to places or activities "associated" with the person in the image. This produces any number of arguments, which are not helped appreciably by the examples, several of which most players (including myself) would not allow if played by an opponent. For example, do we really associate Albert Schweitzer with religion, medicine, *and* music? *I* would allow

Eisenhower "golf," but should Nixon be permitted "football"? To handle challenges of this sort, a file of reference material (dictionaries, encyclopedias, etc.) should be handy, but even that won't entirely solve the problem: something can be *true* without being *significant*. (If a person visits Tijuana, can we properly say he is "associated" with Latin America?) Unfortunately, I have no ready solution to this problem; sooner or later, you and your friends will settle on some ground rules, but that will come only after you've played (and argued) awhile. The ambiguity is just something you'll have to live with if you want to play Image, and, despite its problems, it *is* worth playing.

MONAD®

Monad is a 3M "Gamette," which means that it is smaller than the regular "bookshelf" game and about half as expensive (something of a "paperback" to the other's "hardcover"). The current editions are sturdy and attractive and vastly superior to the old ones, which wouldn't stay closed and were impossible to store.

If its terminology (e.g., "buying" and "trading") and some of its procedures point toward the next chapter, Monad is nonetheless firmly of this one. There are six different kinds of cards, from Commons to Monads; each has a numerical value of slightly more than twice that of the next lower ranking card, and each (except for the black-and-white Monads) comes in six colors. The object is to be the first to acquire a specified number of Monads; this is done in stages, by melding various sets of cards to the board. For example, a pair of one rank (e.g., Commons) in contrasting colors ("hot" and "cool") can be traded for a card of the next higher rank (in this case, a Bi). Alternatively, you can use the numerical value of a series of cards to "buy" other cards, or you can gain progressively higher cards by melding four, five, or six differently colored Commons (a procedure called "leaping"). Which method to use depends more on the availability of cards in your hand and on the board than overall strategic superiority; "leaping" occurs more often with only two players than with more, since with three or four it is very difficult to accumulate enough of the right cards.

I must confess to being underwhelmed with Monad. There are no glaring errors in design; I just don't find it terribly interesting. Although two can play (without any rules changes), it is better for three or four, due to the greater turnover on the board.

CHAPTER 3

Stock Market and Business Games

As of this writing, there is no very good auction game on the market. The auction process *per se* is not sufficiently diverting to constitute a game, and to add interest the designers have come up with nothing more than the simple—and unsatisfying—concept of randomization (i.e., chance).

HIGH BID®

In High Bid (3M), the random factors are special dice. After a property is bought at auction from the block, the high bidder is allowed to sell some of the properties in his hand for a price determined by the dice; he may refuse the "bid," but he cannot then try to sell anything else. If he has been dealt (or has acquired at auction) a Buyer's Card, he can also buy from the Gallery (i.e., from the stock of items previously sold by other players) one to three items—again at a price determined by the dice.

The object is to collect related cards, sets, which are worth more collectively than they are separately; the winner is the first player to achieve a worth of $5,000 in cash and sets. In practice, the completion of one or two medium-value sets is enough to win; the high-value sets take too long to collect. Since only a small dent is made in the pile of cards, the winner is often the only player whose complete set has appeared on the auction block.

MASTERPIECE®

Masterpiece (Parker Brothers) has, if anything, even less to offer an adult. Much of the randomization is built into the board, around which players move according to the roll of a die. The various spaces allow players to open the main auction, take bids on their own property, buy or sell property for a fixed amount, or sell a painting to the bank for its value. More than this, however, the paintings themselves are valued at random; there is a value deck, one card of which is paired with each painting when it is bought. These values range from $1,000,000 to zero—worthless forgeries—so the only thing to go on in bidding for a painting is the statistical distribution of value cards; i.e., you bid the average. Masterpiece is played until all paintings have been bought, at which time each player totals his cash and the value of his paintings, and the high man wins.

The best part of Masterpiece is a totally extraneous set of six "personality cards," fictional bidders at an auction whose identities players can assume for the game. If gratuitous awards for rolling the right number on a die or landing on the proper space is your idea of excitement, then High Bid or Masterpiece may afford you hours of fun. Otherwise, look elsewhere.

DEALER'S CHOICE®

Breathes there a man with soul so dead, who never to himself has said, "I could wheel and deal as well as Jim Moran (the Courtesy Man—remember him?), Ralph Williams, or Cal Worthington (and his dog Spot)"? Such, at least, is the premise of Dealer's Choice (Parker Brothers), a clearly related but far better game than the previous two. Indeed, given the fact that most people (justifiably enough) prefer a Playmate to a Picasso and are more concerned with first gear than first editions, the almost legendary world of the used car dealer seems *prima facie* better grounds for a trading game than art galleries and antique auctions.

The object, as usual, is to accumulate the greatest net wealth, in cash and cars, by the end of the game. The difference, however, is between mediocrity and quality, and extends even to the components. Each player's Blue Book not only gives the value *to him* of each car; it also gives the range of possible real values for each list price, and it includes an outline of the many things a player can do in his turn (draw, play, or replace cards; buy insurance—a potentially valuable but risky purchase, since some of the policies are phony; buy cars from the bank, and make his cars available for purchase by anyone who can be induced to bid on one). All the information, in short, a person needs to play the game is at his fingertips. Another efficient device that could profitably be copied in other games is a round plastic rack called the Organizer, which neatly compartmentalizes all the various sorts of cards involved in the game. The players are not at the mercy of dice and chance landings on spaces; instead, the elements of randomization are the Dealer's Choice Cards, which players accumulate and play at their own discretion.

The crowning touch, however, is the handling of the properties —the automotive stock in trade of each player. The element of uncertainty in Masterpiece has here been tempered by the sound economic principle of differential valuation and refined into a useful and suspenseful game device.* The $6,000 (list price) Jaguar sitting in your lot is in fact worth only $1,500 ("lawnmower engine") *to you;* to someone else it might be worth as much as $12,000 ("playboys only"). If you get a bid of $3,000, do you take it, try for list price, or demand top dollar? If you insist on a higher bid, the buyer may accede (a coup for you—and one he won't even know about), or he may demand to "look under the hood" (i.e., examine *your* Blue Book on the car), which in this case means that he would get the car for $1,500 (*your* value), and

---

* In brief, the principle states that the value of any object is not absolute but relative, not intrinsic but relative to human beings, *each of whom will value it somewhat differently*. Some gross examples: a fan of Alice Cooper would gladly buy a new album for $6.00 while to most people the record wouldn't be worth $.06. Similarly, I wouldn't take a ticket to the World Series if someone tried to give it to me; yet, a real baseball fan might sell his spouse into slavery for the same ticket. It is curious that this fact of human behavior, without which all forms of trade would be impossible, should be so commonly overlooked in trading games.

you would have to pay him a $2,000 fine to boot. If the price you asked did *not* exceed your Blue Book, the buyer would be stuck with the high price (your Blue Book price), and would have to pay *you* $2,000 for besmirching the name of Honest Jim/Ralph/Cal/Josephine. Unlike other games with similar claims, in Dealer's Choice bluffing—and the ability to see through an opponent's bluff—is a significant factor in determining your success. Without "looking under the hood" you have no way of knowing what any car is worth to anyone else; that $4,000 tank on Hortense's lot is worth list price to you (as a "getaway car"), but do you dare put in a low bid? It might be junk to her, but she might have recognized it as a "camouflaged Cadillac" worth $8,000—and, naturally, she'll want to extract every penny if you open your mouth. (Incidentally, if you're wondering what a tank is doing in a used car lot, you haven't been paying attention to the "full-sized" cars Detroit has been marketing for the last decade or so.)

A really greedy player might, after being challenged, sell a 1925 Mercedes-Benz for $12,000 ("best in show") and then, on a later turn, buy it back from his victim (whose Blue Book says, "$5,000: Berlin Taxi") for considerably less, with the hope of selling it *again* for top dollar either to the bank or (via the right Dealer's Choice Card) to a "forced" buyer. This, however, can backfire: another player might play a "Fire" or "Theft" card on the car, resulting in a total loss (unless it was protected by the proper insurance). For this reason, it is a good idea to get rid of a car whose high value (to you) is known to other players.

While best for five people, Dealer's Choice is an enjoyable game for three or four as well.

BILLIONAIRE® AND VENTURE®

The best thing about Billionaire (Parker Brothers) is its packaging: although the box is (as usual) larger than necessary, there are handy plastic racks for all five sorts of cards; the "Analyzer" does not look as if it will fall apart the second time it's used, and the playing pieces—large upright dollar signs mounted on a base—are a pleasant change from the usual tokens. Unfortunately, Billionaire is a prime example of the Macbeth syndrome: "full of sound and fury, signifying nothing." Those who have been lucky enough to read some of the Oz books (or unfortunate enough to sit through the movie, *Zardoz*) may identify the problem with the Wizard of Oz: beneath the hype and the glossy image sits a humbug. A basically simple (and relatively unexciting) concept has been ornamented with more randomizing elements than a Las Vegas casino: dice, chance (power play) cards, the "Analyzer." The simple board is very reminiscent of Masterpiece's and is equally gratuitous; its only function is to keep players from conducting their affairs in a more straightforward fashion.

Venture (3M) is almost embarrassingly similar to Billionaire—minus the extraneous nonsense. Instead of money, both games employ profit cards, which the players use to buy corporations (also represented by cards). In Venture, profit cards accrue regularly each turn; in Billionaire, they are obtained only by landing on the proper space. Billionaire ends when a player achieves a worth of a billion dollars; Venture continues until all corporations are bought. In both cases, of course, the richest player wins.

Both games have mechanisms by which one player can obtain a corporation belonging to another. In Venture, this is done by means of a proxy card from the resource (i.e., profit) deck; if used, the player pays 50, 100, or 150 percent of the face value of the corporation (depending on the card), but he can only take the top card of a conglomerate. There is a similar restriction on the use of the "Analyzer" (Billionaire's chief method for such piracy), which is no more than a toy whose spinners determine the result: the corporation may change hands, or profit cards may be drawn and/or exchanged. I hope you sense a difference in the principles involved in the two methods.

Both games supplement the basic value of their profit cards for trading purposes; in Billionaire, the investments themselves have a trading value (equal to 10 percent of their ultimate value) which can be used to purchase more valuable corporations. This is the game's best feature, as it forces a player to *plan*—to weigh short-term good against long-term good. In Venture, certain sets of cards marked with the same symbol are worth extra money.

Aside from surface complexities, Venture is basically a more involved game than Billionaire. The corporations themselves are more complicated; they are divided "horizontally" into six industries (each identified by a particular color) and "vertically" into groups bearing one, two, three, four, or five of six possible letters. The cost of each ranges from $8 to $24 million, depending on the number of letters on the card. Corporations score not on the basis of their face value (as in Billionaire) but on their arrangement into conglomerates, each of which is a group of corporations from different industries with one or more letters in common. The longer the conglomerate, and the more letters in common, the higher the value.

Although within each group industries and individual letters are distributed evenly, the *groups* of letters are not. Only six three-letter combinations can be made into conglomerates of maximum (six-card) size—ABD, ACF, ADE, BCE, BEF, CDF—none of which could exceed a length of three corporations without the addition of the right three five-letter cards. The most common two-letter combinations (none of which require five-letter cards to form conglomerates of maximum length) are AD, BE, and CF.

My major complaint with Venture is that too much emphasis is placed on quantity instead of quality: a five-card, two-letter conglomerate is worth less than one of six cards with only a single letter in common; yet the latter is easier to obtain than the former. It seems to me that a considerable adjustment in the scoring is called for.

Venture can be played by two to six players but is probably best for a number somewhere in the middle. While it is not a short game, and some have found it dull, I have always rather liked it. Certainly, I much prefer it to Monad or (as should be obvious) Billionaire, which, as far as I can see, is not for adults.

CARTEL® AND ACQUIRE®

Two better games which focus on the joining of companies into conglomerates are Cartel (Gamut of Games) and Acquire (3M). In both, each company (in Cartel) or hotel (in Acquire) has a specific location on the board and is further represented by a card (in the former) or a tile (in the latter). In both, each player has a hand (of tiles or cards) from which, each turn (usually), he plays and to which he adds one element. In Acquire, tiles adjacent on the board form a chain; the tiles, *per se*, are unowned, but players may buy shares of stock in any of the chains. In Cartel, players buy the individual companies; two or more adjacent companies owned by the same player give him extra profits. Such a group is called—with a cavalier disregard for dictionaries or economics texts—a "cartel."*

A Cartel player can buy companies with cash, bonds (long-term loans which halve the profits of the company purchased—though without effect on special, conglomerate, profits), or some of his limited amount of stock. Since the value of the stock increases along with the size of his holdings, he must decide whether to sell stock early, to buy companies and increase profits quickly, or to save it for later use when the shares are worth more. Bonds allow early purchases but cut into long-term profits. Some players have won without using bonds at all; their use, at least, should be restricted to quick expansion early in the game or to companies whose *special* profits are more significant than the profits of the company itself.

Similarly, the cost of stock in a hotel chain in Acquire rises as the chain increases in size, so that there is an obvious incentive to "get in on the ground floor" when things, of course, are most uncertain. Chains are merged when a tile is played which is adjacent to both of them; when such an event occurs, stockholders in the smaller chain can sell their stock for cash, trade it in (two-for-one) for shares of the larger chain, or save it with the intention of starting another chain of the same name. (This last course should *not* be taken late in the game.) This is the only time players can get more cash (to buy *other* stock). For short-term profit (and future investment purposes), it pays to hold stock in the "merged" chain; for long-term standing, it is good to hold stock in the "merging" (i.e., larger) chain. In either case, because of the majority shareholder bonuses, it is *very* important to be one of the two largest stockholders in a chain. A well-managed portfolio is intensive rather than extensive; the ideal holding is one in which you

---

* The game defines a cartel as a group of companies whose collective worth is greater than the sum of the parts. In its most common usage, a cartel is a group of *related* businesses or organizations which (usually with government aid or "regulation") act jointly to displace prices from their open market level: e.g., the NCAA (which maintains the "wages" of college athletes at a level below what they would obtain in a free market), the Mideast oil bloc, "public utilities," the airlines, unions, etc. Common ownership of a supermarket and a firm of architects, regardless of the game rules, is not a "cartel."

have one more share of stock than anyone else—in as many chains as possible. Tiles which form or merge chains should be played when and only when such transactions will do *you* the most good: merge a small chain you control before someone else can challenge that control; given a choice, merge it with a large chain controlled by you rather than one controlled by your opponents.

Timing is also important in proper Cartel play. If you hold several adjacent cards in your hand, and another is on the board, unbought, try to obtain the latter *first;* not knowing its value, the other players will not be so interested in thwarting you, and you will be able to buy it for less. After that, they will be unable to keep you from completing your group. Also, be aware of the stock price schedule. Because the relation of a company's net worth to the value of its stock is not simply linear, a $1 million difference in the value of two companies can mean a $10 or $20 million difference in the value of your stock; so buy accordingly.

Although Cartel is ostensibly for two to four players and Acquire for two to six, neither is very good for two. With that exception, both games are enjoyable and stimulating, easy to learn, and can be played repeatedly. Playing time depends largely on how long each player ponders his move; the first occasion is usually the longest. Neither game can drag on the way Risk or Monopoly often does; two hours is perhaps a reasonable estimate for an average game.

If Acquire has an edge, it is in the quality of its components. Cartel's board is more colorful, but it is far less sturdy and tends to warp badly, and the ownership markers (smaller versions of Billionaire's dollar sign tokens without bases) don't always stay in place. Acquire's higher price is unquestionably reflected in its packaging and presentation, but *both* games deserve a place in your game library.

STOCKS AND BONDS® AND
THE STOCK MARKET GAME®

The stock market is well represented in the game field, and unlike the auction games at the beginning of the chapter, the basic concept here is interesting and sound enough so that the game designers, in general, did not find it necessary to garble it up. Stocks and

Bonds (3M) and Avalon Hill's The Stock Market Game are typical of the "pure" type, and are very similar. Both are packaged in the familiar "bookcase" format, both are relatively short games (ten turns for the former, twelve for the latter), both consist of nothing more than buying and selling stock and recording the prices on the boards, and both can be played by any number.

In Stocks and Bonds, a card is drawn to determine whether the market is bull (up) or bear (down); then dice are rolled, and the number is cross-referenced with the appropriate bull or bear chart to determine the fluctuation of each stock for that turn. Buy and sell orders are written in secret and then revealed simultaneously.* After all stock transactions have been settled, a new card and dice roll determine the new stock prices.

The Stock Market Game determines stock prices slightly differently. As before, a card is drawn, which indicates the market— bear, bull, or mixed—and includes a minichart of stock movements which is cross-referenced not to dice but to the net difference between all "buy" and "sell" orders for each stock. These are *not* written in secret but are posted, via markers, on an appropriate section of the board.

It is hard to say which method is more realistic. In the real market, the fluctuations of each stock represent nothing more than the collective willingness of individuals to buy and sell. Stocks and Bonds assumes (reasonably enough) that the actions of the players represent too small a portion of the total market to affect stock prices. The Stock Market Game attempts to connect the actions of the players in some way with those prices. Both are partly correct: you don't buy and sell in a vacuum, and yet the Avalon Hill game at times allows the players too great a control over the total market. For example, it's not hard to corner the market on warrants and continue to drive the price up by placing "buy" markers even when there is no stock to be bought. For that matter, if most players are buying, their stock is virtually guaranteed to go up. The best counters to these flaws are to use the "selling short" option (not available in S & B), to give some players an incentive to drive the market down, and to use S & B's method of secret orders

---

* The rules here are slightly ambiguous, but this is the procedure that should be followed.

simultaneously revealed, which would allow (and encourage) one member of such a collusive group to sell out at a high price and destroy the stock's price supports.

In The Stock Market Game, the stocks to buy are the cheap ones—speculative and warrants—because their greater fluctuation allows the possibility of greater profits. In Stocks and Bonds, United Auto, Uranium Enterprises, and Stryker Drilling (in order) are increasingly speculative; they offer the greatest chance for making large sums but are also the riskiest. When they get *very* low (25 or so), they should be bought, despite the risk of bankruptcy, because of the enormous potential profit—100-300 percent or more. Tri City Transit, followed by Metro and Growth, is the steadiest and best long-term gainer; similar in character but inferior are Valley Power and Pioneer. The game's "Securities Review" is not, actually, a bad guide.

Both games offer margin buying as an option; it doesn't change the basic character of either, but I don't suggest it for the first time. The Stock Market Game has a number of other options. I don't suggest using those in Game II (the conversions) unless the limitations in the optional rules are also used. Additionally, there is a 1929 "crash" version and a corresponding "explanation" of the famous stock market crash. Unfortunately, it is filled with ridiculous claptrap designed to cover up the fact that the author has not the foggiest notion of the causes of the crash and the depression that followed.

Disregarding the worthless "explanatory notes" and adopting the changes I suggest, you will find little to choose between the two games. With Stocks and Bonds, all transactions take place on paper, which simplifies and hastens matters if all the players can add, subtract, and multiply. If the subject matter appeals to you, neither game would be a bad choice, though buying both would probably be superfluous.

STOCK MARKET GAME®

Whitman's Stock Market Game resembles the games of the following chapter, in that players move tokens around a board according to the roll of the dice. The spaces they land on move the stock price index up or down. They may sell any stock for the price listed on the board, but they may only buy the stock printed on the space on which they have landed.

There are four pairs of identical but differently named stocks; when the four stocks on one side of the index (i.e., one of each pair) rise, the four stocks on the other side drop by an exactly corresponding amount. Unlike the two previous games, therefore, neither any stock in particular nor the "board" in general has a long-term tendency to go up. Making money is thus not a matter of sound long-term investment but of buying stocks when one side/ group is low and selling when they are high.

More important, however, are stock splits. In the real world, if you have 100 shares of stock valued at $100 apiece and the stock splits, you end up with 200 shares valued at $50 apiece; *the worth of your investment is unchanged.* This is *not* the case in this game. If you own a share of the appropriate stock, you can duck into side paths which ostensibly represent shareholders' meetings (much like entering a career in Careers, discussed in the next chapter) and which can multiply your holdings in that stock many times.

The method of raising money at the beginning of the game (which is too tedious to explain) can easily be dispensed with by starting everyone with $1,000. If you follow the rules, don't pick "Prospector" for your occupation; you'll get your $1,000 faster by being a Deep Sea Diver or a Doctor.

Despite the fact that it bears almost no relation to reality, Whitman's game is, perhaps surprisingly, quite enjoyable, and younger players might well prefer it to the previous two. Like them, it can be played by almost any number (including two), though it is a somewhat longer game than either of the others.

CHAPTER 4

Family Games

MONOPOLY®

Although Monopoly (Parker Brothers) is responsible for numerous half-truths, distortions, and outright myths about the subject of economics in general and capitalism in particular, it remains the most popular board game invented in modern times. Perhaps the major reason for its enduring popularity is that people of almost any age can play, and children can compete on a more or less even footing with adults, chance usually being as much a factor as wisdom or experience. Too, many people like long, involved games upon occasion, and few know of or care for more challenging and deterministic games like 4000 A.D., Diplomacy, or Avalon Hill's line of war games. Despite the element of chance in Monopoly, it is possible to improve considerably the odds in your favor through knowledge and the application of the proper strategies.

The Importance of Boardwalk and Park Place

Among Monopoly players it is a truism that he who controls Boardwalk and Park Place controls the game. Certainly the crux

of the game is the precise nature of the monopolies involved, and
to begin our analysis of Monopoly—and the Boardwalk problem
—we will have recourse to the following table:

Color	Property	A	B	C	D	E	F
Purple	Baltic and Mediterranean	$ 620	$ 450	$ 250	73%	40%	113%
Light blue	Connecticut, Vermont, and Oriental	$1070	$ 600	$ 550	56%	51%	159%
Fuchsia	Virginia, States, and St. Charles	$1940	$ 900	$ 750	47%	39%	124%
Orange	New York, Tennessee, and St. James	$2060	$1000	$ 950	49%	46%	141%
Red	Illinois, Indiana, and Kentucky	$2930	$1100	$1050	38%	36%	109%
Yellow	Atlantic, Ventnor, and Marvin Gardens	$3050	$1200	$1150	39%	38%	115%
Green	Pennsylvania, North Carolina, and Pacific	$3920	$1400	$1275	36%	33%	101%
Blue	Boardwalk and Park Place	$2750	$2000	$1500	73%	55%	128%
	Railroads	$ 800	$ 200	$ 200	25%	25%	100%
	Utilities	$ 300	$ 120	$ 20	40%	7%	47%

A=Total cost (cost of properties and hotels on each)
B=Rent with hotel on most expensive property
C=Rent with hotel on least expensive property
D=B/A (highest rent as a percentage of total cost)
E=C/A (lowest rent as a percentage of total cost)
F=Total rent as a percentage of total cost
For Utilities, figures D and E are for high roll and low roll

If we look at the data in the last column of the table, we note
that while the return for Boardwalk and Park Place (128%) is
good—third best on the board—it is not spectacular. The dominance of this monopoly is, however, real, as any number of players
will attest, and the reason lies in the other columns. From "A" we
see that the total cost of full development of the whole monopoly
—the actual capital investment—is lower than any other monopoly on the expensive half of the board; yet the rent is the highest
on the board. It is certainly to this latter fact that is owed the
familiar feeling of dread experienced by opposing players headed

down the "back stretch." Two thousand dollars puts a dent in the wealthiest player's account, and the poor unfortunate who lands successively on a fully developed Park Place and Boardwalk has lost the game, whether or not he can manage by some miracle to scrape together the rent. In a conventional game, no player can recover from a $3,500 loss. The final important fact—more significant, perhaps, for the owner than for the other players—comes from Column D: an opponent landing on a hotel on Boardwalk will return, in that one play, almost three-fourths of the total cost of developing the entire monopoly.

Compare this with the real sinkhole of the game, the greens: putting a hotel on Pennsylvania, North Carolina, and Pacific requires more than a thousand dollars more in total investment, and in order to get that money back, other players must do the equivalent of landing on all three of the properties. And that is just to break even! The reds and the yellows are a little better, but not much.

An obvious aim, then, is to gain ownership of Boardwalk and Park Place, but this can be done only by one player. What of everyone else? Should they all resign? It could be suggested that if, in the first trip or two around the board, one player does manage to get both Boardwalk and Park Place, the rational thing for everyone else to do might be just that: give up. (I am, as you can see, being candid.) However, lest I be accused of defeatism, let me hasten to add that, under most other circumstances, there are viable and more desirable alternatives.

The Monopolies

Discussion of some of these alternatives must be left to later sections, but for the moment let us look at one of the more obvious: other property. I presume everyone has noticed that the buildable monopolies (i.e., all but the Railroads and the Utilities) increase in cost and rent in order as one proceeds about the board. Thus, despite the fact that (as the table shows) return on investment does not obey this orderly ascendance, the unfortunates who do not manage to obtain Boardwalk and Park Place usually scramble for control of the greens, yellows, and reds—most often in that order.

As I have indicated above, the greens—Pennsylvania Avenue et al—cannot by any means be considered much of a bargain. True, their rent is high (as are the others', to a slightly lesser extent), but because of the enormous investment involved, hotels appear on them (if they ever do) only in very late stages of advanced games. This is bad for two reasons: first, the eventual winner has probably already had time to achieve dominance over the game; and second, the odds are considerably reduced that the hotels will ever manage to pay for themselves. The value of the high-cost/high-rent properties is directly related to the amount of time they exist in fully developed form (i.e., with hotels on them). The odds that the opposing players will land on your property three or four (or more) times in one or two rounds are obviously much less than the odds they will do so over a period of half a dozen or more trips around the board.

In this regard, a specific example may be helpful. Using the data of the first three columns of the table to compare the greens with the reds, and assuming that players land on both monopolies with the same frequency,* the green monopoly will have to be landed on at least four times before its real return begins to exceed the reds'. Compared to the yellows, which offer a better return than the reds, the greens look even more dubious. All three monopolies, however, suffer from the same flaws: high cost and low percentage return, counterbalanced only by a high *long-term* return.

If the reds, yellows, and greens are not the answer, what is? Let us consider the other properties in turn, noting first that all but Baltic and Mediterranean show a better average short-term return than the three monopolies just discussed.

B & M owe much of their poor reputation to their low rent, of course, but even here most of the blame rests with Mediterranean, which alone of all the buildable properties on the board does no more than pay for itself when another player lands on a hotel there. Baltic, on the other hand, shares with Boardwalk itself the distinction of having the highest percentage return on investment. Granted that no one ever won a game solely on the strength of the

---

* A logical but not quite valid assumption; see the later discussion on the effects of the "Go to Jail" space.

"little two," there is a valid place for them, particularly in the earlier stages of the game, as I will suggest in a bit.

The monopoly of Connecticut, Vermont, and Oriental can be considered the best bargain on the board (see Column F); it is cheap, but the rent is not to be sneered at. More specifically, its total cost is barely more than half that of the next-cheapest monopoly, the fuchsias (Virginia, States, and St. Charles), but its rent is two-thirds of theirs.

Not so strong a case can be made for the aforementioned fuchsias as for the monopolies on either side; yet they are worthy of consideration. Their Column F percentage is decent if unspectacular; it would fare better were it not for the wide divergence between the high and low rents. However, their total cost is a thousand dollars less than the reds', while the high rent is only two hundred dollars different.

The real gem in the rough is almost certainly the oranges, with the second-highest overall percentage return in the game. New York Avenue, despite certain differences in rental structure, can be considered a half-price Boardwalk (e.g., initial cost of property $200 vs. $400, cost of houses $100 vs. $200, maximum rent $1,000 vs. $2,000). A comparison with the reds is simply devastating: a nearly nine hundred dollar difference in investment yields a mere hundred dollar difference in maximum rent. That means that, if the odds for landing on both were approximately equal, opposing players would have to land on the reds (with hotels) *nine times* before they returned more money than the oranges. When was the last time *that* happened?

Further, the oranges have certain incomparable advantages of *position*. Although there is no "chance" card which directs a player to advance his token to New York Avenue (as there is for Illinois Avenue, St. Charles Place, and Boardwalk), anyone who "takes a ride on the Reading" has perhaps a one-in-three chance of landing on the oranges in his next few turns. The same one-in-three chance applies to whoever draws the "Go back three spaces" card, since there are only three "chance" spaces on the board, and one of them is three spaces ahead of New York. These, however, are essentially trifling matters (though they may not seem so to a player landing on a hotel in the oranges because of them); the oranges' chief advantage in this regard lies in their relation to the Jail.

Note first the obvious fact that, because of the "Go to Jail" space between Marvin Gardens and Pacific Avenue, as well as such lesser factors as "Go to Jail" cards and the hazards of too many doubles, a player is more than twice as likely to land on the Jail space as any other (his status—prisoner or visitor—is irrelevant for our present purposes).* Subsequently, if he leaves Jail on a roll of doubles, his chances of landing directly on Tennessee or St. James are one in three. More significantly, the chances are *nearly even* that any player leaving the Jail space will not pass the oranges without landing on one of them; if you own the oranges, you can look forward to greeting one out of every two players stopping on the Jail space.

There are two conclusions to be drawn from the preceding three paragraphs: first, a player is more likely to land on the oranges than on any other monopoly; and second, the oranges are a desirable monopoly second to none—not even, perhaps, to Boardwalk and Park Place!

A word in passing about the Railroads and Utilities. More truly so than the oft-maligned Baltic and Mediterranean, the Utilities (the Water Works and the Electric Company) are the least valuable properties on the board, partly because of their miserable percentage return and partly because it is impossible to imagine them significantly affecting the outcome of the game. The Railroads are unique in that a player may acquire a "partial" monopoly: he doubles the rent on each Railroad he owns every time he buys another. The advantages of further acquisition, however, are so great that the drive to monopolize completely is almost as great as with other properties. For example, in going from ownership of two Railroads to three, at an increase in cost of 50 percent (assuming, as throughout the discussion so far, a purchase at the "face value" of the property—an assumption we will examine shortly), the player has doubled the rent on all his Railroads and

---

* This "Go to Jail" space also means that the half of the board between that space and the Jail—i.e., the half occupied in part by the greens, the blues, the purples, and the light blues—will receive in the course of the game approximately one-seventh less traffic than the other half of the board.

simultaneously increased the chances that other players will land on at least one of them by approximately 50 percent—thus essentially *tripling* his revenue. Despite an unimpressive percentage return, there are several advantages to the Railroads: they are relatively inexpensive,* are not subject to "street repair" costs, and offer a relatively steady income, which, if unspectacular, can be of some benefit in the early and middle stages of the game.

Stages of the Game

For purposes of analysis, a typical game of Monopoly can be said to have three stages: early—in which the players advance around the board, buying unowned property; middle—in which all property has been acquired by someone, and players trade, consolidate their holdings, and scramble to build on their monopolies; and late—characterized by the existence of developed monopolies belonging to each player, many hotels, and possible building shortages. Games which reach the late stage (and not all do so) may be called advanced games; those which do not I will term basic games.

My first suggestion in this regard is that many and possibly most advanced games should have—and, with proper play, could have been—ended in the middle stage. If a player has an overwhelming overall advantage (in a multiplayer game, Boardwalk and Park Place, the oranges, any other developable monopoly, and money), there is no point to delaying the *coup de grace*. Such a player will *probably* lose nothing in permitting the game to develop into the late stage, but why take the chance, however slight, of losing when victory is within your grasp?

More significantly, a player who could force a victory in the middle stage may well lose an advanced game, because of the changing values of the monopolies. I cannot overemphasize this. The table to which we have referred so often might, with a little latitude, be considered a table of middle game values (especially if we include the late middle game). Unless you are forced by circumstance to tear down and rebuild (i.e., sell houses to the bank

---

* But note that the Baltic and Mediterranean monopoly is cheaper, even in fully developed form, and with hotels has a 75 percent higher average rent.

to raise cash), the cost of a monopoly is effectively a one-time thing, even though it will usually be paid over a period of time. Revenue—rent—however, is a continuing affair. Thus, as I have mentioned before, the longer the game goes on, the better the expensive properties (the reds, yellows, and greens) will do. A player who owns the oranges and the light blues—and none of the more expensive monopolies—has an excellent chance of winning the basic game. Unless, however, there are four or more players and the expensive monopolies are divided equally among the others, that same player will probably lose the advanced game. If you do not have one of the most expensive monopolies—and do not have a good chance of getting one—do not let the game progress into the late stage.

We have already noted that property values change according to the stage of development of the game. Let me say further that the importance of any one monopoly—whether it be Boardwalk and Park Place, Baltic and Mediterranean, the oranges, or whatever— varies directly with the number of players in the game and inversely with the lateness of the game. When there are few players, or when the game is in its later stages, a player's overall holdings —his total monopolies—are relatively more important.

Except in the case of the more expensive properties, which tend to become more valuable in the advanced game, the foregoing is an additional reason for "making hay while the sun shines"—i.e., in the early and middle stages of the game. The unique value of Boardwalk and Park Place lies in the fact that their higher percentage return makes them a good bargain for the middle game, while their high rent makes them a good bet in the advanced game.

If, following the above guidelines, you decide your best chances lie in the advanced game, there are several things you can do to help the game move in that direction. Generally, the more money in circulation (including money going into building), the greater the impetus toward the advanced game; and the more players, the more money there is in circulation. Consequently, you should be very careful about helping to eliminate anyone early in the game. Rather than make him mortgage heavily (making his chances for lengthy survival almost nil), you should consider allowing a player who owes you rent to give you property (preferably a monopoly, of course) instead of cash, even if the face value of the property is less than the amount of rent owed. Of course, if he has vast amounts of property, and the required rent would completely bankrupt him (rather than merely crippling him), by all means foreclose.

If you are determined that it will be "advanced game or bust," consider building one or two houses on each of your properties rather than building hotels on one monopoly and leaving the others bare. While this tactic will not increase your stature in the mid-game,* it will tend to prolong the game into the late stage. Why? Because you are keeping the rent down to affordable amounts, and you are, in the long run, spreading the impact of the rents to more people. A hotel rent of $1,000, payable in one chunk by one player, will, in the basic game, probably cripple or bankrupt him. Four players paying $250 apiece (or even two paying $500 apiece) on various house rentals will survive long enough for the game to become advanced.

A more preliminary step involves delaying the formation of monopolies in the early stages of the game, at least until all (or very nearly all) properties have been bought by someone. That is, if it looks as if the monopolies you will end up with are of the high-cost, low-percentage-return variety (reds, yellows, and greens), delay a trade that would give you and the other player monopolies if *his* monopoly is of the low-cost, high-percentage-return sort. In fact, be as obstructionist as possible for *all* trades (many trades involve three-player swaps or are at least conditional upon the cooperation of more than two players). Rarely, if ever, should you sell properties for cash; more generally, do not give up long-term good for short-term good.

To bring the game to a conclusion in the middle stage, you can, in general, reverse the procedures outlined above. In a larger sense, the thrust of the main strategies discussed throughout the Monopoly section is to achieve a victory in the basic game. If, however, you find yourself inexorably bound for, say, the yellows and the greens (and nothing else), the measures just discussed *may* enable you to overcome your disadvantages.

---

* See the later section on building strategies.

The Market for Property

The face price of a property is only the price the player who first lands on it must pay to the bank if he wishes to have immediate, clear title to the property. The property may later be bought or sold at any price mutually agreeable to buyer and seller. For that matter, the original lander may decline to buy at the face price, with the result that the property will be put up for auction.

Generally, the face price is below the actual market value of the property; so it is wise to buy as much property as you can in the early stage of the game. Do not put up property for auction if you can avoid it (even if you are not planning to keep it), unless you are fairly certain you can buy it at a reduced rate. To veteran players I need hardly say that this rarely happens.

You are probably familiar with the plight of the fellow in the multiplayer game who manages to follow in the tracks of someone else, perpetually landing on owned property, with the result that after twice circling the board he is the richest player in the game (in strict cash terms) but has only two or three properties, while everyone else has half a dozen or more. His cash to the contrary notwithstanding, that person is in bad shape, and unless drastic action is taken he will be the first player to go bankrupt.* Such a player should act to convert some of his cash to property, preferably as soon as he feels his rate of acquisition is significantly behind everyone else's and *before* all the properties are bought. Buying property from other players outright at that stage of the game will not be easy; to do so the player may well have to offer what some might consider extravagant amounts. Unfortunately, he has little or no choice in the matter. I suggest trying to buy one of the four cheapest developable monopolies; along with Boardwalk and Park Place (and who is going to sell *them?*), they are the best bets for the basic game, and they are generally considered less important and less valuable than the more expensive monopolies. Ninety-nine players out of a hundred (unless they have read this book) would sooner part with the oranges—even in the early stage of the game—than the greens, and I have been in many games in

---

* Unless he happens to own both Boardwalk and Park Place and promptly builds on them, which would make for a novel and interesting game.

which Baltic and Mediterranean have almost literally been given away.

The most likely target in such a case is perhaps the light blues; their building costs are half the fuchsias' or the oranges' (and the oranges are much less likely to be available, anyway), and the rent and likelihood of landing on them are greater than that of Baltic and Mediterranean. If you manage to obtain a monopoly, build as much as you can; with a little luck, a bankruptcy or two will give you all the property you need.

Much of the above advice can be utilized by those who are not in such dire straights. Try to obtain a good monopoly before all the properties are bought. The first player to monopolize has a distinct advantage not often fully exploited. Again, this is difficult but not impossible to accomplish; most players are not going after the same properties you are.

Some examples: you own New York, Tennessee, and Pennsylvania; Jackie owns St. James Place and Pacific Avenue. North Carolina is as yet unowned. Jackie might offer you St. James in a straight swap for Pennsylvania, pointing out that the difference in face price was negated by the fact that you were getting a monopoly. Admittedly, the foregoing trade is more likely to occur if Barbara owns North Carolina, and Jackie and Barbara have a trade planned that is conditional upon the deal for the oranges; but in either event, run—do not walk—to the other side of the board and accept the trade before Jackie changes her mind.

Another example: you have two yellows and an orange; Phil has two oranges and a yellow. Instead of making the obvious trade (and probably being made to pay additional cash), suggest that Phil give you his two oranges and take your two yellows. If you request a "suitable" cash compensation (because you are giving him a monopoly with a higher face value)—even if negotiation "forces" you to lessen or eliminate outright this proviso—you can probably bring this trade off. And Phil will be convinced that *he* got the best of the bargain.

Most players prefer property to money and are loath to give up an acquisition except in trade. There is nothing drastically wrong with this tendency, but there are circumstances in which a smart player might sell a piece of property. Example: you have a monopoly on the oranges but lack money to develop them; you also own one of the greens. Al, who has the other two greens, offers you $600—all his cash—for the third green. Unless you feel he will have more money shortly, and will be willing to pay more, go ahead and sell. Without a great deal of cash he will be unable to develop the greens, and six houses on the oranges will be a good start on further development. The sale should probably still be made if circumstances were a little different: e.g., if he also had the fuchsias and you also had the light blues, especially if he had not already developed the fuchsias considerably.* The presence of cash and an undeveloped cheaper monopoly would indicate he was interested in getting—*and developing*—the more expensive one. For reasons which may already be clear and for others which will be elaborated in the next paragraph, such a player is no threat to you.

The following example will probably be viewed as heretical by most Monopoly players: you are in the early stages of the mid-game and own several monopolies, including the oranges, the greens, and at least one other developable (and essentially undeveloped) monopoly. The wealthiest player in the game, who owns one or more monopolies (the exact number is almost irrelevant, unless he owns more property than everyone else put together), and has perhaps $2,000 or more in cash, is interested in (or can be interested in) purchasing outright the monopoly of the greens for, say, $1,500. Take it and use the proceeds to buy hotels on all three of the oranges.

This sale could by itself take victory from his hands and put it into yours. Consider: you are given a good income property (i.e., the developed oranges). Assuming he has taken the rest of his money to build houses on the greens, it will cost you *at most* $150 to land on his property (which formerly would have cost you nothing); on the other hand, if he lands on the oranges (and the odds, as we have seen, are that he will land on them more often than you will land on the greens), he owes you *at least* $950. It is surely superfluous to point out who is profiting from this sort of exchange. Note also that, as a result of the sale, the other player

---

* However, your disposition of the proceeds would be different, assuming you had not yet built on either monopoly. See the section on building strategies.

can no longer afford the rent on the oranges, and to pay it should he land there will require the resale of houses to the bank and probably the mortgaging of property. Reselling the houses he had just built on the greens and mortgaging his just-acquired monopoly will not be enough for even one payment. In fact, unless he can hang on and draw the game out to great length, the more money he has sunk into houses on the greens, the worse off he will be!

Now is perhaps a good time to discuss Boardwalk and Park Place from the standpoint of buying and selling them. Usually the two properties are divided in the early stage, with each owner unwilling to give the monopoly to the other. This is essentially a reasonable attitude, since the monopoly of Boardwalk and Park Place is, to use a bit of pro football parlance, a "game-breaker." Assuming you own one of the two properties, should you keep trying to buy the other or give up and sell the one you have?

Generally, a delay in settling the problem (or a total absence of such a settlement) benefits the other players in the game; it means the temporary (or permanent) absence of a monopoly which would otherwise be a drain on their financial resources. Most particularly, such a delay benefits most the player with an otherwise dominant position in the game, since the monopoly in question is almost certainly the most powerful force in the game and is easily capable of tipping the scales away from that player. If he is *you*, you should be in no great hurry to reach a settlement. On the other hand, if a third party is, in effect, winning the game, then it is to your advantage to come to terms, even if it means that the other fellow involved in the trade gets the Boardwalk and Park Place monopoly.

It is impossible to set an unvarying price tag on one of the blues. If a one-for-one swap were contemplated, the accompanying cash compensation would have to be high (more, certainly, than the difference in face values). On a strict cash basis, $1,000 might be a suitable figure; half that would surely be too low, twice that much too high. It depends on your circumstances, on what you need most. Players will pay high prices in order to acquire the monopoly, and you should be ready and willing to demand them.

The basic question is how much are you willing to pay—either in cash or property—to get Boardwalk (or Park Place), and how much is the other player willing to pay to get Park Place (or Boardwalk). To determine this means considering not only your immediate cash position, but also the other player's, your other monopolies (and his), and your chances of winning the basic game with and without the monopoly in question. For example, it is not a good idea to permit a player to acquire Boardwalk and Park Place if he has the money to develop them immediately, but there may be no way to avoid it. In the final analysis, whoever is willing to offer more will—and "ought to"—get the monopoly.

If, as was suggested previously, you own two of the Railroads, the benefits to be derived from obtaining one or both of the others are great. Conversely, if, after the early stage of the game is over, you have only one Railroad, there is little point to hanging onto it (unless you can get the others); its value alone to you is small, whereas its value to the collector of the Railroads may be quite large.* This means that he should be willing to offer a price in cash or property distinctly in excess of what it would be worth for you to keep it.

Building: The Coup de Grace

Since the basic monopoly rent even of Boardwalk is only $100, and since this sum is hardly enough to bankrupt anyone, it is obvious that the key to eliminating an opponent lies in the high rents afforded by building houses and hotels. Even the worst Monopoly player knows enough to build on his properties—at least some of them.

This leads us to one of the more common errors in playing: most people tend to develop their more expensive properties first. This is not in accord with the basic economics of the game.

Examine the following table:

---

* The principle of differential valuation, again.

Monopoly   Building Investment

	$300	$400	$600	$900	$1200	$1500	
Purples (Baltic and Mediterranean)	$270	$480	$ 700+	—	—	—	
Light blues (Connecticut, Vermont, and Oriental)	$280	$480	$1250	$1700+	—	—	
Fuchsias (Virginia, States, and St. Charles)	$160	$280	$ 480	$1400	$1950	$2400	Maximum Total Rent
Oranges (New York, Tennessee, and St. James)	$220	$360	$ 620	$1700	$2300	$2900	
Reds (Illinois, Indiana, and Kentucky)	$226	$226+	$ 480	$ 800	$1700	$2325	
Yellows (Atlantic, Ventnor, and Marvin Gardens)	$274	$274+	$ 580	$1020	$1980	$2625	
Greens (Pennsylvania, North Carolina, and Pacific)	$254+	$332	$ 410	$ 710+	$1230	$1780+	
Blues (Boardwalk and Park Place)	$275+	$375	$ 775	$1100+	$2500	$2800+	

For reds, yellows, greens, and blues, figures include, where relevant, rent on undeveloped property. "+" indicates cash left over.

Let us grant immediately what everyone already knows: the second property on each side of the board is a better investment than the first, and therefore it is intelligent to develop the second one ahead of the first. (Note in passing, however, that the *average* rent for a fixed investment is higher on Baltic and Mediterranean, because there are only two of them, than on the light blues.) However, in the more usual case in which a player has monopolies from two or more sides of the board, it is generally a good idea to develop the less expensive monopoly first. The usual tendency to the contrary is just bad policy. Witness the astonishing fact that $400 spent on houses on Baltic and Mediterranean (supposedly the worst of the developable monopolies) gives a better return than $400 spent on houses on Boardwalk and Park Place!

For the perpetual doubters, let us examine the following detailed comparison of the results of two development strategies for the same two monopolies: the light blues and the yellows. The first set of figures (A) shows the total rents on all six properties when a player follows the traditional policy of building first on the yellows until hotels have been established there. The second set (B) shows the results when the reverse strategy is adopted. Both sets include the rents from the properties which have not yet been developed. The bottom line shows the gains or losses at each stage from following the suggested strategy.

Building Investment

	$300	$ 600	$ 900	$1200	$1500	$1800	$2100	$2400	$2700	$3000
A:	$314	$ 620	$1060	$2020	$2665	$3015	$3365	$3600	$4340	$5200
B:	$416	$1386	$1908	$2040	$2500	$3210	$4150	$4500	$4850	$5200
Net:	$102	$ 766	$ 848	$ 20	−$ 165	+$ 195	$ 785	$ 900	$ 510	—

Only at one brief stage does the traditional strategy yield a higher return, and in fact the average gain in rent provided by the reverse is a whopping $440! And this, remember, is with the same properties and identical investments.

Let me point out, for those who have not already noticed, the one exception to the general theory: Boardwalk and Park Place (surprise!). The "big two" should be developed before all but the $50-a-house monopolies and possibly the oranges.

Having settled the problem of which monopolies to develop first, we come to the problem of how to develop a monopoly. Frequently, a player is not able to build evenly and one property ends up with one house more or less than the others. Which one? While everyone has his own preference, mine is this: build so as to maximize the total rent of the monopoly. Normally, this means building the "extra" house on the more expensive property, but there are exceptions: e.g., if you have only $200 to spend on the blues, the total rent—and also the average rent—is higher if you build the first house on Park Place rather than Boardwalk. If it makes no difference to the total, maximize your minimum rent and build last on the most expensive property. Example: you have three houses apiece on the yellows and have $300 to build two more. It makes no difference to the total (or average) rent where you build, so ignore Marvin Gardens and build on Ventnor and Atlantic. That way you will get at least $850 if someone lands on your least developed property, whereas if you build differently someone could get by for only $800.

There are several other considerations involved in development theory. The first is that there is no point in building beyond the point at which the wealthiest player in the game cannot afford to pay the rent. For example, if the richest player can come up with no more than $1,500, counting cash on hand and money from reselling houses and mortgaging property, you can build a hotel on

Park Place, but there is no point in building more than four houses on Boardwalk. Use the other $200 to build elsewhere or keep it on hand for emergencies.

Similarly, there is no point to building on Boardwalk and Park Place if your opponents have all just passed Go. You might as well wait for them to reach, say, the vicinity of the B & O Railroad. The houses do not do any good until someone comes close enough to land on them, and in the meantime you may land on someone else's property and need the money to pay the rent. Conversely, of course, the best time to build is when your opponents are five to ten spaces in front of your monopoly.

Finally, there is the concept of marginal revenue, which in this context we may define as the net increase in rent provided by the addition of one house to the property. An examination of the deeds of the various properties will show that the marginal revenue for any of them is neither constant nor proportional to either total or marginal cost. For example (in case I have managed to confuse some of you), the rent on Boardwalk with one house is $200; the marginal cost is $200 (the cost of the house), and the marginal revenue is only $100 (its rent with one house minus its undeveloped rent, $100). The cost of a second house is still $200 (for the moment let us ignore the fact that we must be building on Park Place, also; it will do no harm to our calculations), but the marginal revenue is $400 ($600−$200, the rent with one house). More amazingly, the marginal revenue with the third house is $800—four times the marginal cost. However, the upward trend does not continue: marginal revenue for four houses is only $300; ditto for a hotel.

In fact, nearly all properties show a marginal revenue peak at the level of three houses (the exceptions are Baltic, peaking at four houses, and its partner, Mediterranean, which does not peak until a hotel is built), although it is not quite so pronounced as Boardwalk's.

All this may be very interesting, at best (you may be thinking), but what good is it? Just this: a question plaguing any player with $100 or more in cash is, do I build with it or do I hold onto it for use in emergencies? A decision must take into account many factors, not least of which, as has been suggested, is the positions of the players on the board. Another major factor is the marginal revenue involved; since the addition of one house can result in a rental increase out of all proportion to the actual cost of the house, it is intelligent to gamble on building when the rewards (i.e., the marginal revenue) are high, and perhaps to save your money when the prospective increase in rent is not particularly large. Specifically, this means that a short-range goal of three houses is not a bad idea and is in fact almost certainly worth going short on cash or even mortgaging undeveloped property.

Do not be afraid to mortgage. Obviously, the more properties you have mortgaged, the less likely that someone will land on a paying property. On the other hand, no one goes bankrupt by paying ordinary rents, either, and you are in the game to win— which means to bankrupt other players. The few dollars in rent lost by mortgaged property is normally more than balanced by the hundreds or thousands of dollars of rent created by the building of a few houses.

The standard game of monopoly is subject to building shortages, especially near the onset of the late stage. Like most of the other aspects of the game, this, too, is a fruitful subject for analysis and use. Most players can detect the imminence of a building shortage; fewer act to minimize their losses therefrom, and fewer still take positive advantage of it.

To begin with, building shortages do not just "happen." They are caused by the actions of the players, and there is no reason why one particular player—*you*—cannot be the prime mover. If you own the oranges, the light blues, and Baltic and Mediterranean, and have $2,200, you yourself can create a housing shortage by building four houses on each property. If, in fact, you can do this, it would be the sheerest folly to do otherwise. If all the houses are "in use," players can build only by paying the large sum necessary to build a hotel (that is, without the intermediate steps of one, two, three, and four houses). This is not likely to be the case, particularly if their properties are expensive (i.e., $150 or $200 a house). Nor are they likely to be able to accumulate the money, with your high rents draining their funds and their own extremely low rents and $200 salary their own sources of income.

It would be naive to protest that a hotel would give a higher rent than four houses. It is true, of course, but the additional one or two hundred dollars of rent per property is more than offset by the hundreds and hundreds of dollars in rent thereby available to the other players.

Building shortages are easier to bring about if houses already exist on various properties, but the benefits for you are reduced. It is important to realize that, just as it is easiest to create a housing shortage if you own the less expensive properties, so is it vital, if you own those properties, to be on the "inside" rather than the "outside" of a shortage. In such a situation, the few houses (if there are any) available from the bank must be sold at auction; obviously the owner of a $50-a-house monopoly will have trouble competing on even terms with the owner of a $200-a-house monopoly. A bid of $200 for a house is nothing more than normal in the one case, but in the other is four times the customary cost.

In general, a building shortage not controlled or initiated by one particular player will be hardest on the owners of undeveloped properties in general and undeveloped expensive monopolies in particular; on the other hand, if the shortage is not total, and if some houses are available, the owner of the inexpensive monopolies will lose some of his advantage. Note, however, that because of the general pattern of marginal revenue, the owner of an inexpensive monopoly who had two houses already on his properties might reasonably be able to outbid the owner of a more expensive monopoly who was just beginning to build.

Rules Variations

There are several fairly common variations from the standard game of Monopoly, some of them sanctioned by the publisher, some not. All of them in varying degrees affect the play of the game and, therefore, affect the strategies involved.

Parker Brothers suggests two short games, one (in which the game ends after the second bankruptcy) which, following their usage, we shall term the "short" game; the other we shall call the "time limit" game, for the obvious reason that it is played only for a certain length of time. The general effect of both variants is to reduce the possibility that the game will reach the late stage; in this regard they merely reinforce the strategies discussed heretofore. The short game, in particular, because of the three-house rule (which allows jumping from three houses to a hotel, and which, incidentally, drastically reduces the possibility of a building short-age), increases the advantage of whoever can monopolize and develop first. However, both variants do have one factor mitigating against the previously recommended strategy of obtaining and de-veloping the less expensive monopolies first: because neither game is played to a conclusion, the winner is determined by a compara-tive assessment of wealth, including the face value of his property and buildings. The difficulty here is that such assessment can be said to measure input, not output: i.e., it measures how much money a player has put into a property; it does not measure (ex-cept indirectly and partially) what he has gotten out of it. For instance, the face value assessment of two houses on New York Avenue would be the same ($200) as one house on Pennsylvania Avenue, despite the fact that the rent would be higher in the first case ($220) than in the second ($150). The judgment structure of the short and time limit games is effectively biased toward the theoretical, traditional value of properties and against what I am suggesting is the "real" value (at least in games which do not last a very long time).

Another fairly common variant is designed to bypass the early stage of the game entirely and get down to the "nitty gritty" imme-diately. This is accomplished by dealing out all the properties to the players. There may or may not be a token payment, but in any case the players do not usually (and, often, cannot) pay for all the properties. Generally, a flurry of trading precedes the first roll of the dice, and houses are ubiquitous before the first round is over. The tendency to equalize properties, monopolies, and money obvi-ously goes against standard early and middle stage strategy, and in fact the coupling of the omnipresence of simultaneously develop-able monopolies and a high cash flow tends to bring on the late stage quickly, thus shifting considerable value toward the expen-sive monopolies (the familiar reds, yellows, and greens). This, obviously, has dire consequences for general property theory, and you must adjust your strategies accordingly. Building strategies and many other aspects of the general discussion remain un-changed, however.

A variant that occurs most often when two Monopoly sets are available entails the possibility of building a hotel *and* four houses on a given property (i.e., after a hotel is built, you can add up to four houses; rent is simply the sum of the hotel and house rent figures). If this variant is played using only one set, it seems to have precisely the opposite effect of the variation mentioned in the paragraph above; and even if two sets are used, allowing increased building should reinforce the advantages of the low-investment, high-return properties. It should be mentioned in passing that if two Monopoly sets are used, building shortages do not, in practice, occur.

The selling or granting of immunities usually occurs in connection with one of two distinctly different events. Often, when a player lands on a property whose rent he cannot easily afford (when it would either bankrupt him completely or merely force him to sell back houses or mortgage properties), he may offer, in lieu of full payment in cash, the privilege of landing rent-free on certain (or all) of his properties for some specified time period. This notion has been implicitly discussed before: allowing an opponent to mitigate the effects of paying rent is *not* going to maximize your chances for winning the game. On the other hand, if positions are reversed, it is often not a bad idea to grant some sort of immunity rather than take a double loss from turning in buildings, particularly if it is a multiplayer game or if your overall property situation is much better than the other player's, or both.

The granting of immunities also may occur when a player sells a piece of property to another player. If the owner of Park Place, for instance, is selling out to the player who owns Boardwalk, the receipt of an immunity for either or both properties will obviously lessen the advantage of the player who will be getting the monopoly. Such immunities, however or whenever granted, are not true variations in that while they are not expressly mentioned in the rules, neither is there anything in the rules which would tend to exclude them.

Something else which is not explicitly covered in the rules, but should be added, regards bankruptcy. Often, a player who is bankrupted by landing on a high-rent property will either sell his remaining property for a pittance to a third party (rather than let it fall into the hands of the player who delivered the *coup de grace*) or will mortgage it all before turning it over to his creditor (thus costing the creditor an additional 10–20 percent of the property's mortgage value). Such practices would not be permitted in real life, are contrary to the spirit of the game, and should be prohibited.* As long as a player is a free agent, he can deal with his property as he sees fit, mortgaging it or not, or even selling it to Joe for less than Jeff has bid—if such is his desire. However, when his debts exceed his cash on hand and the potential mortgaged value of his property, he is no longer a free agent, and he cannot legitimately sell a property for less than its mortgage value or, in fact, less than his creditor is willing to bid for it.

Perhaps the most common rule variation is one which many players believe is the ordinary way to play, despite the explicit paragraph in the rules to the contrary. This involves "Free Parking." According to the rules, this is an empty space; a player landing thereon pays no fines or rents and receives no rewards of any kind (hence the title "*Free* Parking"). Many people, nonetheless, believe that fines and taxes (but not money paid to buy property or build houses) paid to the bank ought to go instead into a pot which would be won by whoever landed on "Free Parking." In the long run, disregarding lucky streaks, the net effect of this "bingo" rule is to increase the amount of cash available to the players; it increases everyone's net wealth. In the short run, this may benefit most the person in the best position to utilize these funds (the first person to monopolize, or the person with the best early investment structure), but it is in the short run that the effects of chance are strongest. In general, the more money in circulation at any time, the greater the chances that the game will proceed into the late stage and the smaller the advantage provided by following the general strategy.

More than this, however, the addition of any further element of chance will tend to minimize the degree to which a player can improve his position by using *any* strategy or plan. Obviously, a player landing on "Free Parking" is, in the above variant, gaining money he has not earned through superior play, greater intelligence, or a better strategy. There is little point to injecting any additional elements of luck—as opposed to skill—in a game played by adults.

---

* This applies to certain other games in this chapter as well.

FINANCE® AND EASY MONEY®

Monopoly addicts will find themselves in familiar territory with Finance (Parker Brothers) and Easy Money (Milton Bradley); players move tokens around boards which are similar but even more archaic in appearance according to the roll of the dice, buy and sell properties, collect rent, build houses, and draw chance cards (called "Give and Take" cards in Easy Money). Nonetheless, there are differences significant enough to affect proper strategy.

The most obvious difference is a lack of monopolies. The closest thing to it in either game is a rule in Easy Money which stipulates that players cannot develop their property until they have one property on each side of the board. Moreover, a player cannot purchase additional property until he *does* own something on all four sides of the board. The purpose of this "Rule of Four" is, presumably, to minimize the effect of chance (which, in Monopoly, can lead in the early game to players' owning widely disproportionate amounts of property); however, as is so often the case in real life, the effect of the rule is considerably different from its apparent intention: the person who is first to acquire his fourth property (possibly at an "auction" in which he is the only player eligible to bid!) can wield a power over his rivals that would shame the most hardened Monopoly tyrant. It is not merely that he is the only one who can build houses (though this in itself, of course, is often fatal to some of his adversaries); worse, perhaps, his presence at the frequent auctions gives him the choice of most of the board's properties and ensures that, if an opponent does obtain his fourth property, it is at so dear a cost that his development is throttled at the outset.

The directions state that the "Rule of Four" should be ignored when more than six play, but I suggest that you ignore it when more than *four* play. Or, if that seems too drastic, then change the "Rule of Four" to a "Rule of Three": i.e., a player can build houses and acquire additional property as soon as he owns properties on any three sides. While keeping the apparent aims of the original rule, this change should minimize its abuses.

Finance is, in effect, Easy Money without the "Rule of Four." The only restriction on building is that no one may build until he

has gone around the board once. The first player around, therefore, should immediately erect houses on a property he owns on
the first row (if he has one) and hope to wipe out one or more of
the other players as they pass Go (Start) before they can retaliate.
The single largest factor of chance in the game is the identity of the
first player to circle the board, but it is up to him to take full
advantage of it.

In both games, as in Monopoly, it pays to build intensively, but
unlike the restrictions in Monopoly, in either of these games a
player can sell or trade *developed* properties, complete with
houses. Indeed, it often pays to do so. There is no "mortgaging" in
Finance. A player may resell property and houses to the bank for
half-price, but he does not retain title to the property; as a conse-
quence, he can usually get a better deal from another player. There
are mortgages in Easy Money, but to a Monopoly habitué they will
seem peculiar: the mortgage is *higher* than the theoretical purchase
price (which, of course, makes buying any property for less than
its mortgage value worthwhile), but it is not affected by extra
houses, which *cannot* be sold back to the bank. There is a strong
incentive, therefore, to mortgage properties early in the game (to
get the cash required to develop other property), but to *sell* developed property rather than mortgage it.

With this in mind, it would seem at first glance that the opportunities for trading are wider in these games than in Monopoly,
but, unfortunately, such is not the case. In general, in a game or
elsewhere, you only trade (or buy or sell—a "trade" for money)
when you believe you will benefit from the transaction. Since this
is equally true of everyone else, a trade can be consummated only
because of the principle of differential valuation (introduced in
chapter 3). For obvious reasons, a property in Monopoly which
gives me a monopoly is worth far more *to me* than an "odd"
property of similar face value; similarly, I would prefer the
oranges to the reds, whereas a Monopoly traditionalist would
rather have the latter than the former. While the basic property
structure of both games is like Monopoly's (i.e., the properties get
progressively more expensive as you proceed around the board),
there is in Finance and Easy Money no such difference between
the apparent, or traditional, value, and the "real" value. In the
former game those values coincide (the expensive properties offer

the best return); in the latter, because of the fixed relationship between price and rent, there is little to choose between properties. Nor is it possible, because of the restrictions of the "Rule of Four" on extra property, to have a trade in which both players get monopolies. As a result, trading is limited primarily to the final stages of both games, as players attempt to stave off bankruptcy by selling their property outright or trading it for something less expensive.

Easy Money's superficially greater complexity is largely illusory, but there is an element of *tactical* complexity owing to the game's biggest difference from Monopoly or Finance: a game of Easy Money ends after the *first* bankruptcy. This is more significant than it looks. For example: if you are not ahead, you don't *want* to bankrupt anyone—a fact which may influence how many houses you put on a property. Further, if it looks as if one player is in imminent danger of bankruptcy, it will pay you to buy any developed and mortgaged property you can get your hands on, unmortgage it, and increase your score when the end comes.

In fact, since bankruptcies can occur suddenly and without warning, and since good *playing* tactics are not necessarily the same as good *scoring* tactics, I suggest, as a house rule, that all players be allowed to mortgage and/or unmortgage whatever property they wish after the bankruptcy occurs and before tallying the score. (Public Buildings should at this time be mortgaged and developed properties unmortgaged whenever possible.)

Of the two, Easy Money has the advantage that no one is left out of the game after going bankrupt, but it is slow-paced and dull until play has reached the "building" stage—which takes a while. Finance develops much faster and play proceeds more quickly throughout than either Easy Money or Monopoly—at least until there are only two players left, when the prohibition against owning more than eight properties acts to postpone the end somewhat. On balance, I have a marginal preference for Finance over Easy Money (although the latest edition of the latter game, with its plastic trays and money rack, is a model of what internal packaging should be); but if the "Rule of Four" were relaxed, there would be little to choose between them. Lacking the scope and complexity of Monopoly, both games are certain to remain "poor relations" at best, and Monopoly fans who are looking for a little variety might do better to pick from one of the other games in this chapter.

CAREERS®

Careers (Parker Brothers) has always seemed to me to be under-rated as a family game, though I have no idea why this should be so. It is a friendly game, not at all cutthroat; no one is eliminated due to bankruptcies, and since the specific success formulae are secret, suspense and hope are maintained to the end. The rules are lengthy, but the game is easily understood, and Junior can play on fairly even terms with Mom and Dad. The players are sufficiently independent of each other that one person's blunders will not materially hinder or help anyone else, and, indeed, the players play as much "against" the game as their opponents.

For newcomers to Careers, it should be explained that the winner of the game is the first person to achieve a success formula he or she has fixed: it is a mixture of money, fame, and happiness in any ratio as long as the total adds up to 60 points—e.g., $20,000, twenty fame units (stars), and twenty happiness units (hearts). A player accumulates these points by traveling around the board in the usual fashion, but there are opportunities for side trips along various "career" subpaths. The notion of controlling your own destiny—setting your own standards for success and choosing whatever careers you fancy—is, unfortunately, unusual in a board game, but it's a good one.

This leads us to the obvious question: is one success formula better than another? As far as I can tell (and I have played the game for many years), there is no surefire winning formula. On the other hand, there are some *losing* ones: 60-0-0 (regardless of the categories involved), for instance. As a rough guideline, the largest category should probably have no more than 30 and the smallest no less than 10. A first-time player is probably as well off with the common 20-20-20 success formula as any other, until he develops his own preferences in careers. The major element of strategy in the game lies in pursuing a choice of careers suitable to whatever formula you have devised.

Careers has recently undergone a substantial face lifting: the board has been redesigned, new careers have been substituted for some of the old ones (e.g., Going to Sea is now Teaching), and although the rewards or punishments doled out on each square are identical in almost all cases, there is a whole new set of captions.

Toward these changes I remain neutral. Some are obvious and, if anything, overdue; running away to seek passage on a tramp steamer is, to say the least, *passé* (although the carryover requirement of $100 for union dues—instead of a college degree—may seem too painfully timely to be amusing). The change from Hollywood to The Arts, on the other hand, seems gratuitous, and the rewards of Uranium Prospecting look rather strange wrapped in the mantle of its successor, Sports. In real life, professional athletes achieve a fame second only to politicians and movie stars (and, for better or worse, considerably ahead of astronauts); yet, on the new board, Sports offers the niggardly total of two stars while Space boasts no fewer than forty! The change from Prospecting to Sports did have some far-reaching consequences, but to deal with them we must first examine a player's choice of careers.

A player's opportunities to enter careers are to some degree dependent on chance (as well as his ability to trade "opportunity" cards with other players), but generally he will choose to enter those careers which will make the most progress toward achieving his success formula. Farming (now Ecology) and Going to Sea were easy to enter; both gave hearts and little else. The more expensive and valuable careers lay on the far side of the board (as usual), which held a near-monopoly on fame. Specifically, Uranium Prospecting (for money and happiness) and the Expedition to the Moon—now Space—(for fame and money) were most often the keys to victory. The cheapest way to enter these most expensive careers (except for the lucky draw of the right "special opportunity" card) was to go to College and get the proper degree: Engineering (for Prospecting) or Science (for the Moon).

But now comes the change. Since anyone knows it is unnecessary to have an engineering degree to be an athlete, the game designers shifted that degree to Space and the science degree to Ecology, and allowed entrance into Sports with *any* degree. Not at all unreasonable, except that, where there were formerly three valuable degrees, there are now but two (Engineering and Law—the latter for those inclined toward Politics). The first player into college will take the engineering degree, and the others can take their time about getting an education (there is no duplication of the "specialized" degrees, you see, but *any* degree will get you into Sports). Thus, in a roundabout fashion, going to College has been de-emphasized.

Space is undoubtedly the most attractive single career, offering a total of $15,000, 40 stars, and 20 hearts. It is also the most hazardous, however; so it should be approached carefully (especially if you are considering a second trip through). A few "experience" cards (which can be substituted for throws of the dice) would come in particularly handy. These are collected upon completion of any career, and a skillful player may repeatedly utilize a cheap career like Ecology or Teaching primarily for the cards gained thereby.

Armed with these tips, a decent success formula, and an intelligent playing strategy, you will win your share and more, but if the dice are going against you (for the element of luck in the game *is* strong), relax and enjoy the game; there's always next time.

RATRACE®

Ratrace (House of Games) has many of the virtues of Careers: it's a friendly game, it doesn't take too long (an hour or so), and no one is eliminated (players who go bankrupt can start over, and are not necessarily hopelessly out of the running).

The game is played on a board with three concentric paths (traversed, as usual, via rolls of the dice), each representing a different social class. In order to change classes (and paths) and eventually win the game, a player must have an increasing amount of cash, the proper social connections, and status symbols of the appropriate class. Players are not required to advance to the Upper Class, but in practice to do otherwise is a losing course.

Each player owns a business (all of which are equal in value); when other players land on the business they must pay "rent" in the form of a purchase, which may be a cheap, ordinary item or a higher-priced "status symbol." Since these last are necessary for social advancement, the cheaper alternative cannot always be chosen. Although the social aspects of the game may seem quaint,* the flavor of the economics is more pleasant—and more realistic—than Monopoly's. In order to get ahead, you must, perforce, help others to get ahead; every time you spend money, it must, by definition, end up in someone else's hands—a fact ignored by critics of lunar landings and rich men's extravagances.

There are six businesses, one for each possible player; when fewer people play, the bank runs the extra ones. By buying status symbols from these bank-owned businesses, you *can* keep your money out of the pockets of your opponents—a sneaky trick, but only partially effective. You need four status symbols, and the bank would at most own two (when three play, each owns two businesses); so you still have to get some of them elsewhere. Moreover, if you determine to wait until you can buy from the bank's businesses, uncooperative dice rolls may keep you in the same class long after your more easy-going competitors have "moved up."

It pays to be the first to change classes at either level: not only do you get the jump on your opponents, but also you can sell them your old status symbols (and regain thereby some of their cost). This effect reaches the point of diminishing returns after the second or third player moves up (depending on the number in the game), by which point the number of bidders for your discarded status symbols is so few that the return is minimal.

The real way to make money in the game, regardless of status, is through the two great gambling opportunities: the Racetrack and the Stock Market. Both of them are prejudiced *in favor* of the player; i.e., both are winning propositions. You will lose sometimes, but in the long run you should at least double your money.

The Stock Market's bias is not hard to discern. Seven, the most common as well as the average roll (i.e., the median, the mode, *and* the mean), is the break-even point. However, the worst that can happen is that you lose your investment; the best is not that it will double (an even-money proposition) but that it will yield an elevenfold return. Thus, while there is, on a single dice roll, an equal chance of gaining or losing *something*, the rewards will, over time, greatly exceed the losses. However, you are not limited to a

---

* The people I know have about as much interest in status symbols as my cats, but then maybe they're unusually sane.

single throw at a time; if unsatisfied with the first throw, you can continue for as many times as there are other players in the game. The combination of factors makes this as close to a sure thing as you are likely to find.

What follows is a table of acceptable rolls—i.e., those throws of the dice on which you should take your winnings and stop gambling. There are two sets of figures given, for two different investment personalities: the "liberal" is concerned solely with maximizing his long-term gains (even at the risk of some short-term losses); the "conservative" wants to make money, of course, but he also wants to minimize the chance that he will lose any part of his investment. Choose the one that suits you. The conservative will lose money somewhat less often; the liberal will make more money in the long run. "Rolls left" simply means the number of people not yet tried—the number of chances remaining after the roll in question.

Rolls Left:	Four	Three	Two	One	
	10	9	8	8	Conservative
Acceptable Roll:					
	10	10	10	9	Liberal

The Racetrack is a little riskier but still worth the gamble. I will go a bit more into probability theory in the next chapter, but for now let me point out a few facts about dice and the laws of chance, or probability. As is fairly obvious, if you roll a single die, the odds that a particular number will come up are one in six (which can also be expressed as "five to one against"). What some people don't realize is that, with *two* dice, the total is equally predictable but much less even. For example, a seven will come up six times as often as a two. Indeed, if you graphed the results of a large number of throws, you would find the numbers formed a pyramid (an angular version of the famous bell-shaped curve beloved of teachers everywhere), with seven at the top and in the center, and two and twelve at the bottom, at either end.

Taking this into account, the Ratrace Racetrack has weighted the outcomes, making an unlikely roll more rewarding, to even things up.* They were not altogether successful at this, however. First, by giving the player three chances, they tipped the scales considerably in his favor. Second, since the rewards involved are not *exactly* inversely proportional to the likelihood of their occurrence, some numbers *are* better than others. The Stock Market conservative will bet on seven (and win more *often* than anyone else), but the liberal will win about 20 percent *more* in the long run by betting on five or nine.

In sum, don't be afraid to buy on credit (but don't go overboard); buy higher-class status symbols if you happen to have the money (but don't worry if you don't); and, while you shouldn't risk anything you can't afford to lose, put as much as you can (as often as you can) into the Stock Market and the Racetrack.

MOVIE MOGULS®

Movie Moguls (RGI/Athol) is Monopoly's West Coast relative— its Hollywood cousin, so to speak. The "properties" are famous movies (*Boom Town, High Noon, A Night at the Opera*); the "houses" which are added to increase the rent are the stars of the movie—three per picture (e.g., Tyrone Power, Linda Darnell, and Rita Hayworth for *Blood and Sand*). A player landing on a Star Agency space (or his own production) can draw the top several cards from the "star" pile and purchase any which belong to his movies (or, failing that, one which strikes his fancy, for sale or trade later on) for an amount equal to $100,000 times the roll of two dice. Since each player starts out with only a few million dollars, acquiring a movie and its stars can be a relatively expensive proposition.

This, in fact, is one of the game's major difficulties; there is no real cash inflow (you don't collect a salary for passing Go, for instance). Thus, on average, everyone gets progressively poorer as the game progresses. There are two sets of "chance" cards, but the production and publicity cards actually drain off more money than they pour out, and it can be *hours* before the Awards cards are available.

---

* A similar thing was done with the "occupations" in Whitman's Stock Market Game, discussed in the last chapter.

In the long run, the expensive properties are the most valuable, since the overall cost is mainly proportional to the expense of acquiring the stars, but the return is proportional to the "production cost" (i.e., the purchase price). On the other hand, it is always worthwhile to buy any movie property at auction for less than 80 percent of its "face value," since you can always sell it back to the bank for that much. Building extensively versus building intensively (that is, having a star of each of several movies as opposed to having all three stars of a single movie) is not usually a matter of choice; nor does it make a difference in the total rent involved. However, you only become eligible for the Awards (which involve cash bonuses as well as increased rent) when you have a "completed production" (a movie with all three stars). Unfortunately, getting to that point generally takes a while.

The packaging could certainly be improved (punching out all four sets of cards is a real drag), but slow development is the biggest flaw of Movie Moguls. It is not a bad game, and despite its torpid pace the novelty of play and the subject matter will carry you through the first hour or two, but only insomniacs, lovers of the Late Show, and hardened game fanatics are likely to get much beyond that point.

Variations for a quicker game are included in the rules, but Speed Game No. 2 ("Financial Success Winner") is no help at all because, as I have noted, players get progressively poorer; and the choice of a winner after a reasonable time limit (Speed Game No. 3) is apt to seem distinctly arbitrary. Only Speed Game No. 1, which calls for an initial auction of some of the production cards, is likely to help, but don't expect a miracle cure.

AIRPORT®

Airport (Dynamic Design) suffers from some of the same problems of pace as Movie Moguls; it is difficult for one player to get significantly ahead of his opponents, and the game tends to drag on forever. In physics terms, both games lack negative entropy (something that would cause significant change or progress).

In Airport, players buy or lease jets, which they place on a variety of cross-country routes between key U.S. cities. Each route is composed of a series of circles with numbers ("fares") printed on them; when a player lands on the appropriate space on the main (outside) path of the board, the bank pays all players with jets on the route a fare based on the numbered circle occupied by the last jet in line. (The numbers usually diminish.) Picking the best routes for your jets may seem obvious: find the route with the highest-numbered circle still available and place your jet thereon. Child's play.

Fortunately (for it would otherwise be a very dull game), it is not quite so simple. Some routes (e.g., LAX-DAL or LAX-NYC) have more squares on the main path than others and, consequently, pay off more often. To get a more accurate picture, the printed fare must be "weighted"—that is, multiplied by the number of route squares for that route. Thus, the low-priced ($10,-000) Los Angeles–San Francisco corridor (LAX-SFO), due to its multiplicity of squares, has an expected return (or "weighted fare") of $40,000—making it the equal of anything on the board except the very lucrative Los Angeles–New York run.

I suspect that some of you are looking rather smug at this point, having deduced all this the moment you set eyes on the board. My congratulations. Of course, you *have* considered the problem of marginal revenue, haven't you?* (Was that a groan from the back row?)

Consider a simple example: the first circle of the LAX-DAL route is marked $35 (all such figures are in thousands though, to be more realistic, they should be in millions; all the game's figures are too small by an approximate factor of a thousand), and the second is marked $20. Since there are *two* corresponding squares on the main path, the expected return is therefore $70 and $40, respectively. Suppose you occupied the first circle at the beginning of the game (not, by the way, a bad move), and now, at a later point, you see that nowhere else on the board is there an open circle which would give you an expected return as high as $40. So you place a second jet on the LAX-DAL route. A mistake. With one jet on the first circle, your expected return was $70; with two jets, your *net* expected return is only $80—$20 (the rent under the last, or second, circle) times two (the number of squares on the

---

* Laggards can reread the section on Monopoly.

board) times two (the number of your jets on the route)—an actual increase in revenue of only $10 (again, thousands)! You could hardly do worse!*

Suitably chastened, you transfer your jet to a more rewarding position, only to be genuinely annoyed when another player places his jet on the very circle you abandoned as not being worthwhile. A blunder on his part? Not at all. From his point of view, such a move represents a clear gain of $40, with the added bonus that it reduces *your* revenue on the route from $70 to $40—an irresistible combination. All routes—except LAX-SFO and CHI-NYC (the fares of which remain constant regardless of the number of jets on them)—have points at which it does not pay an occupant of the route to add a jet, but it does pay an outsider to play there. Differential valuation, again.

As a general rule, anything promising a net expected return of less than $20,000 is a dubious proposition, and a jet getting a fare of only $10,000 will probably never pay for itself.

The question of leasing versus buying jets confronts a player throughout the game, and if its importance is overshadowed by proper route selection (and, perhaps, sheer luck), it is certainly material. Perhaps the best policy is leasing judiciously at the beginning and then converting to ownership as soon as possible. To this basic idea, however, can be added a number of helpful hints. It's generally reasonable to lease just *after* passing "Start" (to get the most for your money) and to buy just *before;* since you must pass "Start" twice between the time you order the jets and the time you actually get them, this minimizes the actual time/distance involved.

On the turn that you pass Start, you receive (and finish paying for) jets from the factory, pay interest, and renew leases; however, there is nothing in the rules which states the *order* in which these operations are to be done. Moreover, you can retire a lease at any time by turning in a lease card and one jet (N.B.: *any* jet). If you have reached the stage that conversion from leasing to owning looks desirable, there seems to be no reason for not paying for your new jets and using them at once to retire your leases—thus

---

* Actually, you *could* do worse; in some situations, the addition of a jet to a route will actually *decrease* your revenue!

avoiding what would be, in effect, the double payment cost of renewing those leases.

Another interesting variation on this ploy can be used to get around the most troublesome squares on the board, the Maintenance Bases. When a player lands on one of these, he has to take a jet off each route indicated and leave it marooned on the Maintenance Base until he can get entirely around the board again and put it back into service. When this happens, use these "out-of-service" jets to retire any leases you may have—at once! Then lease new jets and put them back on the routes where they will do you some good. If you own all of your jets, you can lease one, put it in service, and "retire" one of your stranded jets (and the lease) —continuing the process until all the jets in question have been "rescued" thereby. It will cost you, but it is usually worth it.

Unlike many games in this chapter, no more than four people can play Airport. If you play long enough to achieve the victory criterion prescribed in the rules, you're likely to get so bored that, afterward, the game will sit on the shelf and collect dust. If, instead, you set a time limit for the session (two hours might be a reasonable period) and stop playing before you get tired of it, you will be much more willing to play it again another day.

THE GAME OF LIFE®

A friend of mine once observed that one way to tell a bad game was to visit the second-hand stores a short time after a major holiday, to see what newly bought gifts were discarded. Nine times out of ten, the winner of this "unpopularity" poll was The Game of Life (Milton Bradley). Which perhaps shows that people have more taste than is often thought.

The game is so dominated by chance that it provides little challenge for a thinking young person, much less an adult, but this is not, to my mind, its major offense. Ostensibly mirroring reality, the game in fact propagates all the worst values of the 1950s-era middle class (as a matter of course, all players in the game get married, have children, buy cars and houses, and take out life insurance), and is not only *un*realistic but often *anti*-realistic. At the end of the game, for example, each player gets a large monetary bonus from the bank *for having children*. There are, for some people, considerable rewards in raising children, but (unless you're Rodney Allen Rippy's mother), they aren't monetary. Children cost—and more than just money. The contrary idea (or the equally hare-brained notion that the worth of a man—or a woman —is somehow measured by the number of his children) is exactly the sort of idiocy that leads to population problems.

Life is an insult to an adult and a meretricious influence on impressionable children. Would that the game had been aborted; as it is, it's a long overdue candidate for euthanasia.

BOTTOMS UP®

Despite its dubious dress and tawdry company (it is usually found with such games as Seduction, Adultery, etc.), Bottoms Up (Taurus Creations, manufactured by Golden's) is a rather straightforward example of the sort of game covered in the rest of this chapter. The motif is college; in the course of their travels around the board (attending classes or campus events), the players try to accumulate points (credits) by answering questions. Sample: "Name ten NFL teams in ten seconds." If you cannot answer correctly, you must pay a forfeit (like taking a drink). The game can go on until one player has reached 30 points (or credit hours—i.e., one year) or, for long games, 120 points (4 years and a degree).

The problem, as you might guess from the sample, is that the questions are not at all easy, even without any alcohol in your system. With the addition of the drinks—even small ones—the game tends to go on for hours before one player gets within shooting range of even thirty points, and everyone is either frustrated or smashed, or both.

BEAT DETROIT®

In their different ways, Beat Detroit (Dynamic Design), Woman & Man (Dynamic Design), and Anti-Monopoly (Anti-Monopoly, Inc.) are typical of the spate of "contemporary" or "cause"-oriented games to have hit the market in recent years. As games, they range from flawed to unplayable. Often, they are little more than propaganda devices for whatever cause they happen to be pushing.

Beat Detroit is a light-hearted game, enjoyable for a while, though not the sort that you would play very often. Each player starts with a new car and tries to be the first one to go 50,000 miles (five times around the board) while running a disheartening gauntlet of accidents, tolls, fines, and astronomical repair bills. Like The Peter Principle Game (which we'll get to shortly), Beat Detroit is less a race than a survival test. Illustrative of the flavor of the game as well as the authors' biases is the fact (noted by others) that the only place on the board where nothing happens is the square marked "Write a Letter to Detroit."

Be warned: it is a *long* game, and there are few opportunities for tactical skill and decision-making. Luck is overwhelmingly important. For those who wish to indulge in this mildly enjoyable masochism, I will offer a few tips.

When in a new car, always challenge the "Big 3" (the "independent" service stations, which, in effect, often pad the bill). In a used car, challenge them whenever the basic (untripled) service charge is $120 or more. Otherwise don't fight them; countersuit will cost you more in the long run than you would save in repair bills. Don't use your warranty coupons for "cheap" repairs (save them for parts bills of $100 or more).

Being forced to buy an extra car (to "keep up with the Joneses") can be a pain, but it should make you money if you don't sell until you roll doubles and can get $1,000 for it. Try to hold out unless you're desperately short of cash. In case of an accident, you can sell the car instead of suing, but it's still better to sue now and sell later. Finally, the crush at the beginning of the game is not the only time it's handy to have insurance; get it and keep it.

WOMAN & MAN®

Woman & Man (like its predecessor from the same publisher, Blacks & Whites, a *Psychology Today* game) is a race to be the first to cross the finish line with 100 status points. Since you can't get past a certain point without the proper score, this requires several circuits of the board. Supposedly in order to explore the "problem" of the equality of the sexes, the game is biased heavily against women (or against players of either sex who take female roles in the game); there are two sets of each of the several "chance" cards—one "male" and the other "female"—and the rewards of each square vary according to sex.

This bias ruins the game as a contest. The setup strongly encourages the women to team up (while forbidding men to do so), but to win a woman would have to (a) team up, (b) be incredibly lucky, and (c) win an overwhelming majority of her "confrontations." Confrontations are contests for points and are of two sorts: either a high-card "showdown" with the "confrontation" decks (with the odds, of course, against the woman) or a quiz based on a flock of esoteric questions the answers to which are likely to be known (if at all) only by the most ardent women's-libber.

Despite the cartoons and captions on the board, Woman & Man seems to take itself with incredible seriousness. There is even a section in the rules calling for a serious postgame discussion of such burning "issues" as "Should husband and wife share equally the chores of bringing up children?" or "Women and men should dress alike, to eliminate all artificial sex differences." At the risk of seeming naive, I still have trouble believing these are really *issues*. It seems to me as self-evident that it is not *ipso facto* a *mother*'s duty to do the chores as it is obvious that it is not *my* business to tell another married couple how they should be raising their children. And anyone who thinks "clothes make the woman" hasn't taken a good look at a well-developed female in a T-shirt!

Nor do I agree that "only by confronting our myths and assumptions about the sexes can we be free of them." I'd rather not perpetuate the myths at all. In the game, there are only two stereotypes available: you can be a "male chauvinist pig" and win, or you can be a "mere female" and lose. Not only is this unrealistic, but it would seem to be directly contrary to the point the game is ostensibly trying to make; if male chauvinist pig-ism were in fact the only way to win at the "game" of life, then it would be a reasonable—and blameless—policy to adopt.

Woman & Man might be amusing if played by a mixture of repressed females, their "superior" husbands, and a "libber" or two, but the people who are more likely to play it (e.g., you and I) will find it dull, stupid, and patronizing.

ANTI-MONOPOLY®

If Monopoly can be criticized for being unrealistic in its economics, it is fair to say Anti-Monopoly bears no relation to reality whatsoever. In some games—checkers, say, or parcheesi—this is irrelevant, but Anti-Monopoly is obviously set up as a real-life "answer" to Monopoly. The board is a slavish imitation of the parent game, but the names of the properties are no more than thinly veiled references to contemporary institutions: there is a "Nazareth" and a "USA Steel"; the oil companies are "Stundart," "Egson," and "Techsico," and so on.

Like Woman & Man, this game takes itself very seriously. On the front page of the instructions we are told (at length) what's wrong with monopolies, complete with allusions to the Sherman and Clayton Anti-Trust acts, and the back page is filled with more of the game designer's simple-minded definitions. And there, as Shakespeare said, is the rub. Monopolies, we are told, charge "unreasonably high prices" and make "exorbitant profits." Such terms, like cotton candy, look nice, but when you chew on them awhile, you find there's nothing substantial there. In practice, an "unreasonably high price" is simply one that's higher than you'd like to pay (but not so high that you won't pay it) and an "exorbitant profit" is more money than *you* happen to be making.

Depending upon your personality (and your political inclinations), the notion of a Monopoly-in-reverse, in which the players ("trustbusters") break up monopolies instead of establishing them, may seem novel, silly, or even virtuous. After examining the game, I can't decide whether it's more funny or pathetic. The author assures us that monopolies are bad because they have "total control over a market" and "hence" can keep competitors out of the market and "prey" on consumers. But there is no need to worry; when the game's monopolies are "trustbusted," they become virtuous, government-regulated monopolies—like those paragons of efficiency, low prices, free enterprise, and open competition, your local phone and power companies, Amtrak, and the Postal Service.

Worse, this blind hypocrisy carries into the basic structure of the game, the chief aim of which is to establish monopolies over the supposed monopolies! Players who attain partial (an "assigned case") or complete ("trustbusting") monopolies charge rent (called "fines" in the first case and "supervisory payments" in the second) to players landing thereon, get paid bonuses by the bank, and accumulate "social credits" (whatever they are)—the primary victory criteria. If such feedback existed outside the game, it might be possible for the government to know what it was doing, but like so much else, the game's "social credits" have no basis in reality.

Let it not be thought that I am glossing over any hidden virtues in the play of the game. When at length you see through the disguise of the author's doubletalk to the underlying concepts of ownership and rent, what is visible is a pale copy of Monopoly which lacks the skill and the fun of the original.

The subject matter of the games below is often as contemporary as it was in the foregoing, but here the tone is definitely tongue-in-cheek. Lacking depth and an opportunity for truly skillful play, they are not the sort you would play all the time, but in the right company an occasional game can range from mildly amusing to completely hilarious. Note well: in the following descriptions rules are often skimmed, paraphrased, or totally ignored. Don't concern yourself with the rules here; half the fun of these games comes from reading the instructions aloud and in detail.

KOMMISSAR®

An enjoyable take-off on Monopoly is Kommissar (Selchow & Righter), something of a pseudo-Communist parody of the Parker Brothers classic. It is theoretically limited to four players (the fifth token being the Kommissar, a sort of roving secret agent), but more can play if you borrow pieces from some other game (in which case you should probably reduce the amount of money needed to win). Players go around the board in the usual fashion, "donating" and "collecting" money and drawing cards from two decks. The Kommissar deck contains only Party cards; the people's deck contains a mixture of Party cards and "forbidden items" (ranging from comic books and skateboards to shares of stock and a book called *How to Make Money*). The forbidden items can be exchanged for cash at the People's Hock Shop; with enough cash, the player can leave the country—and thereby win the game.

Any player can attempt to expose one of his opponents by challenging him with a Party card (or, indirectly, by maneuvering the Kommissar into the other fellow's path—always a good idea when someone is approaching the Hock Shop); as long as the challenged player can show a Party card in response, he can proceed along his way. If, however, he is forced to turn over a *verboten* item, he loses the item, pays his challenger a fine, and is sent to Siberia via the Trans-Siberia Railroad. If he has any cards left, the unfortunate victim is inevitably challenged by every other player in the game, until he is devoid of cards (and, often, cash) and is allowed back onto the board's main path. Progress thus tends to be cyclical, and the ultimate winner often escapes because no one (including himself) has noticed how much money he has accumulated.

There is little strategy involved (except the obvious), but (rather like Ratrace) "people's roulette" is a good way to get ahead. The key is knowing when to stop: get two or three cards and leave. Trying for more is just pushing your luck.

LIE, CHEAT & STEAL®

A game which has considerable similarities in play to Kommissar is Lie, Cheat & Steal: The Game of Political Power (Dynamic Design), which gives "you and one to five of your shifty friends" the chance to "get in on the dirty-dealing, back-stabbing and thinly disguised thievery that make up the real political world." Like other election games, this one is a contest for votes, but unlike the hopelessly naive pre-Watergate variety, Lie, Cheat & Steal focuses on the *real* political system; players can buy votes from the Chicago Machine, get bribed, cheat on their tax returns, libel other players, or, worst of all, send them to the Witness Stand.

There are three decks of chance cards. "Black eye" cards allow you to libel your rivals; "feather-in-your-cap" cards grant you some measure of protection from the depredations of your opponents. Cards displaying a dollar sign (the third deck) levy fines or pay rewards, but you need not be honest about them, so long as you aren't challenged by a player in a Press Box square. Most players simply reverse the signs for penalty cards and take what they are supposed to be paying. Particularly if this is a large amount, they run a considerable risk of being challenged. A more conservative—and more subtle—approach is minimizing large losses: i.e., declaring a "Pay $100,000" card to be, instead, a "Pay $10,000" card. Done in a properly innocent manner, this should keep you free of suspicion.

The game is full of "sad but true" touches. For example, the fine print on the vote cards reveals that "Organized Labor Will Deliver 100 Votes"; "Big Business" means but 20, and "The Intellectuals" can promise only 5 votes. The dollar sign cards yield similar gems: "You administer a $100,000 poverty grant: Collect $80,000," says one. "Your textile investment is enhanced by a new restrictive trade bill: Collect $90,000," reads another. A third: "Your friend on the Highway Commission builds a freeway past your land: Collect $40,000." My favorite, though, is probably "You are appointed to head a commission to study the high cost of commission studies: Collect $50,000."

Like Kommissar, the game often lasts a long time, as anyone who shows signs of getting close to victory becomes the target of the other players' concerted malice. If nothing else, it gives you the chance to laugh at a subject that would otherwise make you cry.

THE PETER PRINCIPLE GAME®

The Peter Principle Game (Skor-Mor) is a uniquely successful attempt to transfer a book to a game format: it's all there, from Final Placement Syndrome cards to the techniques of Percussive Sublimation or the Lateral Arabesque. If you liked the book, you can't help but like the game.

It is short (reading the directions takes longer than playing but don't skip them), and, despite the elaborate explanations, so simple to play that even non-game lovers can manage. The winner is the last one to survive, and, in accordance with Peter's thesis, the easiest way to accomplish this is to avoid promotion at all costs. As you rise in the hierarchy, there are fewer havens of safety (i.e., blank spaces), and after two promotions you must switch from the Minor Decision deck (which has a majority of "right" decisions) to the Major Decision deck (in which "wrongs" outnumber "rights" three to two). Worse, you can be promoted and have nowhere to go because of people above you, resulting in that quick trip to suicide known as "Peter's Parry" (in which, however it may appear, the odds are distinctly against you), or you may be found incompetent (by having more "wrong" decision cards than "right" ones), which will put you out of the game.

One major problem is that the basic winning strategy is to do nothing and avoid change of any sort; thus, it is more interesting to follow a losing course. Despite this, and despite the fact that the rules booklet discusses a number of the finer points of strategy, I will offer a few hints for more positive action. Start, if possible, from a central position (rather than either end); this should keep you from being blocked from above. Ditto if promoted to Midwig. If blocked, investigate the possibility of moving by means of "Peter's Circumambulation" *before* you land on a promotion space and are forced to attempt Peter's Parry. Keep rolling until you land on a blank space, and stop when you do; despite appearances, the odds that you will hit a blank on one of your three rolls are nearly three and a half to one in your favor. If you chicken out, a Final Placement Syndrome space is preferable to a Minor Decision, but if you do draw a "wrong" decision, aim for the Minor Decision space next time. Hopefully you will draw a "right" card and be safe; being incompetent is dangerous at any time.

As in the two games previously discussed, there are "challenges" in The Peter Principle Game, too. They are risky—if you wrongly accuse someone of imcompetence, you're out of the game —and can be (and should be) avoided so long as you're safely a Wig. However, if you get promoted well beyond your peers, your only real chance for victory is to eliminate them by challenges. Remember that the more Minor Decision cards a player has, the more likely he is to be competent; the more Major Decision cards he has, the greater the chance he will be incompetent. In either case, since competence is assumed in the case of ties, a player is more likely to be incompetent when he holds an odd number of cards than when he holds an even number. Finally, don't forget that, regardless of the number of cards he holds (unless he's cheating), any player who lands on an FPS space and rolls again *must be competent* or he would have to pick an FPS card.

It's not the sort of game you'd play till dawn, but it's kind of fun and should go over well with anyone in the business world. Not a bad gift for your favorite executive.

CHUTZPAH®

If you're playing Chutzpah (The Middle Earth Company) with someone who's Jewish, you may find it tolerable; if you happen to be "into" Jewish humor, you may find it uproarious—at least for the first hour or two. If you're not in either of those categories, proceed at once (do not pass Go; do not collect $200) to some other game.

The layout is standard. The properties proceed in straight ascending order around the board, from the $70 "One Room Walk-up Cold-Water Flat" past the $1,000 "5 Weeks in Miami" to the $20,000 (down) "14 Room 3 Acre Estate with 5 Baths." Like Easy Money (and with the same consequences), the rent on each property is directly proportional to its cost; so it really makes very little difference what properties you buy. Further, you can't trade and can only sell to other players under the incredibly dictatorial direction of the Banker. Make no mistake: this is not a game of skill. There are no less than four decks of chance cards. Two (marked "Shlemazel" and "Shlemiel") are bad; one ("Chutzpah") is good, and the fourth ("You want to take a gamble?") is full of fifty-fifty propositions, some of which, in the long run, pay more than they take. While there is a fairly simple formula for finding the precise value of such cards (in case you are thinking of buying or selling them), it would be out of place in a discussion of this sort of game.

The quintessential "Shlemazel" card reads: "You call your son-the-doctor. He asks you how you feel. You tell him. He sends you a bill for $50. You call your son-the-lawyer. He asks you what's wrong, you don't sound so good. You ask him if his brother the doctor can do such a thing. He says 'yes' and sends you a bill for $100. Pay pushka $150 for having such smart children." If this sort of thing has you rolling in the aisles, then by all means get some of your friends together and give it a try; three to six can play as individuals, but experienced players insist that it's more fun played by couples, in which case up to eight can play.

PRIME TIME®

Prime Time (Skor-Mor) is designed by the same wacky duo responsible for The Peter Principle Game and Beat Detroit. The instruction booklet, which deliberately resembles *TV Guide*, features a bogus program section (sample: "O. N. Marshall: Counselor at Camp—Drama. Otis befriends a boy who is tied to a cement block and thrown in the swimming pool by other campers as a practical joke.") and the rules themselves.

As they go around the board, players purchase programs and collect sponsors in an attempt to assemble a complete prime time lineup. The first player to do so receives a substantial bonus ($500,000) from the bank, but this is outweighed in amount and significance by the Emmy Award, which can give a lucky player $1,000,000. Players do not collect rent; instead, they collect profits from their sponsored programing whenever they pass Go.

The programs range from sitcoms (e.g., "My Mother, the L-1011") to specials ("Sing Along with Joe Valachi"). Sponsors, each of which will go with only certain types of programing, are, typically, Arooma Furniture, Ahilla Beans, and Aloafa Bread. The single exception to such amiable silliness is Phil Baumann's Garage. If you're wondering how *that* got in, dig up a copy of Beat Detroit: by examining the board carefully, you will note that one of the independent service stations thereon (the "Big 3" mentioned earlier) is the very same Phil Baumann's Garage.

The real maneuvering of the game involves the ratings. Cards are dealt randomly from the rating deck, which matches the program deck in all but shape and color, to fill the five rated slots and the Emmy Award envelope. The owners of rated programs, if sponsored, get bonuses every turn. However, no two rated programs can occupy the same time slot; if they do, the lower-rated program is immediately dropped from the ratings and replaced. Every time a player passes Go, he can rearrange his programming, which in practice means that he shifts *his* rated program to place it in competition with an opponent's lower-rated program. The no. 1 rating is thus far more valuable than any of the others, in part because of the greater monetary bonus, but more because it enables its owner to eliminate all rival programs from the ratings. It is, therefore, the inevitable target of anyone landing on the space marked "Steal a Show."

Stealing a show in the later stages of a game, when players have a more or less full lineup, is particularly sneaky; since the only available slot for the abandoned ("stranded") sponsor is apt to be next to the pirated program, it is often possible to steal both program and sponsor!

The principles of good play are fairly obvious. Among the programs, movies don't pay much, but in the early stages you just buy what you can. Later on, voluntarily or not, you can change your lineup. If forced to give up a program, the best choice is one which just won an Emmy (which seems true to life, somehow) or just lost out in the ratings, since its rating cards won't be coming up for a while.

When arranging or rearranging programing, it is not usually a good idea to leave open two nonadjacent half-hour slots; it's better to have them next to each other, where they can be filled by an hour program, if you happen to draw one. On the other hand, if you have two rated shows, don't put them next to each other if there exists a higher-rated hour show; the opponent could (and should) rearrange his programing and knock *both* your shows from the ratings.

The game moves along well until each player's Schedule Board is filled up, when it begins to slow somewhat. As was the case with Airport, and despite the importance of luck (a single Emmy Award can counterbalance perfect programing and the no. 1 rating), Prime Time is a game that you can play repeatedly, provided you don't overdo it in a single session. Set a time limit (try two hours for a start) and stick to it.

It should, by now, be unnecessary to state that Monopoly is not going to be replaced by any of the other games in this chapter, but for those people looking for humor or variety, there is plenty to choose from.

CHAPTER 5

Abstract Circular Race Games

DICE AND THE LAWS OF PROBABILITY

To play well at any game that includes dice (like those of the preceding chapter), it helps to know something about the laws of probability and their relation to the rolling of the dice. For backgammon or parcheesi, such knowledge is essential. While we can, in the space available, do no more than survey the tip of this particular iceberg, the subject does bear examination.

Theory first: it is fairly simple to determine the probability of one particular outcome occurring in a finite series of events. The odds that a flipped coin will come up "heads" is $\frac{1}{2}$; that a given number will appear on a single die roll is $\frac{1}{6}$; and that a particular number will come up on a roulette wheel is $\frac{1}{36}$ (if we discount 0 and 00). Unfortunately, most problems in probability are more complicated; they usually involve a combination, or series, of outcomes: e.g., what are the odds that a particular number will appear on either of two dice? On both dice?

The first step is to determine the range of possible outcomes. For a series of events, this is done by multiplying the number of possible outcomes from each event. Thus there are four (two times two) possible ways two flipped coins could land, and eight (two times two times two) ways (i.e., permutations, not combinations) three coins could land. Similarly, there are thirty-six (six times six) possible outcomes when two dice are rolled. Even this small amount of information is enough to solve some problems—for example, the odds of rolling doubles. Since there are, obviously, six possible doubles (one for each number on the face of a die) out of thirty-six possible outcomes, the odds of rolling doubles are $\frac{6}{36}$, or one in six.

To find the odds that two separate events will *both* occur, their individual probabilities are multiplied. If we wish to find, for example, the likelihood that we can roll the number 1 on both of two die rolls, we simply multiply the probability that it will occur on one die (i.e., $\frac{1}{6}$) by the probability that it will occur on the other die (that same $\frac{1}{6}$, even if it is the same die thrown twice in succession; contrary to the opinion of some bad gamblers, dice—like roulette wheels—have no memory). You will have the chance to check the answer ($\frac{1}{36}$) for yourself, shortly.

To find the odds that *neither* of two events will occur, a similar procedure is followed. This time, however, we multiply the probability that each event *won't* occur by itself—in the case of two dice and the number 1, that's $\frac{5}{6}$ ($1-\frac{1}{6}$) times $\frac{5}{6}$—to get the answer ($\frac{25}{36}$, in this case).

Finding the probability that *either* of two *mutually exclusive* events will occur is simplest of all, involving no more than simple addition. If the probability that the LA Rams will win the Western Division of the NFC is $\frac{1}{2}$, and the probability that the Falcons will win is $\frac{1}{4}$, then the probability that either one or the other will win the division is $\frac{1}{2}+\frac{1}{4}=\frac{3}{4}$. Unfortunately, the behavior of dice does not, for all purposes, fit this pattern. If we consider simply the total of the two dice, there is no problem, but if we consider the individual numbers on the faces of each die (as, in the games we are about to consider, we do), the situation gets more complicated. To find, for instance, the odds that a given number (let's be consistent and say 1) will appear on either or both of two dice, there are two main ways of arriving at the solution: you can add together the chances that it will occur on the first die but not the second, the second but not the first, and on both dice—and get the answer; but this frequently presupposes the possession of the same sort of information we're trying to find. So, the easier, and more usual, course (in theory) is to first find the odds that *neither* die will show a 1—which, you recall, we did in the previous paragraph—and then subtract that figure from 1 (unity, 100%): i.e., $1 - {}^{25}\!/_{36} = {}^{11}\!/_{36}$.

For those of you who are finding all this a bit hard to digest and are looking about for an exit, relax; the worst is behind you. I will now present the same information, applied specifically to dice, in a form you should find much easier to swallow.

We have already noted that when you roll two dice, there are thirty-six possible outcomes. Specifically, there are the six doubles (1-1, 2-2, 3-3, 4-4, 5-5, and 6-6) and fifteen pairs of the other possible combinations (1-2 and 2-1, 1-3 and 3-1, 1-4 and 4-1, 1-5 and 5-1, 1-6 and 6-1, 2-3 and 3-2, 2-4 and 4-2, 2-5 and 5-2, 2-6 and 6-2, 3-4 and 4-3, 3-5 and 5-3, 3-6 and 6-3, 4-5 and 5-4, 4-6 and 6-4, and 5-6 and 6-5. If you have trouble seeing that 2-1 and 1-2 actually represent different rolls, take two dice of different colors and work it out for yourself.*

For the nonmathematically inclined, the list of possible outcomes provides an easy (if somewhat tedious) way to get the proper results without going through the same sort of calculations I have been discussing. For example, by inspection we can see that the number of outcomes which include the number 1 (or, for that matter, any other number) is eleven: the five pairs of 1 and each of the other five numbers, plus one double. The odds that a 1 will show up on any given roll are therefore eleven out of thirty-six; comparing "bad" rolls to "good," this can also be expressed as twenty-five to eleven (more than two to one) *against*—which, you may recall, agrees with the answer we arrived at earlier by theoretical means.

The odds that either a 1 or a 2 (or either of any other two numbers) will appear on a roll of two dice is found by adding the two sets of possible individual permutations (i.e., eleven plus eleven), subtracting the overlap (i.e., the pair in common to both —1-2 and 2-1) and dividing, as usual, by thirty-six. The answer is ${}^{20}\!/_{36}$, or ${}^{5}\!/_{9}$—just over 50 percent. For any such combination,

---

* 1-2 and 2-1 represent different *permutations* but the same *combination*; thus there are, with two dice, thirty-six permutations but only twenty-one combinations.

you can determine the answer by going over the list, but there is an easier way: the numbers form a readily memorizable series—11 + 9 + 7 + 5 + 3 + 1 (totaling 36, unsurprisingly). The odds that you will roll a 1, 2, or 3 are obtained simply by adding 11 + 9 + 7 and dividing the result by 36. Conversely—and of equal importance —the odds that you won't roll, say, either a 1 or a 2 are found by subtracting 11 + 9 from 36 (or, instead, taking 1 + 3 + 5 + 7) and dividing the result by 36, as always.

Similarly, it is possible to find out the odds of rolling any given number as the *total* of the dice by looking at the list of the 36 permutations, but it is easier to use the following table:

Number:	2	3	4	5	6	7	8	9	10	11	12
Permutations:	1	2	3	4	5	6	5	4	3	2	1

Find the number you want in the top row (7, say), and divide the number below it in the second row (6) by 36. The odds for rolling a 7 are thus $\frac{6}{36}$, or one-sixth. To find the possibility that a small number will be rolled on either die or as the total of both dice in combination, combine this method with that of the previous paragraph. Take 6 as an example. There are eleven ways that a 6 can show up individually; adding the five ways it shows up as the total of both dice (from the table above), we find that sixteen of the thirty-six rolls will give us a 6 of some kind. If we count both single numbers and combinations, a 6 will, in fact, show up more often than any other number. This information can be summarized in our final table, which shows the total number of rolls (out of the thirty-six possible) which will produce—in some way—any given number.

Number:	1	2	3	4	5	6	7	8	9	10	11	12
Rolls:	11	12	13	14	15	16	6	5	4	3	2	1

The practical application to backgammon or parcheesi should be obvious. Since, in either game, a single, unprotected man (called a "blot" in backgammon), if hit by an opponent's piece, must start over again, it follows that the last place on the board to leave such a man is on a space six squares from an opponent. In general, you want to stay as far away from a potential attacker as possible, or, failing that, to get as close as possible.

BACKGAMMON

It may seem peculiar to begin the section on parcheesi and its variants with backgammon, a game played by a different number of players with a different number of pieces on a different board. However, though authorities disagree on exactly who begat whom, there is no question that the two games are related. Backgammon is, moreover, very much the "in" game these days, and in the space of a few years has gone from an anonymous existence on the back of cheap chess boards to its present position as the most famous of this group.

The board does look strange (and looks nothing at all like a parcheesi board), as can be seen by examining Diagram 5-1. As

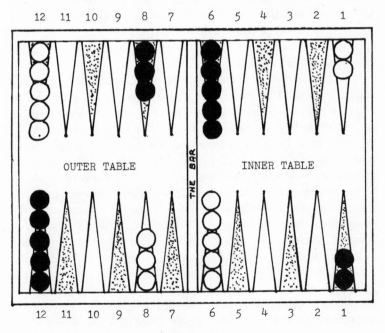

Diagram 5-1

you can probably surmise, there are two players, each with fifteen pieces, or "men." In the diagram, White goes counterclockwise, from top to bottom; Black goes clockwise, from bottom to top. It may be helpful to remember that the pair of men on the opponent's 1 point (the ones sitting off by themselves) have the farthest to go; hence they are called "back men." The triangles, or points, are simply spaces ("squares," in effect, but the term is obviously inappropriate); the colors of the triangles have no real function. Following common backgammon convention, the points are numbered for convenience.

The object is to be the first to move all your men into your own inner table and then "bear them off"—i.e., remove them from the board. In both cases, men are moved conventionally from point to point according to the roll of two dice. A roll of 6-5, for example, would allow White, in the diagram, to move one man from his starting position on the black 1 point eleven spaces forward to the black 12 point. At a later stage of the game, when all White's men were on his inner table, such a roll would allow him to bear off men from the 6 and 5 points. Unlike parcheesi (or Monopoly), a roll of doubles does not grant an extra throw, but it does double the number of spaces to be moved; thus, a double three is effectively a roll of 3-3-3-3.

It is important to note that the two dice are counted separately and may be used to move one or two men. In the previous example, a roll of 6-5 can be used to move two men—one six spaces and the other five—or one man six *and* five spaces. This is not, in the latter case, quite the same as moving the man a simple eleven spaces; nor is the difference trivial. When you have two or more men on a single space, you are said to have "made your point." Not only are such men then safe from attack, but opposing men may not stop on such a point—even if the roll of the other die would allow them to continue. Thus, to return again to our first example, White's man on the black 1 point could move six and five, *but not five and six* (which would cause him to touch on the black 6 point).

For this reason, several consecutive "made" points constitute a formidable barrier against an opponent's progress. Indeed, six such points—called a "prime"—are totally impassable. A glance at the starting position will show the most obvious location for starting such a blockade: the points on either side of the bar (the ridge or line running vertically down the middle of the board). An immediate tactical goal, then, is the occupation of your own 7 point (called the bar point) and 5 point. Similarly, occupying your opponent's 5 point with your two back men puts a crimp in the formation of his own blockade.

The only crucial aspect of the basic game left to mention involves attacking. When a point is occupied by a single man (a "blot"), and an opponent's man can land on that point by the count of either a single die or both dice, the first man is removed from the point and must start over. The mechanics of this are simple: the man is placed on the bar and must enter his opponent's inner table at a point corresponding to the throw of either die. With a roll of 3-4, he can enter on either the opponent's 3 or 4 point, and can then move the number on the other die, if feasible. However, the player cannot make another move until all pieces are brought in from the bar, and if the points corresponding to the roll are blocked (i.e., made), then his throw is lost, and he can do nothing on that turn.

At this point—or perhaps after playing a game—you may be wondering, "What's all the fuss about?" It's no secret that backgammon lacks the color and variety of Monopoly, the complexity of Panzerblitz, and the depth of chess. Indeed, there are many people who would say that the game is "all luck"—a charge that could also be leveled at parcheesi.

There are two responses to this. The first is that one man's "luck" is another's probability. Anyone familiar with probability theory can, in the long run, predict the general behavior of the dice. Further, making the best use of any of the possible rolls in itself calls for a considerable measure of skill.

While there is truth in the above, I have become convinced that a more significant reason behind the current backgammon fad lies in a device called a doubling cube. This is a die with numbers— usually 2, 4, 8, 16, 32, and 64—written on each of its six faces. Using this cube, either player may at any point in the game double the stake for which the game is being played. In a tournament, this would represent points; otherwise, it would be money. The other player can accept the double and play the game for the higher stake or decline the double, forfeit the game, and lose only the original stake. Similarly, a doubled player can redouble, raising the stakes still further. Note that this is exactly like raising, calling, and folding in a poker game; the draw of the cards has been replaced by the roll of the dice. In fact, at the jet set, club, and enthusiast level, modern backgammon is primarily a gambling game.

Since the basic game, as it is learned and played on a more common level, does not use the doubling cube, I will concentrate on the tactics of play and leave most of the ramifications of doubling to other authors. However, one basic point is relevant to material at the beginning of this chapter and elsewhere in the book. That you should double when you are distinctly ahead is obvious; that you should *not* double when too far ahead (but instead play for a gammon) becomes obvious with experience.* However, what seems to make no sense at all is that you should accept an opponent's double even if the odds are up to three to one against you. Here's why: if you decline the double, you have lost the game at the original stake; in four games, this represents a loss of four points (or four dollars, or whatever). If you accept the double, you will, in the long run, lose three of every four games (that's what we mean by saying the odds are three to one against you). Your total losses are six points (three games at two points apiece), and your gains are two points. Your net expected return, therefore, is a loss of four points—*the same as if you had declined the double*. If the odds had been two to one against you, you would have lost three points by declining the double but only two points by accepting it. From this it can be seen that at odds of anything less than three to one, you will lose more by declining than by accepting the double.

Strategic Approaches to Backgammon

There are two basic strategic approaches to backgammon: the running game and the back game. Loosely speaking, you may consider these "attack" and "defense" and not unlike the corre-

---

* A "gammon" is a shutout, in effect. If the loser does not manage to bear off a single man, the winner scores double the stake.

sponding basic and advanced game strategies in Monopoly or the "attack" and "stonewall" methods of playing Scrabble. Some authorities suggest a third strategy, the block game, aimed at making primes and blocking the opponent, but this usually appears in conjunction with one of the other two and is perhaps more properly considered a tactic rather than a strategy.

The running game simply involves bringing your men forward as fast as possible and trying to outrun your opponent. The pure running game occurs when your rearmost men have passed your opponent's rearmost men, so that there is no longer any possibility of either side hitting the other's blots. It is nothing more than a race. This is fine if—because of better rolls or hitting your opponent's blots—your men are, in the aggregate, closer to home than your opponent's men or, at worst, are not far behind.

If, on the other hand, you find yourself falling distinctly behind your opponent in the early stages of a running game, you should consider shifting to a back game. This involves slowing the progress of your forward men, exposing blots, and building up a strike force of four or five men in your opponent's inner table. As your opponent gathers his men in his inner table and bears them off, he will probably be forced to expose a blot (and usually more than one); ideally, your back men are in a position to hit those blots, and your forward men can either prevent his men from coming in off the bar or hit them as soon as they do. To do this properly, both your groups of men should be as far back as possible: the back men ideally on your opponent's 1 and 2 points, and your forward men scattered along your outer table and the upper points of your inner table. If your advance men are too far forward (concentrated on your 1, 2, and 3 points, for example), the opponent's men can freely enter from the bar behind your men and proceed unmolested on their way, forcing you to move your back men and expose them to attack. A good, well-developed back game will win more often than not, but *if* it loses, it will probably lose a gammon—a loss which counts double. So don't go for a back game if you have any other feasible alternative.

Don't commit yourself too early to a specific strategy. It is a good idea in the early and middle game to maintain a position such that, if you find yourself ahead in a potential running game, you can move up your rearmost men and move into a pure running game; if you find yourself falling behind in a potential running game, you can shift to a full back game.

Backgammon Tactics

From strategy we now turn to tactics. Some general principles—like leaving a blot as far from (or as close to) a potential attack as possible, and making your 5 and bar points—have already been mentioned. Another is an axiom of aggressive players: if you must leave a blot, leave it where it will do the most good if it doesn't get hit (your 5 point, for example).

Move your back men together, if possible, especially if you can get them to the enemy 5 point or beyond. If you split them, go to extremes or not at all: that is, if you can move one man all the way out to the safety of the enemy 12 point (which you already occupy)—or close to it—do so; or consider a tiny split, moving one man to the adjacent 2 point (doubling your chances of hitting an enemy blot). Anything in between offers too tempting (and too easy) a target for your opponent.

The five men on the enemy 12 point are primarily builders; bring them down to make (or help make) the 5, 7, and 9 points. The 6 and 8 points should be maintained; the extra men on them should be used (with the builders just mentioned) to make points at the upper end of the inner table. Except for the extreme late stages of the game, don't move them too far forward, where they will be effectively out of play. The 4 and 3 points are the farthest forward you should consider, and these should probably be ignored until you control your bar and 5 points.

On every roll, consider the points that might be made. Except in the very late stages, doubles are almost always used to move *pairs* of men, automatically making points. With nondoubles, subtract the smaller number in the die roll from the larger, and look for men that number of spaces apart; if there are any, you can make a point by moving the forward man the lesser number and the rearward man the greater. For example, with a 5-3, look for men two points apart; with a 6-2, look for men four points apart. Making points in such a fashion is often the best move (as with the initial rolls of 6-1, 4-2, and 3-1), and it is *always* worth considering.

It is impossible to describe how best to play each one of the twenty-one dice combinations in every situation. However, I will relate the favored ways to play those rolls at the beginning of the game. Keep in mind that, unless it is the first roll, preceding moves on the part of either player may make the recommended plays impossible or undesirable.

A traditional way to play 6-5, 6-4, 6-3, and 6-2 is to use the entire roll to bring one back man up from the opposing 1 point. While 6-5 is undeniably strong, in keeping with the principle discussed earlier, succeeding rolls in that series are progressively weaker, making the alternative—using the six to move one back man to the enemy bar point and using the other number to bring down a builder from the enemy 12 point—increasingly attractive.

With 5-4, 5-3, 5-2, 4-3, and 3-2, bring forward two builders from the enemy 12 point. With 5-1, 4-1, and 2-1, split the back men with the 1 and use the higher number to bring down a builder.

With a 6-1, make your bar point with a man from your 8 point and a builder from the enemy 12 point. With a 4-2, make your 4 point with a man from your 8 point and a man from your 6 point. With a 3-1—the best ordinary opening—make your 5 point with men from the 8 and 6 points.

With a 6-6, make the enemy bar point with your back men and your own bar point (with two builders from the enemy 12 point). With a 5-5, there's little alternative to the uninspiring prospect of making your 3 point with two builders. With a 4-4, on the other hand, there are a multitude of pleasant alternatives: best, perhaps, is either making your 5 point with two builders from the enemy 12 point, or making your 9 point with two builders and the enemy 5 point with your two back men. Again, 3-3 offers a good choice: either make your 5 and 3 points with men from your 8 and 6 points, respectively, or make your bar point with two builders from the 12. With 2-2, make your 4 point with two men from your 6 point and bring two builders down to your 11 point. With a 1-1, make your bar and 5 points with two men from the 8 and 6 points, respectively.

The above is offered as no more than a general guideline; no two experts will agree on how all rolls should be played, and about half the plays suggested have alternatives approximately as good. Nonetheless, the choices given *are* viable and will not get you into trouble. As important, however, they fall into fairly obvious groupings and illustrate certain of the basic principles discussed earlier. At this stage it is easier to know the reasons behind an uncomplicated set of moves, than it is to try to memorize the dozens of exceptions and alternatives which have *some* merit in *some* circumstances. Using these examples and the general principles discussed throughout the section, you should be able to hold your own against all but veteran players.

I will not claim that backgammon is one of my favorite games. It isn't. Since I am not a gambling man, that aspect of the game does not exert on me the irresistible attraction it does for many *aficionados*, and as a game of skill I would just as soon play Ploy, Diplomacy, or bridge. On the other hand, it is, on its own terms, by no means a bad game; it certainly has its fans, and it takes no more than an hour to play. If you decide to try it (and everyone else seems to be doing so), you will find that backgammon sets range from the $1.50 dime store variety to the sort of elaborate, hand-carved works of art you can find at a place like Chess & Games Unlimited, for $1,500. Your own choice, obviously, will depend on personal taste and the amount of money in your wallet. Not a bad selection for a newcomer is Backgammon, B.C.® (Gamut of Games), an inexpensive, compact set that includes not only the complete rules but also tips on play by John R. Crawford, an expert at the game (and coauthor of *The Backgammon Book*).

PARCHEESI

The main difference between modern parcheesi (variously spelled) and the game played in India a millennium or two ago is the use of six-sided dice to determine the moves; formerly, four-sided, rectangular dice or cowrie shells were used. The basics of play and the design of the board, however, remain essentially unchanged.

The first problem encountered in a discussion of parcheesi is the lack of standardization of the rules; no two editions of the game—no two authorities—agree on all particulars. Some specifics, therefore, are clearly in order.

In brief, the game is for two to four players, best for four (or two playing two sets of men, as teams). Each player has four pieces, or men, which can leave their starting space and enter the main path of the board only on a roll of 5 (on either die or as the

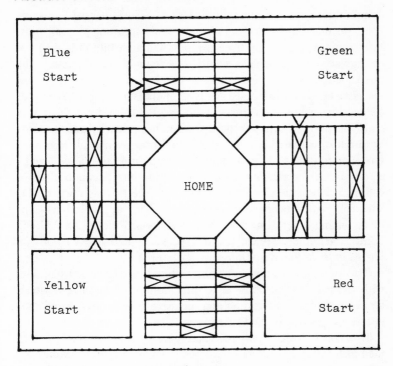

Diagram 5-2

sum of both dice). From the entrance square, men are moved
counterclockwise according to the roll of the dice nearly all the
way around the board, up the home path to the left of their Start,
and thence to Home (see Diagram 5-2). Men may only land on
Home by exact count, but for each one Home a player gets a
bonus move of ten or twenty spaces (depending on the version),
which must be taken at once by any *one* of his remaining men. The
first player to get all four of his men Home wins the game.

As in backgammon, a single man can be hit by an opponent's
man and sent back to Start; the attacking player gets a bonus of
twenty (sometimes eight or ten), which can be used by any one of
his men. A man is safe from such attack, however, on his home
path and on the twelve safety spaces, except for an opposing piece

coming from Start to his entrance space. Two men of the same color on the same space constitute a blockade; not only are they safe from attack, but no piece can pass them. A blockade may not be moved as a blockade (unlike backgammon); however, the blockade can be split on one roll and then moved back together on the next (even if both rolls are part of the same turn). A roll of doubles grants an extra throw; however, the third double in a row ends the player's turn (without further movement), and he must send back to Start his man closest to Home. When all four men have entered the main path, the pips on the top *and the bottom* of a roll of doubles are counted (as in Russian backgammon); thus a roll of 5-5 becomes, effectively, 5-5-2-2 (the total is always 14). This roll can be taken by one man or divided up, as in backgammon, among several men. Note that all bonus moves (the Home bonus, the capture bonus, and the special doubles move) *must be played in their entirety or not at all*.

The rules given above in abbreviated form agree substantially with those of the Selchow & Righter edition of parcheesi, which contains the most interesting and inclusive rules for the game as it is currently played in the United States.

It is not difficult to play the game well. You attack the opposing men in front of you whenever you can, while you protect your own rear with blockades, distance (remember the tables at the beginning of the chapter), and safety squares. Keeping your men together in a tight mass makes retaliation easier, but it isn't really practical: you'll miss the use of Home bonuses at crucial stages of play, you'll present too many targets, and the attack bonuses will tend to separate your men anyway.

A blockade composed of your rearmost men has many virtues, particularly if the player behind you has been getting better rolls than you have. It slows and bunches his men up and protects your own more advanced men. Generally, a blockade should be maintained long enough to have the other players gnashing their teeth in frustration. Knowing when to quit is important, though; as long as you hold a blockade, your choice of plays is limited to two men, not four. A good time to break a blockade is with a bonus move, allowing one or both blockading pieces to get some distance ahead of their pursuit, or with a roll that would allow one or both to get to nearby safety squares. For this reason a blockade on a safety zone is advantageous and one on your entrance square is ideal (providing all your men are out); a roll of 7 or 12 can move one man to one of the next two safety squares, and the remaining man is safe where he is.

Regardless of the rules you play, I favor using the two rearward men to delay and the two forward men to run. The greater the bonus for getting a man Home, the more strung out your men should be. With no Home bonus, there is little point in rushing to get a man there; it gets him to safety but decreases your options. Attack an unprotected man whenever possible, unless there are strong reasons for doing otherwise (such as building a blockade or splitting one safely); the greater the bonus, of course, the stronger the incentive to attack. Avoid attacking when there is a good chance you will be hit in return; in a four-person game, you are simply helping the two players not involved.

Try to make sure your men are placed so that they can take advantage of bonuses; don't rush a man Home if the resulting bonus will be lost or wasted. Be especially wary when you have a man nearing your Home path; if he is attacked and sent back to Start, it would be a heavy and possibly fatal blow.

The best game for two is for each player to take two sets of men, located opposite each other, and play until one player gets one set (of four men of the same color) Home. Using these rules, use one set of men for offense and one for defense. The defenders set up interminable blockades (maintained longer than they would be were they played independently) and harass and delay opponents wherever possible, regardless of cost to themselves; they never attack their "teammates," regardless of benefits. The running set (the ones you are trying to get Home first) will not maintain blockades overlong, will be a little more wary of retaliation, and will attack even their defensive "teammates" for the resulting bonuses.

Because of the larger board, greater number of players, and difficulty of entering men from Start, parcheesi tends to last a bit longer than backgammon—an hour or two, perhaps, in total.

All of the parcheesi variants which follow use different boards, but the goal and general methods of play are the same: the object is to be the first to get all your men around the board to Home.

Like parcheesi, all (except for some editions of Aggravation) are theoretically for two to four people. In practice, this usually means four. When three play, the one "in the middle" is at a disadvantage, being delayed by the men in front and attacked by the men behind. This is, of course, true of the parent game as well.

AGGRAVATION®

Aggravation (Lakeside) is the simplest variant with any claim on adults. A single die is used for movement; there are neither blockades, safety zones, nor bonuses, and the only real element of skill comes from the existence of "shortcuts." A piece ending its turn on one of the inner "points" of the track can, on its next turn, move along these points instead of around the main path, reducing the distance required for a circuit of the board enormously. Unless you're almost home anyway, these points should be used whenever possible, especially if the roll gives you a chance to "Aggravate" someone (i.e., send him back to Start). These points are popular, and the odds of getting "Aggravated" are fairly good, but such a fate does not represent the loss it would in parcheesi, and it can often be made up quickly. On the other hand, the center space "shortcut" should in most circumstances be avoided: it is too hard to leave (you have to throw a 1), and you're too much of a target for too long.

One version of the game can be played by six (or three, without the usual drawbacks). Another, newer six-player version is called Split-Level Aggravation®, in which the playing board is set on two levels. The basics of strategy and play, however, are unchanged. Both are easy to learn (even for children) and can be fun for casual players, but I wouldn't recommend either for serious gamers.

SORRY!®

Sorry! (Parker Brothers) is a surprisingly enjoyable game; it is, in fact, probably the fastest-moving and most fun of all the games in this chapter. It is a game my wife consistently wins. (I don't know why. She may cheat.) While there are, again, neither blockades nor bonuses, the two factors which distinguish Sorry! from other parcheesi variants are the Slides and the use of cards instead of dice.

The Slides are simple but rather neat devices. There are eight of them, two on each side of the square main path, color coded to match the four sets of playing pieces. When a man lands by exact count on the head of a Slide (except one of his own color), he "slides" forward four spaces to the foot of the Slide. It is more than just a way of getting extra spaces from a move, however: such a play sends back to Start any man of any color anywhere on the Slide. Tactically, then, an obvious goal is to maximize the use of the Slides.

Instead of rolling dice, each player in turn draws a card and moves a man (only with a 7 is there an option of moving two men) according to the directions on the card. With some of the cards only a move straight forward is possible, but with many, things are more complicated. A man can leave Start with a 1, 2, or Sorry! card (though in somewhat different ways) and can move *backwards* with a 4 or 10.

Making the best use of the cards is, of course, the element of skill in the game. The ideal use of the 4 is to move a man from his entrance space backward along the main path, *past* his Home path (called the "Safety Zone"), so that on the next turn he can move forward into the Safety Zone without having to circuit the board. For this reason, it pays not to be too hasty in moving a man away from his entrance space. On the other hand, that entrance space is also the foot of a Slide; so there is a certain danger involved. If you have a man on the entrance space, it usually is advantageous to use the 10 to move him back a space, for the same reasons.

Similarly, there is a certain incentive to keep at least one man in Start because of the Sorry! cards, which allow you to take a man from Start and use him to attack any opponent's man anywhere on the board. Besides frustrating your opponent, this can result in a considerable "shortcut" for your man. The 11 is usually used to change places with an opponent's man; if the men involved are diagonally across from each other, *both* men may be helped by this maneuver. A better play is to use the exchange to shorten the distance your man has to travel while lengthening the distance between the other man and his Home. An ideal example is to exchange with a man *behind* you who is nearly Home, giving youself but a short distance to go while forcing him to traverse most of the board again. This can be an excellent blocking move, if there is danger of an imminent win by another player: a shift of three or four spaces at the right point can put him the entire board away from Home.

There is an "adult" version in the rules, in which each player maintains a hand, from which in his turn he plays a card. Curiously enough, this procedure, obviously designed to minimize the element of luck, does not markedly improve the game.

SHAKESPEARE®

Shakespeare (Avalon Hill) is a literary parcheesi. The four middle sections of the main path of the board and the four players' Home paths are labeled with nearly scene-by-scene summaries of eight of Shakespeare's plays. The other spaces on the board are captioned with titles of his other works. Additionally, many of the squares have instructions on them ("Advance 7 Spaces," "Pick Card," "Return to *Othello*"), which a player must follow if one of his three (not four) pieces lands thereon. In this game, in fact, there are even "chance" cards ("Quotation Cards"); so you know there is a good deal of luck involved.

The basic game is 100 percent luck and is not worth playing even as an introduction to the more complicated versions. Even in the advanced game players are not allowed to split the roll of the dice; instead, the total must be taken by one man. Attacking an opponent's man merely moves the victim back four spaces and gives the attacking *piece* (not the player) a four-space bonus. Attacking, therefore, is not a primary objective, and a good move is simply the one that makes the best use of the various "gimmick" spaces. Tactical skill is involved, but it is on a fairly obvious level.

In neither of those two versions is knowledge of Shakespeare required or rewarded. The Quotation Cards are pleasant versions of chance cards, especially if you have a weakness for Shakespearean quotes; the game's designers did an admirable job of matching the quotes to suitable moves. While neither version is really challenging, the cards and the board design are worth the price of admission for anyone with an interest in English literature.

The tournament game is another matter entirely. Played with these rules, Shakespeare becomes as much a game of knowledge as of skill. A player can move forward additional spaces if he can name characters from the play on which his piece landed. The Quotation Cards are used in a similar fashion: the player gets a bonus of five spaces if he can identify the quote correctly (by common agreement, players can make this identification as general as the play from which it comes or as specific as act, scene, and line). Other players can challenge either characters or quotes, with the prize an extra turn and the penalty the loss of a turn. When played by Shakespeare buffs, this can make for a very challenging game, indeed. Of course, the reward is more for knowledge of the subject matter than game-playing skill, and for this reason it is impossible for an English major to find opponents (except other English majors). It seems to do no good to point out that most people know more Shakespeare than they think, and that you can absorb a good portion of the required knowledge just by playing the game a few times.

There is, additionally, a solitaire game seemingly designed for someone studying for a final exam; and, indeed, Shakespeare in all its versions seems aimed at an audience as interested in literature as in games. Not a bad way to introduce young people to Shakespeare, or to brush up on a subject you've probably been neglecting.

THE GOD GAME®

Despite the outlandish packaging, The God Game (American Publishing) has nothing to do with religion and everything to do with parcheesi. Under its garish disguise, it is in most respects less complex than the parent game. Except for the Home path to each Heaven and a corresponding one from each Hell (i.e., Start), there are only two safety spaces on the board; there are no bonuses for attacking, and the complicated roll rules are gone (a man can begin the journey around the board on *any* roll). However, besides the four traditional men for each player (called "Followers" in The God Game), there are two other double-strength men ("Disciples") apiece. The rules for attacks and blockades have been modified to allow any number of men of the same color on a space, and a larger concentration of force on a space sends the lesser back to Start. That is, a blue Disciple would make a red Follower on the same space go to Hell, but a green Disciple and Follower could attack a lone Disciple of another color.

This change introduces an element of tactics not found in any of the other variants. Combined with the lack of bonuses (either for attacking or getting a man Home) and the ease of leaving Start, this means that a player's entire force sticks pretty close together. At most it will split in two groups, with a Disciple leading each. A Follower by himself is a sitting duck, and while two Disciples traveling together can make real pests of themselves for a while, their abandoned Followers will suffer for it eventually.

If the game has a fault, it is in the very conservative play it fosters. Attacks are hard to manage in general, and particularly hard to manage without getting immediately attacked in return; and with the absence of bonuses and the flow of pieces out of Start, the benefits are often small. The ultracautious approach thus encouraged can make the game boring. This is not a game for two: if each plays a single set of men, there will be a total lack of interaction between the opposing pieces; if they use two sets, the torpid pace and double dose of conservatism will do them in.

The casual player can readily be enticed into a game by the iconoclasm of the approach and the simplicity of play, but midway through he is likely to get restless, and he may not return for a second game. On the other hand, the "deep" player is apt to dismiss its nonsensical facade as unworthy of his attention, but if he is induced to give it a try, he is far more likely than the other sort to enjoy the particular tactics involved enough to keep coming back.

EXORCISM®

Regardless of the title, the circular board, and the various concessions to the current occult fad, Exorcism (Playwrite Company) is The God Game taken several steps too far. Each of the four possible players has *ten* (!) pieces, five of which must reach the inner circle (Home) to win. The "Disciples" in this game are pieces "possessed by the devil," which are, in effect, more powerful than ordinary pieces. "Selling a piece to the devil" is simply a means by which you can attempt to knock opposing pieces out of the game.

There are a number of reasons why the game doesn't work. The rules are *too* concise and leave too much to implication. Despite the multiplicity of pieces, few are on the board at any time: it is harder to start pieces than in most parcheesi games; some are eliminated by Devils, and captured pieces are not sent back to their home base but are instead imprisoned in their captor's base, where they remain unless their owner has the desire—and gets the opportunity—to try saving them in a double-or-nothing gamble. Since Devils move on a special roll, they lack direction and usually are halted outside the inner circle because of an inability to enter by exact count. When two or more are controlled by a single player, however, he can split up the Devil roll as he wishes and so exert a measure of control over their individual destinations. A piece entering a space occupied by an opposing piece does not necessarily capture it; that depends on the player's willingness to gamble on a die roll in which the low roller's piece is taken. The more such chance elements exist in a game, the less room there is for strategy and calculation; a game based on dice in the first place simply cannot afford additional elements of luck.

All these factors combine to make Exorcism tedious, dull, and overlong. Conjure up something else.

CHAPTER 6

Sports Games

The sports games probably most accessible—and most interesting—to the nonfan are those which deal with automobile racing. Speed Circuit (3M), Le Mans (Avalon Hill but, as of this writing, temporarily out of print), and U.S.A.C. Auto Racing Game (Statis-Pro, formerly known as Midwest Research) are typical of the spectrum of approaches to racing games in particular and sports games in general.

U.S.A.C. AUTO RACING GAME®

The U.S.A.C. Auto Racing Game is essentially a solitaire simulation of the Indianapolis 500, involving as many as thirty-three cars (the full field at Indy). The race may be run for a shorter distance—and/or with fewer cars—at the player's discretion. There is no formal provision in the rules for competition among several players, but it's not impossible; the most logical arrangement would have each player control a team of cars.

Statis-Pro employs a probabilistic approach: each car is controlled by a card on which is printed a "speed" (the number of squares it can move) for each one of the possible rolls of the dice. These are based on the actual performance of the car and driver in the year in question. For example, using the cards for the 1972 race, a roll of 4 would move A. J. Foyt's car fourteen spaces, Gordon Johncock's car fifteen spaces, or Bill Vukovich's car thirteen spaces; a roll of 2 would move Johncock seventeen spaces. Although the basic edition uses the results of a single year, cards for ten years' worth of races are available.

On all sets and for all cars, a roll of 12 causes a second roll, which is cross-referenced to a Trouble Chart—which can mean anything from a temporary loss of speed to a blown engine (and a quick exit from the race). There is a similar chart for time spent in pit stops (three are required in the full 500). In a long race, quite a few of the starters will succumb to one problem or another.

In this sort of game, the race—complete with varying speeds, accidents, and pit stops—almost runs itself, and the player is little more than a spectator. Elaborate races can be confusing (since the blue plastic cars are alike except for their identifying numbers) and definitely take time. Since this game is not really a contest of skill, it is of least interest to the nonfan.

SPEED CIRCUIT®

Speed Circuit is at the opposite end of the spectrum: there are no dice, and no luck is involved (except for unexpected behavior on the part of another player). While it can be played solitaire, it is primarily intended for multiplayer competition. All six cars should be in use; so the game is better for two or three (with each player racing more than one car) than four or five; the ideal is, of course, six players—one per car.

Each car is a unique combination of five elements: Start Speed, Acceleration, Deceleration, Top Speed, and Wear. The first four are in increments of twenty mph. The cars move around one of three tracks provided on the two-sided board (Monza, Monaco, and Watkins Glen)* at the rate of one space per twenty mph.

---

* The packaging of the "3M Sports Games" is unique: the plastic laminated board comes wrapped around the *outside* of the box.

Each player sets the speed of his own car—subject to its specified limits and the allowable speed in corners—on a Speedometer, a simple device formed of two concentric circles of cardboard fastened at their centers, which is, unfortunately, awkward to use and of questionable durability. The speeds are revealed simultaneously and can produce unpleasant surprises for drivers in the rear who have miscalculated where or how fast the front runners are going.

An optional rule allows each player to design his own car's specifications, according to a set of guidelines which attempts to equate the variations in each of the five elements, but for the basic game, Speed Circuit's designer, Bob Eckert, is dissatisfied with the specifications listed and suggests replacing them according to the following chart:

Car	Start Speed	Acceleration	Deceleration	Top Speed	Wear
# 1	60	40	40	180	4
# 2	40	40	40	180	5
# 3	60	60	40	160	4
# 4	40	60	40	180	4
# 5	40	60	40	160	5
# 6	60	40	40	160	5

Use of the above figures results in a very close, even contest for the two-lap races Eckert favors. Tactics on the straightaway are fairly obvious. The advantage lies with the faster, inside cars, but outguessing your opponents in the corners—deciding when to stay on the outside and keep your speed up, when to cut inside, and when to use your wear allowance—is a real challenge.

LE MANS®

Le Mans lies somewhere between the other two games: it can be played satisfactorily solitaire or by as many as twelve persons, but it is best for a few players racing teams of three or four cars. The abilities of each car are controlled by individual specification cards which list the speed (in spaces) the cars can go in each of six gears. The player determines the gear his car is in (and therefore the speed it is going) much as in Speed Circuit, operating under similar limitations of acceleration (one gear per turn for all cars) and deceleration. Record-keeping on prepared sheets of paper is surprisingly easy. Corners in Le Mans limit—not speed directly— but the gear in which they can be taken. Although Hard Braking (for extra deceleration) is like the previous game's Wear, the price for going into a corner a gear high is a gamble with a die to determine whether the car spins out or not.

Again, there is a choice of tracks: Monte Carlo (the same as Speed Circuit's Monaco) and Le Mans.* Using unmodified specifications and the basic rules, the two fast Class C cars, the Ford GT (Car # 1) and the Ferrari (# 2), usually run away from the field on the long straightaways of Le Mans; only the BRM (# 6), with its fantastic second gear, can make up enough ground in the turns to make it a race. Although the BRM pretty much "owns" Monte Carlo, the slower, curvier track makes for better competition between classes. On either track, the "slipstreaming" and "bonus move" options and the use of a large number of cars tend to mitigate the advantages of the faster cars and induce a closer contest.

There are specification cards for three cars in each of four classes: $C, D, E,$ and F. Unfortunately, the cars are balanced neither within classes nor between classes.† The Ds can compete against Cs, and the Fs, curiously enough, can often nudge out the Es, but the two groups can't really go head to head. Even within classes, some cars are obviously worse (or better) than others: the Jaguar is more hippo than jaguar (in no gear does its speed exceed that of any other D); the Elva is the slowest of the Fs, and the Alfa is the class of its class. None are so *déclassé* as the halting Corvette, which would make only a second-rate D; as a C, it's no better than a hay wagon. If you don't want to junk it completely, drop the 'Vette a class or two (against Cs and Ds, you might try running it as an E; against the slower cars, treat it as a D).

To replace the Corvette at the top, to increase competition in

---

* In fact, originally the game was to have been titled Grand Prix and to have included the Watkins Glen course, but Avalon Hill management, cringing at the thought of their title being mispronounced, changed the track and the title to Le Mans.

† There may well be other sets of cars: the ones included in my copy of the game are not the same as those discussed in the instructions or illustrated in the diagrams.

the upper classes, and to even the teams when several persons are playing, supplement the field with some of the following cars:

Car No.	Class	Speed (Spaces Moved in Various Gears)					
13	C	6th/22	5th/18	4th/14	3rd/10	2nd/6	1st/3
14	C	6th/20	5th/18	4th/15	3rd/10	2nd/7	1st/5
15	C	6th/19	5th/15	4th/13	3rd/12	2nd/7	1st/4
16	C	6th/17	5th/16	4th/14	3rd/10	2nd/8	1st/7
17	C/D	6th/16	5th/14	4th/12	3rd/10	2nd/8	1st/6
18	D	6th/16	5th/12	4th/10	3rd/9	2nd/7	1st/3
19	D	6th/15	5th/14	4th/12	3rd/9	2nd/6	1st/5
20	D	6th/15	5th/13	4th/11	3rd/9	2nd/7	1st/5
21	D	6th/14	5th/12	4th/11	3rd/10	2nd/8	1st/6
22	E	6th/14	5th/12	4th/10	3rd/8	2nd/6	1st/4
23	E	6th/13	5th/12	4th/11	3rd/10	2nd/6	1st/3

Copy the information on the backs of the existing cards˒ or get blank three by five-inch index cards. Call the cars Lotuses, Matras, Panteras, or anything else that strikes your fancy.

For the sake of better balance, I also suggest altering the specifications of the *E-* and *F*-class cars in accordance with the following table:

Car No.	Car Name	Changed Speeds for Various Gears		
		3rd (Old/New)	4th (Old/New)	5th (Old/New)
7	Alfa Romeo GTZ	Same	10/9	Same
8	Mercedes 230 SL	7/8	9/10	Same
	or:	Same	9/11	11/12
9	Porsche	Same	9/10	Same
10	Triumph TR-4A	Same	Same	10/11
11	Elva Courier	6/8	Same	Same

Having balanced the entries in the field to your satisfaction, choose cars which appeal to you, and "drive" accordingly. Deciding whether to take corners safely or to risk the Chance Table depends as much on the car as the circumstances. With its splendid second gear, the BRM should rarely (if ever) gamble, and the Ferrari should move almost as conservatively. The Corvette, on the other hand, or the Ford GT, with wide gaps between second and third gears, should risk the turns more often. In general, gamble only when there is a distinct advantage to doing so, or you'll spend more time in first gear than in fifth.

All three are good, competently designed games; one or more should suit the taste of any racing buff. If all three of them seem too involved, Gridgames sells (by mail) a game called Race-course®, which requires no more than a differently colored pen for each player. Up to four people (more can play, but things become pretty crowded) can "drive" a single car apiece over a variety of courses in a challenging pen-and-paper version of Grand Prix racing.

Monday morning quarterbacks can choose from almost literally dozens of board game versions of their favorite sport, but nearly all adopt one of two approaches. In the first approach on each turn the offensive and defensive players secretly select a play and a formation, respectively, from a limited number of possibilities; their choices, revealed simultaneously, are cross-indexed to determine the result of the play. Stripped of superfluities, the second group differs from the first only in that a chance device—usually dice—introduces an element of randomization to the results of the players' choices.

This difference illustrates the recurring clash between game (or contest) and simulation. There is obviously far more to a real football game (i.e., the sporting event) than just calling the plays: slight differences in personnel, timing, effort, and so on yield an infinite variety of results from the most limited number of plays. Yet, as a battle of wits between two gamesters, the more chance elements, the less the result will reflect the knowledge and skill of the two players. It would be gratuitous for me to make a decision for *you* in such a matter; it depends on what you are looking for in a game.

FOOTBALL STRATEGY®

Representative of the first group are two of the older football games extant: Football Strategy (Avalon Hill) and Cadaco's Foto-Electric Football (now subtitled National Pro Football Hall of Fame Game). Despite the considerable difference in presentation, these two games are identical in principle. Typically, the offensive player in Football Strategy picks from twenty plays, while the player currently on defense has a choice of ten alternatives ranging from an eight-man line to a three-man-rush "prevent" defense. All the possible results of every combination of choices are within view of both players at all times—an excellent feature for this sort of game.

FOTO-ELECTRIC FOOTBALL®

In Foto-Electric Football, the offensive player picks from twelve plays and the defender from six formations; these are represented on cards, which can be placed in a variety of alignments (which act to vary the results) on top of one another on the board. As a concealing screen is withdrawn, light from a bulb underneath illuminates a glowing line that represents the development of the play; the "ball carrier," in effect, progresses until his path is intersected by a tackler.

Although either game is simple enough to be played by football fans of any age, the format of Foto-Electric Football appeals to a somewhat younger audience, and planning is a bit more uncertain than in Football Strategy, since (except for the general advice on the defensive formation cards) there is no way of knowing beforehand the range of possible outcomes for each play. Foto-Electric Football's cards could be visually updated: although most of the offensive choices are pass plays (indicating a "pro" orientation), the offensive formation depicted is the old split-T. Further, the defensive formation *shown* (which, admittedly, has nothing to do with the action) is the same for all the defensive cards. Surely it would be no great strain to present things so that a 4-3-4 *looks* like a 4-3-4 (and not a 6-2-2-1). On the other hand, Avalon Hill has made a change in the newer editions of their game: besides the original set of choices, the offensive player can pick from one of two new sets: one a passing offense, the other a ball-control offense.

VINCE LOMBARDI'S GAME OF PRO FOOTBALL®
AND THE SPORTS ILLUSTRATED PRO FOOTBALL GAME®

The simulation games as a group are more complicated, require more preparation time, and take longer to play. The Basic Game (Version I) of Vince Lombardi's Game of Pro Football (RGI/Athol), which offers twenty-two offensive plays and nine defensive formations, is much like a Football Strategy with dice: the play is cross-indexed with the formation, and the result is matched with the dice roll. Versions II and III, however, more closely resemble the Sports Illustrated Pro Football Game (Time, Inc.), in that all three are based on the actual, statistical play of real professional football teams. In all three cases, each player first picks a team and then plays the game. The choice of teams will affect the success of every play (e.g., if you favor a passing game, don't take the Bears of the Bobby Douglass period).*

Playing one of these simulations is much like watching a football game on TV, especially in the case of the Sports Illustrated game. For one thing, the defensive player has very little to do: he can choose from six defenses, but these merely modify the results of the play called by the offensive player (who is really running the show), and in any case his choice of formation is much less important than his choice of *team* (which is absolutely vital for both players). It is more than discouraging to observe, for example, that the Steeler defensive unit, even with a six- or seven-man line, will probably not even *slow down*—much less stop—the very play which it presumably opposes: i.e., a simple line plunge. (This is true, at least, of the edition I have, which was apparently based on the 1970-71 season.)

Beware of the "Analysis" at the bottom of each chart; without venturing an opinion as to its accuracy as compared with the real life performance of the teams in question, I would have to say that it is a dubious guide for the *game* strategy.

Further, because special, nonstandard dice are used, the graph-

---

* The data in my edition of Vince Lombardi's Game—which seems to date from just before the 1973 season—is more current than my copy of the Sports Illustrated game, but *any* such simulation quickly becomes dated in the rapidly changing world of pro sport, though the playing qualities of the game remain unaffected. Publishers, of course, periodically counter with new editions. In fact, since the Sports Illustrated game was received and reviewed, Time, Inc. has come out with a new version, now called Paydirt.

ics are deceiving; the dice numbers are *not* equally likely to turn up. On defense, for example, the odds of rolling a 1, 2, 3, 4, or 5 are, respectively, $\frac{1}{3}$, $\frac{11}{36}$, $\frac{1}{4}$, $\frac{1}{12}$, and $\frac{1}{36}$. That is, the first three are roughly even and are several times likelier than the last two. The offensive picture is even more confusing; the visual impression of equity is strongly belied by the facts. On average, out of six rolls, one will be in the "tens," two will be in the "twenties," and three will be in the "thirties." Further, the middle numbers of each group of ten are more likely to occur than the ends.* Keeping this information in mind will insulate you from results which would otherwise be shocking and inexplicable. Even with these warnings, however, it is sufficiently difficult to assimilate all the data involved that the results of each play—and each game —remain, in practice, all but unpredictable.

The strength of teams and the anticipated results are less deceiving in Vince Lombardi's Game—at least in Version II. In this variation, the ability of a given team to execute each particular play is compared, numerically, with an overall defensive rating given each team's defense. The net numerical difference, positive or negative, is used to affect the dice roll for the play.

Version III gives a numerical rating to each man on the complete squads of all twenty-six NFL teams; each player, therefore, can choose not only his team but also his starting lineup. This arrangement necessitates more bookkeeping, since he must add up all the individual factors to come up with a composite rating something like that of Version II (although, curiously enough, no possible defensive lineup for any team—including Version II's top-ranked Miami unit—can manage the highest category listed in Version III). For some enthusiasts, this may be fun in itself, but for me it seems a waste of time; it's simpler and no less accurate to use Version II.

Version III includes the use of alphabetic as well as numerical factors for all ball-barriers; the alphabetic factor (properly cross-indexed on a numerical chart) of the ball-carrier on each play is used much like the Offensive Play Factors of Version II to affect the dice roll. Granted that any evaluation of a particular player is

---

* Specifically, the second ("ones") digits and the chances (out of 36) of their occurring are as follows: 0—2, 1—3, 2—4, 3—5, 4—6, 5—6, 6—4, 7—3, 8—2, and 9—1.

bound to be subjective and open to dispute, there is nonetheless something very strange here. One particularly mystifying example: on the basis of the numerical ratings, at least, the game favors Roger Staubach over Craig Morton and Greg Landry over Bill Munson; regardless of where you stand on these perpetually disputed pairs, even their most ardent proponents would not claim that Morton and Munson were the better *runners*—as their alphabetic factors clearly imply. The answer to such anomalies (and there are a number of them) is either to play around with the factors until they fit your own prejudices, or stick with the more reasonable Version II.

If I had to recommend *one* game for the average football fan looking for a board game version of his favorite sport, it would probably be Vince Lombardi's Game, because of its flexibility: it offers a greater choice of plays than the other strategic games; its various versions allow prospective buyers the greatest chance they will find a variation to suit their taste, and it alone features a solitaire scenario, in which a solo player can, with the use of a randomizer, match his coaching strategy with Vince Lombardi's.

SCRIMMAGE®

To my knowledge, the only *tactical* football game currently available is Scrimmage (SPI), which employs an entirely different approach from any previously discussed. Scrimmage is, in effect, football as war game: the Avalon Hill/SPI war game methodology applied to the gridiron. Each of the two game-players manipulates an entire team of eleven men, each of which runs, blocks, and tackles in a fashion appropriate to its real-life counterpart: backs, being faster than linemen, can move more spaces; the linemen, conversely, are better blockers. The "war in the trenches" is resolved by die rolls cross-indexed to the power factors of the men involved.

I confess to considerable sympathy for the concept; I devised a similar game for my own amusement some six years ago. It allows an armchair quarterback a completely free hand in devising not only a "game plan" but the plays themselves. It has obvious uses as a teaching or coaching device, since it affords a chance to evaluate realistically the potential of a new play or formation (which, for some strange reason, always works when diagramed on a chalkboard). As presently constituted, each player's team represents a standardized pro team, but with slight changes in the factors involved, the characteristics of each team could be tailored to fit any particular team, even in the college ranks.*

Scrimmage does have its problems. It is appropriately titled; a "play" or two is as much as you are likely to manage in a single session. Simulating an entire game would take not hours but days. Further, the rules are written for war game nuts who know nothing about football *whatsoever;* the resulting verbiage is as confusing as it is turgid. If you handed a random sampling to George Allen, he could read a whole page of directions without once guessing it was *his* game they were talking about. Since the war-game purists (a narrow-minded bunch, in general) ignore Scrimmage's subject anyway, I cannot urge too strongly that the rules be completely rewritten, so that they are more accessible to the most likely buyer —a fellow who knows a good deal about football but very little, if anything, about SPI's usual game format. At least until such changes are effected (and probably afterward), Scrimmage will not be a game for the average football fan; but for the true fanatic —the person who eats, drinks, and breathes football—Scrimmage is of unique and rewarding interest.

OSCAR ROBERTSON'S FAST BREAK PRO BASKETBALL®
AND THE NBA PLAYERS' ASSOCIATION
BASKETBALL GAME®

There are rumors of a similar tactical basketball game in the offing, but as of this writing nothing has appeared. Typical of the current offerings in the sport are Oscar Robertson's Fast Break Pro Basketball (RGI/Athol) and the NBA Players' Association Basketball Game (Statis-Pro), each of which bears a strong family resemblance to its company's previously mentioned sports game. The latter is primarily a solitaire game, and the former is as at home with solo play as not, but both are simulations with a capital

---

* There is an error in the counters: to conform with contemporary practice, the factors of the cornerbacks and safeties should be interchanged; the faster men are usually cornerbacks, and the stronger, surer tacklers are the safeties, not vice versa.

S. Both involve computer-based team rosters and player ratings, including such obvious factors as shooting and rebounding abilities (and, at least in the Statis-Pro game, more complex factors like guarding ability, as well). You can, of course, quibble with the ratings: despite his unquestioned earlier greatness, for example, I don't think "the Big *O*" was as good in the season in question (both games seem to be based on the 1972-73 season, Chamberlain's last in the NBA) as *his* game, at least, makes it seem—but that's mere nitpicking.

In both games you select the starting matchups and can affect the tempo of the game somewhat; the RGI game, in addition, allows you to choose from three offenses and, if you wish, to use a full-court press on defense. Beyond that point, both games pretty much play themselves, following statistically based randomizing elements: dice cross-referenced to shooting and rebounding charts in Fast Break Basketball and "Fast Action" cards in the NBA Players' Association game. Although the action is invisible (there is a board, for reference, in the RGI game, but it is hardly worth the trouble to use and can easily be ignored), the feel of a real pro game is very much present. Using Chamberlain at the high post and Abdul-Jabbar at the low post, I was able to duplicate the old Lakers-Bucks clashes almost uncannily with Fast Break Basketball. On the other hand, although the RGI timing system is simple, it is also bothersome and easy to forget; the Statis-Pro game times itself (one passage through the "Fast Action" deck constitutes one quarter). If you can exert a little more control in the former, the latter is mechanically simpler; both games take a while to play (and longer than they claim).

Call it a jump ball at center court.

It is a truism, even among baseball fans, that tabletop versions of the sport are generally unsatisfactory. It may be that baseball is not a particularly suitable subject for a board game, or perhaps the problem stems from the fact that baseball is, itself, a dull game. Notwithstanding these difficulties, in the days when baseball was ostensibly the national pastime, the market was deluged with indoor versions of the sport; now that interest has seemingly shifted to football, the former flood has ebbed considerably, but there are still a number of games available, and some of them, at least, have changed a bit since the round-card-and-spinner game I owned in my youth.

MAJOR LEAGUE BASEBALL GAME® AND
SPORTS ILLUSTRATED BASEBALL GAME®

If you must have a simulation of the sport, two of the likelier prospects (despite their prosaic titles) are the Major League Baseball Game (Midwest Research, also known as Statis-Pro) and the Sports Illustrated Baseball Game (Time, Inc.).* The former is set up exactly like the company's basketball game discussed above, and the latter follows a very similar approach to the Sports Illustrated football game. Among the more abstract (i.e., nonsimulation) versions extant, the most unique approach is taken by Sid Sackson's Card Baseball® (included in his book, *A Gamut of Games*), in which the author, using nothing more than an ordinary deck of cards and an elaborate set of rules, succeeds in duplicating every tedious facet of the real game.

Other sports (hockey, golf, tennis, sailing, etc.) are—quantitatively, at least—less well represented, and the choice of the sports' partisans is usually Hobson's. While any particular game may be decent enough, none of them are likely to attract the "mainstream" gamer.

---

* In the latest edition, the Sports Illustrated game is called Pennant Race®.

CHAPTER 7

Games of Detection and Deduction

CLUE®

Clue (Parker Brothers) is the original, and still champion, detective game. I have been playing it for twenty years, and it remains one of my favorites. The rules are simple enough to be understood by eight-year-olds, but there is enough room for logical deduction, decision-making, and risk-taking to please adults. Luck—in the rolls of the dice and the distribution of information—*is* a factor, and the standard procedure is obvious enough to keep most games relatively close, even when played by persons of varied age and ability. Nonetheless, skill makes a subtle but significant difference: in a recent Clue session, against three other intelligent and experienced players, I won three of five games (and lost fifty-fifty gambles in the other two). If those odds aren't good enough for you, go back to chess.

The equipment has been completely redesigned for the new edition. The board is undeniably handsome: each room is represented by a photograph of suitably symbolic material—parquet flooring for the Ballroom, green felt for the Billiard Room, a lace table-cloth for the Dining Room, etc.—and the whole is done in an elegant matte finish. Among the weapons, the "revolver"—for so many years a .45 automatic—is finally represented appropriately; the model is of an antique revolving pistol, to be sure, but at least it's a *revolver*. The suspect cards—now photographs—are certainly improvements over the cartoon figures of the previous edition.

Clue is a game for three to six; each player uses a token which represents one of the six suspects in the murder which forms the background of the contest. The board represents a nine-room house, about which the players move (by rolls of a single die) in search of clues. The rooms are connected by an open network of hallways, and the corner rooms are connected with the rooms diagonally opposite by means of Secret Passages, which, in practice, see considerable use.

There is a deck of cards that includes one for each of six suspects, six weapons, and nine rooms. At the start of the game, one of each sort is taken (face down) and placed in a packet; the object of the game is to correctly identify the contents of the envelope. The other cards are shuffled together and dealt out to each player. If four or five people are playing, some will get more cards—and more initial information—than others. This small difference can be overcome by skillful play and intelligent use of the Detective Notes, but if more than one game is played, the recipients of the extra cards should be varied each time.

Players go from room to room, making "suggestions" (guesses as to the contents of the packet). The first player to the left who can do so must disprove each suggestion by showing the guessing player one of his cards (which must be, therefore, a component of the three-faceted suggestion). The only limitation on such guesses is that they must involve the room in which the player's token rests; if the player directly on your left has the card for the room you're in, you will have to abandon the place for the duration, since you will never get any further useful information there. In part for this reason, and in part because there are more rooms than suspects or weapons, it is usually a good idea to show a room card if you have a choice.

One interesting side-effect of assuming, in the course of the game, the identity of one of the suspects, is that your token can be plucked, willy-nilly, from the space on which it rests, to any room in which someone is making a suggestion involving the suspect you represent. This can be handy, since if your character remains under suspicion, you will not have to spend much time between rooms (and hence unable to make suggestions). On the other hand, you may have trouble getting to the room you're headed for, since the other players may have other destinations in mind. This *is* luck, and there is nothing you can do about it.

There are, however, sound reasons for preferring one character to another. Because of the Secret Passages, the corner rooms (Lounge, Conservatory, Kitchen, and Study) are highly desirable bases of operation; with such a location you can hop back and forth without ever "losing" a turn between rooms. While at the start only eight spaces from the Ballroom, Mr. Green and Mrs. White are farther away from corner rooms than the others; Green is ten away from the Conservatory, and White is an appalling thirteen squares away from the Kitchen. Professor Plum and Miss Scarlet are only eight away from corner rooms, but the characters of choice are the other two: Miss Peacock is only seven spaces out of the Conservatory and nine out of the Ballroom, and Colonel Mustard is eight away from either Lounge or Dining Room. Both characters enjoy the dual advantages of proximity and choice: if they are dealt one of the rooms nearest to them, they can go to the other.

Notwithstanding the advantage of this option, I always leave the corner rooms reluctantly; die-controlled movement between rooms often takes two or three turns—turns which other players can use to gather information. Even if, as Colonel Mustard, I hold the Lounge card, and the Conservatory card turns out to be held by the player on my *right,* I may spend most of the game profitably commuting between the two rooms. I will thereby be able to make a suggestion every turn; since the information I receive will be concentrated among weapons and suspects, I should be able to get ahead of my opponents in those two categories. I can also infer a great deal about the rooms from watching the behavior of the other players. To take an obvious example: if Ken makes the suggestion, "Mr. Green in the Library with the Knife," and has his suggestion disproved, and if he then moves to the Billiard Room, repeats both suspect and weapon, and is again disproved, after which he heads for the Ballroom, I can reasonably assume neither room is the correct location.

An alternative, in case one room's card is held by the player on your *left,* is to travel back and forth between Lounge and Dining Room, Conservatory and Ballroom, or Study and Hall. Though each pair is only four spaces apart, the law of averages will leave you stranded in the hallways half the time; so a Secret Passage "commute" is clearly preferable.

There is nothing in the rules which prevents you from making a suggestion you yourself can disprove. Late in the game, when you are sure of the identity of one of the cards, you can substitute in the suggestion a card you have; this ploy limits the possible responses to those areas in which you lack information and may throw the other players off the scent. Even better, making a suggestion for which you hold *two* cards can rattle the other players completely if it cannot be disproved. Such a procedure can give you the item of information you are missing while leaving the others in the dark. Remember, though, that an "accusation" (your claim to victory, which, unlike a suggestion, carries the ultimate penalty for error) can be made anywhere and does not have to be identical to your just-made suggestion, but it *cannot* follow a *disproved* suggestion.

The main way to adduce information is through the suggestions, but there is more to using the Detective Notes than simply making an X in the appropriate space whenever someone shows you a card. One elementary change is to use the initials of the person showing you the card, for reasons which should be clear in a moment. If a player makes a suggestion that another disproves—and you have two of the three cards involved—you know the third component of the suggestion is also false, and you know who has it. Suppose that Auda suggests that Mrs. White did it with the Rope in the Hall, and Bruce, to Auda's left, disproves it. You hold the Hall card, and you know, from a previous suggestion, that Cindy (to Bruce's left) has the Rope card; obviously, therefore, Bruce has Mrs. White, and you can forget about her.

These examples, while simple enough, are quite typical of actual play; they happen all the time. What really separates the wolves from the sheep is considerably more subtle. Let's say that Auda, the player on your left, makes another suggestion: Prof. Plum with the Candlestick in the Lounge. It is disproved (again) by Bruce. You hold the Lounge card but have no way of knowing immediately whether Bruce has the suspect or the weapon (or, indeed, both); but instead of ignoring the situation, you put Bruce's initial in one corner of each of the two appropriate spaces of your Detective Notes (the same corner, in both cases). This reminds you that Bruce has one or the other card (or both). Bruce's turn follows, but he is left out in the hallway. Cindy reaches the Conservatory and there suggests it was Mrs. White with the Candlestick in the Conservatory. You cannot disprove this suggestion, but Auda can. Now, you know from a previous deduction (in the preceding paragraph) that Bruce has the card for Mrs. White, but since Auda might have shown Cindy either the room or the weapon, you make the same "either/or" notations as before, using a different corner (and Auda's initial) this time. It is now your turn, and you land in the Conservatory and make a suggestion—Colonel Mustard (which you hold), Candlestick, Conservatory—which is immediately disproved by Auda, who shows you the Candlestick, which she had all along. Now, however, you know that if Auda has the Candlestick, Bruce obviously doesn't, which in turn means that Bruce *must* have Professor Plum. Some situations can be even more complicated, but the principle remains the same; one firm clue somewhere along the line can solidify a whole group of suspicions, giving you twice the information anyone else is getting.

Here are a few more tips for advanced players: don't eliminate suspects (or weapons) in the same order every time. If in four games running you use Colonel Mustard in your first suggestion and Professor Plum in your second (or as soon as you have disproved the Colonel), and you open the fifth game by suggesting Professor Plum did it, the more alert players might conclude that you have abandoned Colonel Mustard because you were dealt his card. Don't, in short, be so predictable that you give away free information. Similarly, many players will suggest "Mr. Green, Candlestick, Conservatory," have it disproved by the first player to their left, cross to the Lounge on their next turn, and suggest, "Mr. Green, Candlestick, Lounge." Obviously, the card shown the first time was the Conservatory. Watch for these slips in others, and don't make them yourself; suggest an entirely different group on the following turn, and come back to Mr. Green and the Candlestick at a later time (and preferably separately).

Don't be afraid to make use of the other players' conclusions. If everyone else is suggesting Mrs. White right and left, while you still have three suspects (of whom Mrs. White is one), don't bother going through the tedious process of eliminating each of the others; assume Mrs. White did, indeed, do it, and concentrate on looking for other information (by suggesting Mrs. White or someone whose card you hold, to confuse matters a bit). Conversely, if there is a flurry of interest in Mrs. White followed by a period of universal disdain, it is safe to assume that someone was using Mrs. White as a red herring. To win consistently, you're going to have to gamble when the odds are with you—even to the extent of risking the game on an uncertain accusation. Suppose, for example, you have discovered the suspect and the weapon, and you have narrowed the rooms down to just two: the Library and the Billiard Room (which are only four spaces apart). Unfortunately, you are on the opposite side of the board, and one step from the Library is Joe, whom you have reason to believe has come to the same conclusions you have. If the Library is correct, he will win on his turn; if it is wrong, you will be able to make the correct Accusation (with the Billiard Room) first, on your next turn— unless an intervening player beats you to it. Your odds of guessing now, in your turn, are only fifty-fifty, but your odds of winning the game if you don't guess are not better—and possibly worse. I'd go for it.

Clue is one of the few games I know that can be enjoyed by people of all ages, together or separately. A classic among family games.

WHODUNIT®

It's no secret that Whodunit (Selchow & Righter) owes a good deal to Clue: on a board representing four rooms of a house, players move their tokens according to rolls of the dice, "voice suspicions," and try to solve a murder. To the Clue trio of Suspect,

Weapon, and Room (here, Scene), Whodunit adds a fourth category: Motive.

The solution, however, is quite different. Each suspect (and each weapon, scene, and motive) is a unique combination of three out of a possible five elements. For instance, there are ten suspects, each of which is a unique combination of three of the following five elements: *neat, dark, mean, tall,* and *thin.* Sir Henry Swynford, for example, is *neat, dark,* and *mean,* while Nurse Blanche is *neat, tall,* and *thin.* Three of the elements of each category are placed in a room (e.g., suspect clues in the Parlour, weapon clues in the Trophy Room), and the others—which are, in effect, alibis —are shuffled together. Each player gets one, and the remainder are placed by the Main Entrance, to be picked up, one by one, in the course of the game. Discovering elements of the crime involves landing on the proper squares in the four rooms; if you get all three clues from a particular room, you have solved that category, and can concentrate on the other aspects of the murder.

Voicing suspicions is similar to making a suggestion in Clue, except that first you need to draw the right card, and you can only ask about two elements of the descriptions; on the other hand, you can ask something of everyone, even if one of the players shows you an alibi.

Detective Sheets are used in much the same manner as Clue's Detective Notes. The major thing to remember is to keep straight which elements are clues and which are alibis—that is, which elements must be included in, and which must be excluded from, the description. (I circle the former and cross out the latter.) Since at the beginning of the game, each player has but a single alibi, it is not usually too difficult to deduce what it is, once it has been shown to someone. Remember that two alibis—i.e., two exclusions —in the same category will identify the real suspect, weapon, or whatever as surely as three clues/inclusions.

The use of a set of chance cards—which allow players to voice suspicions, grant or take away turns, and shuttle them back and forth from room to room—makes the luck factor larger than in Clue, but it is still an enjoyable game. Aside from the suspect cards, which are interesting but completely extraneous, the presentation is inferior to the other game's. It is not my first choice for this type of game, but if you already have Clue and like it, give Whodunit a try.

SLEUTH®

Games & Puzzles (which liked it) and Sid Sackson (who invented it) to the contrary, I didn't find Sleuth (3M) all that exciting. As may be obvious to those of you who are familiar with some of his other games (Venture, Acquire, etc.), Sid is no fan of dice. In Sleuth, there are no dice, no tokens, and no board—just two sets of cards and the inevitable "Information Sheets." Its compactness is a virtue—for trips, for example—but unfortunately it's *too* compact; the unnecessarily tiny but thick search deck is all but impossible to shuffle.

The object here is to find the identity of the missing gem, a card taken at random from the gem deck. Each gem is a unique combination of three elements (as in Whodunit): color (red, blue, green, or yellow), number (solitaire, pair, or cluster), and type (diamonds, pearls, or opals). Each player in turn asks some other player about one or two of the possible elements of the description. These elements are determined by the cards of the search deck, four of which are in front of each player (his hand, in effect), while the others constitute a draw-and-discard pile. If the search card played was a one-element card, the asked player merely states aloud to all the players how many cards he has that fit the one-element description (e.g., how many pairs he has, or how many opals); if the card was of two elements, the asked player not only announces the answer as above, but he also shows the appropriate cards (all blue pearls, for example, or diamond clusters) to the questioner.

All information is recorded on the sheets; much of the work is involved (as the game's directions suggest, you must keep track of who can have and who can't have a particular card), but it is not essentially different from the use of the Detective Notes in Clue. Again, the use of "possibles"—"either/or"—is the key. For example, Terry asks Frank for his blue solitaires, and Frank shows him one. You hold the blue diamond solitaire; so you know Frank has either the blue pearl solitaire or the blue opal solitaire, and you should make appropriate notations on your sheet. Also, of course, you should pick the search card—and the person to ask—so as to maximize your information; often, knowing one item of information can allow you to deduce a great deal (as I suggested earlier). The solution can come abruptly. If, for example, in a three-player game, you find that Sandy has no red pearls and Jerry has no pearl clusters, then—assuming you don't have it—the missing gem is the red pearl cluster. Just like that.

Despite its cerebral orientation, the absence of any sort of visual activity makes the game seem—well—dull. It's not bad, but it lacks zing. I'll stick to Clue.

MR. WHO®

Mr. Who (3M) is a game for two to six players; as in Coup d'Etat, there is one round per player. Each person in turn gets a chance to be the criminal, Mr. Who; while the other players try to determine his identity, Mr. Who moves around the board, sporadically raising either his "take" or the reward for his identification. The player who identifies him correctly gets a reward which is inversely proportional to the number of clues required, but, as noted, it can be further affected by Mr. Who's travels. The player with the most money at the end of the complete game wins.

Despite the round-robin format, the short-term goal is identifying the criminal, who is a unique combination of three elements: his hat, his sweater, and his glasses (or lack of them). There are two decks: the suspect cards *picture* the various combinations of three elements; the Mr. Who cards *describe* them. Each player in turn places a suspect card on the board; the Mr. Who for the round accepts it or rejects it depending on whether it agrees with the *appropriate* written element of his secretly chosen Mr. Who card (e.g., if on Space No. 1, the suspect card must agree with the *first* written element of the Mr. Who card). As usual, you have a Deduction Pad to keep track of your guesses and conclusions.

The process of elimination is most efficiently accomplished by changing as many elements as possible on successive questions, regardless of whether the previous suspect was acceptable or not, and the whole thing would be a pretty straightforward process of going from the general to the specific if it weren't for the presence of other players and the fluctuations both of the reward and of Mr. Who's potential gains.

The major problem with Mr. Who is that while a scientific process of elimination is more efficient than random guessing, the skillful player suffers from the poorer players' inefficiency, while they in turn are rewarded by his ability. A guess which narrows five possible suspects to two is a good guess, but it benefits the players who follow more than the person guessing. Mr. Who is essentially passive, and even for the other players in a round there is too great a discrepancy between ability and reward (the two-player game is the most skillful but, unfortunately, the least diverting). The individual does not have sufficient control over his own destiny. This is a flaw in any game at any level (or, for that matter, in any activity whatsoever), but since children are less likely to notice it, they will find Mr. Who more acceptable than adults.

WHY?®

Why? (Milton Bradley) is not a game for adults, either. Indeed, appearances to the contrary notwithstanding, it is not really a detective or deductive game. The skill required, and rewarded, is not deduction but memory. The players move around a board representing yet another mansion, collecting the cards necessary to put together a complete "suspect." As cards are stowed about the house, the trick is to remember what went where. The only real strategy involves *not* going after the "Alfred" and taking advantage of whatever group of cards eventually gets exposed.

Why, indeed?

INSIGHT®

Insight (Games Research) is a game that is less a contest than a means of obtaining information about yourself and the people you know (or think you know). The mechanism is simple enough and is best explained by example: given a choice of four interiors, say, each player secretly marks down the one he prefers and then also picks the ones he thinks each of the other players would choose. Categories range from living quarters to dinner companions to ideas of romance to aspects of personality. When all the choices have been made, the players compare how they see each other with how the individuals see themselves. For the sake of scoring, a player's choice about himself is considered correct; the player with the most "right" answers about the others is the winner.

The game can be sabotaged somewhat by deliberately giving skewed answers about yourself; this helps your chances of "winning" but destroys the purpose of the game. Unlike many other "psychological" games, Insight is not insulting or degrading, but it is absolutely fascinating, and quite informative. It is the best party game I know of, though it cannot be played with strangers unless the people are divided into groups who know each other. However, it can also be played with only two people and is a delightful way to get to know someone.

I do have some complaints about the choices involved. For example, the "modern" interior (Category D, Card One) is so unappealing that many people who (like me) much prefer modern furniture are seriously tempted to choose the less offensive (but more misleading) Card Two. Everyone I know dislikes *both* sets of patterns in Category B. Granted, such preferences are, by definition, matters of taste; but too often there is not a true range of taste involved.

The choices suffer from an overdose of the eastern intellectual establishment, most evident in Categories I (Reading) and G (Conversation). Are we to believe that if they were snowbound in a mountain cabin, nearly half the people in the country would settle down with a volume of Norman Vincent Peale, Charles Darwin, Sigmund Freud, Walt Whitman, William James, Rabelais, Damon Runyon, or the *Wall Street Journal*? Who's kidding whom? The list is too obviously the work of a single person or a small group of very similar people and is a mixture of redundancies and huge gaps. Anyone who would read Darwin would be happy with William James or Freud. The religious have Peale and the Bible; the occult fans have *Astrology* and the *Oracles of Nostradamus*; humorists have a choice of Thurber or Runyon (but not Gahan Wilson or Edward Gorey). For "ordinary reading" we are left only with *Playboy* and Ian Fleming's *The Spy Who Loved Me*, choices which seem, in the context, extremely patronizing—an "intellectual" 's idea of what the common folk might like (an impression reinforced by the fact that the Fleming book is by a considerable margin the poorest and least typical of the James Bond books and was obviously picked ignorantly because the word "spy" was in the title). The exclusion of books like *Stranger in a Strange Land, Lord of the Rings*, or *Atlas Shrugged* is inexcusable, not merely because they are fascinating volumes in themselves but, more importantly (for game purposes, at least), they are the sorts of books which large numbers of people would choose regardless of the alternatives. The Conversation choices are similarly cockeyed: from dozens of examples, I will mention only one: who else but the East Coast intelligentsia would be so enamored of the former "First Lady" to see fit to place Jackie Kennedy Onassis at the same table with Shakespeare, Leonardo da Vinci, and Catherine the Great?

Another, truly boggling omission occurs in Category K, Beauty. There must be someone somewhere who gets turned on by a wheat field, and I suppose some parents find their children beautiful (though I wonder: lovable, maybe, but beautiful?), but 90 percent of the human race finds beauty in attractive members of the opposite sex. You'd never guess it from the choices here, though. As is too often the case, the vast majority has been disenfranchised in favor of some small minorities who apparently fit the designer's taste (or, at best, his rather odd notions of other people's taste).

All questions of taste aside, there is still another problem: many of the images on the Personality cards are vague and don't seem connected, and this helps no one make a good choice. Other cards are, at times, equally ambiguous: does H-10 depict a Peace Corps type instructing the natives or a traveler typing out his experiences?

For all of its difficulties, Insight fascinates everyone introduced to it, including nongamers. Certainly a second edition has plenty of room to improve on the first, but if you get too frustrated with the choices offered, you can always spend a few interesting hours making up your own version.

CHAPTER 8

Word Games

Word games account for a large fraction of the game market, and if Scrabble remains the prince of the realm, it is not for lack of pretenders to the throne. The reasons for the popularity of these games are not hard to find; they are almost invariably easy to learn, and anyone remotely literate usually considers himself *prima facie* an adequate player. People who would not consider playing a board game will play Scrabble or Password at the drop of a hat. Conversely, and perhaps because of a not entirely unjustified feeling that the kind of skill and strategy required in other games is not rewarded in these, word games are perhaps most ignored by hard-core game nuts.

PERQUACKEY®

Lakeside's Perquackey is one of the simplest, though not necessarily the easiest, of word games. It is played with dicelike cubes, on each face of which is printed a letter of the alphabet. Each player in turn rolls the cubes (ten of them at first, later thirteen) and has three minutes to form as many words as possible with the upturned letters. Each letter may be used repeatedly, but no more than five words of each length can be formed. An opponent writes down the words as they are formed; at the end of the time period the words are scored, and it is the next player's turn. At the end of an even number of turns, the highest score over 5,000 points wins.

It is important to get five words in each length formed, because of the scoring bonuses. Very long words score points, but usually take too much time to figure out. The best procedure seems to be to seize upon a particular word length (probably three and four letters to start) and exhaust it before turning to the next (usually larger) one. The simplest and quickest technique involves simple substitution: take a two- or three-letter core, and exchange letters at the beginning, as *r*at-*c*at-*s*at-*b*at-*h*at or *h*eat-*b*eat-*s*eat-*n*eat-*m*eat-*ch*eat, the last being an example of using the same technique to change lengths. Simple stuff, of course, but the way to win. Attacking the cubes haphazardly to make possibly more interesting words of varying lengths may demonstrate erudition, but it won't help your ego much when you wind up at the wrong end of a lopsided score. Don't worry about longer words unless they literally stare you in the face; if so, use them quickly and go back to what you were doing. Otherwise, you might forget them by the time you get to their category.

Spill and Spell® (Parker Brothers), Scrabble Brand Crossword Cubes® (Selchow & Righter), and Tufabet® (Avalon Hill) are much along the same line, except that they all allow the formation of words crossword-style.

ANAGRAMS

In various incarnations, anagrams has been around for years. It is played with letter tiles, but like the previous games does not require a board. It, too, can be played by any number. The object is to be the first to acquire and hold for one round a specified number of words (usually ten). Words are formed from the tiles in a player's hand and from discarded tiles in the center of the table. Words can be stolen from other players, also, and in this piracy lies much of the game's skill and most of its fun; to steal a word, you must add at least one letter to the old word and rearrange all the letters to form a new word. Adding an *s* to form a simple plural is not allowed, but the letter *s* is nonetheless the key to many easy thefts. For one thing, many words are obvious anagrams, and you can use an *s* to form the plural of the anagram: *god + s = dogs; broad + s = boards; rate + s = tears* (*+ s = stares*), and so on. For this reason, it is a good idea to pluralize your words whenever possible. The most common counter to this defense is to shift the *s* to the beginning of a new word (the letter *s* crops up most often either as the first or last letter of a word): *rats + e = stare* (or *+ s = stars*); *loves + h = shovel.*

Protecting your words is a problem not unlike that found in Image (if you can remember all the way back to chapter 2); the solution is similar, too: make each word as long and peculiar as possible. Use those *x*'s, *z*'s, and *q*'s (I know: even *zebra* can be stolen with *brazen*, or *ox* and *axe* with *box* and *waxen*, but try stealing *wax, vixen, zygote,* or *aardvark*; it's the principle that counts).

To be sure, a large vocabulary helps, but a ready wit and plain old practice will do wonders.

TRYCE®, LEXICON®, AND FOIL®

Tryce (a 3M Gamette) is avowedly a rummy variant: the cards are regular playing cards with letters added; melds can be sequences, groups, or words. Also of the rummy/fan tan/crazy eights family is Parker Brothers' classic, Lexicon, but the cards involved feature only letters. From a hand of ten, the object is to be first out of cards by melding words to a crossword layout. As in Scrabble, each letter card has a point value, but here the easy letters score highest, and the object, as in hearts, is to have the *lowest* total when the game is over. The basic game limits melds to four letters, but play is more challenging—and more fun—if the rule is ignored. Foil (another 3M Gamette) is a third variation on this same theme; the twist is that at the end of each hand players scramble their words and try to unscramble those of their opponents.

PROBE®

The classic hidden or scrambled word game is hangman, which Parker Brothers has formalized and elaborated into Probe. Each player thinks of a word, secretly draws the appropriate letter cards, and lays them out in front of him face down. Blanks may be added to either end to disguise the length of the word. Each player in turn tries to guess letters (and eventually the whole words) in opponents' layouts; correct guesses score points and grant extra guesses. There are chance cards to randomize events a bit ("Expose a letter," "Lose a turn," "Double point value of next guess"), but more serious gamers can (and probably will) ignore them.

Novices at the game often try for large words, but this is a dubious tactic; lots of letters mean lots of room for correct guesses, and many large words can be guessed when a few key letters or syllables become visible. Good words are usually of two varieties. The first is often short but composed of groups of letters so common that their presence does not narrow the field appreciably (example: a four- or five-letter word ending *eat*. How much good do those letters do you?). The second variety consists of words of any length whose letters do not obey the normal distributional curve, usually because of an absence of common letters (*e, t, a, n, o, r, s,* etc.) or, less frequently, because of an overabundance of one or more of them (*abba*, say, or *aardvark*). The quintessential word of this type is *syzygy*, a guaranteed winner the first time you spring it in a Probe session. Some short words manage to combine the virtues of both categories, like the three-letter words ending in *y*.

My own feeling is that blanks should be used with very short words (having only three cards showing gives your strategy away too quickly) and *not* with very long words. Most people visualize words of more than six or seven letters as "long"; for them, the difference between a ten- and an eleven-letter word is too subtle to be perceived. Besides, with long words everyone will assume you are using blanks, anyway. Blanks are, in fact, the most popular "letter," and the only real flaw in Probe's equipment is a potentially inadequate supply of them.

PASSWORD®

At the opposite extreme is Password (Milton Bradley), of TV fame. Here, the object is not to hide but to communicate words to your partner. Representatives of each team give clues alternately to their partners; the player who guesses the "password" scores for his team a number of points which decreases according to the number of guesses required. The game can be played to a given point total or, more typically, until the words on one pair of cards are exhausted. If more than one round is played and the contest is too uneven, partners can be switched at the end of each card. This is one of the simplest of all games to pick up; yet it is unquestionably a favorite of adults everywhere.

The best guess is usually the first thing to pop into your head in response to a clue. In turn, the best clue is usually a word which immediately suggests the password: *cat-dog, love-hate, high-low, husband-wife*. Common antonyms are often ideal, but the clue more usually is a synonym. In this case, precision is your aim; try to capture the flavor of the word—not merely the denotation but the connotation as well. A clue of *dirty* should elicit the response *clean*; if something else is desired, try *filthy, sleazy, grungy, tawdry, slimy,* or *obscene* instead. A rhyming word is often helpful as a second or third clue, provided your partner is properly alert (otherwise he will only be thoroughly confused); the ideal first clue would be a rhyming synonym (e.g., *nixie* for *pixie*), but such happy hybrids are almost extinct. People often forget that while proper nouns cannot be passwords, they *can* be clues. Who could miss *vampire* from *dracula, shore* from *Dinah,* or *piano* from *Liberace?* Finally, while gestures are *verboten,* variations in tone and facial expressions are not: a whispered *books* might suggest *library* (while the word alone is too ambiguous); a choked *cough* might elicit *gasp* when nothing else will. The possibilities are limited only by your own imagination.

A variation of Password can accommodate an odd number: one person gives clues to all the other players; the points go to the correct guesser and depend, as usual, on the number of clues required. The same player may be moderator for the entire session, or the job can rotate from person to person (enabling everyone to compete, though it indirectly rewards poor clue-givers as well).

SCRABBLE®

Despite its perennial popularity, most people tend to regard winning a game of Scrabble (Selchow & Righter) as a fortuitous combination of "good" tiles (i.e., lucky draws) and a large vocabulary. The impression is widespread that the skill involved is little more than diligently examining the board to make the best use of the tiles on the rack—"best use" meaning scoring as many points as possible each and every turn.

I am happy to report that both ideas are quite erroneous. A large vocabulary, *per se*, is helpful but certainly not crucial and not, in fact, all that important. If the four-player game is as much a social occasion as a serious contest, there is nonetheless room for considerable skill, and the strategy and tactics possible in the game for two may seem at first glance almost unbelievable.

Consider. The average Scrabble player plays his tiles with a total disregard for his next turn and trades them in only when faced with something like *W-X-L-L-Q-M-M*. He will not let an *X* or a *J* or a *Z* out of his hands unless he can play them on a Double or Triple Letter square, and he will hold onto a *Q* for five turns until he draws a *U* and then wait another two turns until he has an opening on the board to play them. At the same time, without a second thought, he will stick an *S* at the end of the word he is making for the extra one or two points it gives him; a blank will be used to get rid of a few troublesome letters or to stretch a word so that a consonant lands on a Double Letter space. Especially if he is a novice, he will form a word from the tiles in his rack and then look for a place to play it; having found a twenty-point play, it will take an act of Congress to get him to reconsider the hand long enough to find a potentially superior alternative. Usually he will make a single word, intersecting a word on the board; rarely will he form two words by placing a letter at the beginning or end of a previously played word (like placing *audit* so that the *A* makes *jar* into *ajar*). Almost never will he place a new word parallel to an old one, making words in both directions, even though this is the most profitable way to place words. Two-letter words are scarce in his game, as he plays them only when nothing else is available, and they are inevitably of the most common sort: *it, me, to, of, at, in, up*, and so on. Seven-letter words (and fifty point bonuses) are an

Diagram 8-1

impossible dream, and the manufacturer's suggestion of a 500-700 point total for a game seems hopelessly optimistic.

If this hapless fellow sounds a bit like you, you should be able to increase your score at least 100 percent by reading the next few paragraphs.

First, let's compare this average player with his traditional counterpart, the experienced and knowledgeable Scrabbler. His play is characterized by a strong interaction between his rack and the board; he spends as much time examining the board for openings and potential words as he does his own tiles. Facing a layout like the one in Diagram 8-1, he would never play *O-G-A* horizontally to make *toga* when he could use the same letters to make *ago* vertically and *jot* horizontally. With a second *G*, he would of course make *agog, jot*, and *ego*; with an *R*, he would have seen the possibility of *jot, ego, herd*, and *ogre* (for twenty-seven points without bonuses). To get the maximum use of parallel words, he has developed a broad repertoire of two-letter words (the notes of the musical scale, the spelled-out letters of the English and Greek alphabets, etc.). He continually rearranges his tiles, not only to develop longer words, but also to find the anagram which makes best use of the bonus squares, locating the high consonants on the Double and Triple Letter spaces. A major part of his strategy involves using all possible bonuses and denying them to his opponent.

Now the difference between these two traditional representatives of Scrabble players is as much a matter of experience as of aptitude. The Scrabble fanatic probably enjoys crossword puzzles as well, which helps him see those interlocking possibilities and allows him from time to time to come up with words like *aba, jizya,* and *zloty.* He may simply be more literate; unfortunately, developing a facility with language is beyond the scope of this book. However, I would like to suggest that most often today's competent veteran is no more than yesterday's stumbling clod—but with more experience—and the easiest way to get from one category to the other is to practice. More crucially, I would suggest that there is more to Scrabble than *either* traditionalist realizes, and that even the most accomplished veteran can probably add 100 points a game to his score by revising some of his long-cherished notions.

Modern theory distinguishes between two sorts of players: the defensive man and the attacker. The difference between them (and between both of them and the traditionalists) is one of attitude: the average traditionalist will open up a Triple Word Score space for his opponent without noticing it; his more polished counterpart will not do so unless his score for the play is far higher than the other possible outcomes; the true defender will never make a Triple Word Score available regardless of his own score, and the attacker will cheerfully open up such a possibility even if there is a 50 percent chance that his opponent will get to it first.

The aim of the defender is the slow strangulation of his opponent. Rarely will he play more than three or four letters at a time; more rarely still will he leave an inviting opening. He will forego all bonuses without qualm, provided his opponent doesn't get them. He is perfectly happy to win 151-150, even if half the board remains virgin territory. Every play is made with his opponent in mind. Not only will he open with a three-letter word, but, knowing the best response to a short opening is a parallel word, he will be careful to place *cat* with the *A* on the center square, so that his opponent must play mere vowels (worth only one point) on the surrounding Double Letter Score squares. Never would he play an O or *A* in front of a bonus square unless the *X* was out of the way.

If such a style suits you, you are welcome to it. You can win games that way, but for me the essence of Scrabble is scoring. A 700-point game is more fun (it seems to me) than a 300-point game, regardless of who wins. If you win a defensive struggle in which neither of you score more than 200 points, your opponent may grudgingly acknowledge your determination and persistence; if you empty your rack three or four times and score 500 points, your foe will be not only beaten but *dazzled*. And that, I think, is a worthwhile difference.

The essence of attack Scrabble is the single-minded pursuit of fifty-point bonuses; the attacker is perpetually looking for ways to play all of his tiles in one fell swoop. With lesser plays, the attacker is as concerned with the tiles on the rack as he is with those he plays to the board; if the remainder does not constitute a promising core for a new seven-letter word, he will reconsider his play. Any letter that seems out of place will be sacrificed without a second thought. The high-scoring consonants that the traditionalists prize are more often hindrances than helps to the attacker; if he cannot play a *Z*, *X*, or *Q* at once, he will trade it in for letters more to his liking: the one- and two-pointers. For him the prize letters are the *S*'s and blanks: rarely will he part with an *S* without scoring 25-30 points; with a blank, for less than twice that. Indeed, a play that scores less than 20-25 points is hardly worth the bother.

On his first turn, lacking a seven-letter word, the attacker will try for a five-letter word; a lesser word does not open the board enough, and a six-letter word leaves him too much at the mercy of the draw (without the compensation of a fifty point bonus). In response to such a play, he would aim for one (or both) Double Word Score(s) by "capping" the first word, often by pluralizing it with an *S:* making *start* into *starts*, along with a second word vertically. Unlike the defender, he uses two- and three-letter words only as means to an end: either the elimination of troublesome and unwanted consonants, or as anchors for his seven-letter words.

If this sort of wide-open play appeals to you, by all means give it a try; it will do wonders for your game. Before trying it, I rarely scored over 300 and never emptied my rack; the first time I utilized the strategy and psychology of attack Scrabble I scored three 50-point bonuses and broke 400 for the first time.

A Winning Vocabulary

A few words about a few words: while I mentioned at the beginning of this section that a large vocabulary was not essential to good Scrabble playing, a certain kind of vocabulary is, regardless of the style of play you favor. I am speaking most particularly of two-letter words, a knowledge of which is absolutely necessary if you hope to make use of parallel words. Don't be afraid to gamble now and then; there are more two-letter words in your favorite dictionary than you would believe. *Do, re, mi, fa, sol, la,* and *ti* appear in the most modest dictionaries, and *ax, ex, em,* and *en* are quite legitimate. Get to know the ones your dictionary permits.

I must confess to an old-fashioned prejudice against "words" like *ee, ef,* and *aitch* (but not *gee, em, en,* and *ex,* which have other meanings entirely), which are nothing more than spelled-out letters of the alphabet, but if your dictionary lists them (and some do), they are legal for Scrabble purposes. And, though I have nothing against trivia, I admit to a distaste for "crossword English" —the sorts of words that show up in crossword puzzles and nowhere else: outrageously exotic fauna, bizarre foreign implements or coins, terms obsolete since the tenth century, and ridiculously rare variant spellings. Most, thankfully, crop up only in monstrous tomes that cater specifically to crossword addicts.

On the other hand, nearly everyone has a fund of unusual words, and you might as well exploit them. If mythology's your bag, why not use *chimera, roc,* or *djin* (or *jinn, jinni,* and *genie*)? Up on the animal kingdom? Don't forget *gnu, emu, auk, moa,* and *aardwolf,* along with *zebra,* of course (for the Z). Into science? What about *nitric* and *lysergic* (as in acid), *amino, pion,* and *zygote?* Whatever your job, hobby, or field of interest, you can use its terminology to advantage.

I have referred to "your" dictionary. You should settle on one for Scrabble purposes and get used to its idiosyncracies. If a high score is your only concern (and you lack my prejudices), you may want the largest dictionary you can find. Unfortunately, the Oxford English Dictionary capitalizes each entry (a nuisance, as it makes it impossible to tell which words are naturally capitalized—and illegal), and some other unabridged dictionaries do not adequately distinguish foreign words and phrases. My own recommendation for "real" English (i.e., those words in remotely common usage) would be a standard college edition; the new Random House has a good reputation, and I still get considerable mileage out of my twenty-year-old Merriam-Webster.

If you want to practice, there are several solitaire Scrabble variants. You can play a one-person game, or you can take the part of several players, moving from rack to rack around the board. Or you can simply turn all the tiles face up and see what kind of high-scoring combinations you can come up with: done in this fashion, people have actually scored more than 1,500 points on a single seven-tile play (late in the game, of course).

R S V P® AND R P M®

R S V P (Selchow & Righter) is a sort of vertical Scrabble for two players. The board is an upright, open grid; the letter tiles are two-sided and played one at a time, as each player tries to form words on his side while blocking his opponent from doing so. R P M (Selchow & Righter, again) is, in some respects, less a rotating Scrabble than a rotating Image, though it is played with letter tiles and the object is to form words. The "board" rotates at a fixed rate, and every player can add to each portion of the layout as it passes in front of him, starting or building up groups of letters that will eventually form words. As in Image, the person who finishes off the word gets credit for it. Demanding quick thinking and decision-making, R P M is not as hard as it seems on a first try. It's for two to four players.

SYNTACTICS®

Syntactics (marketed by Gameophiles Unlimited) is Scrabble with sentences. The "tiles" are pieces of heavy cardboard with words on them, and the object is to make intelligible sentences out of the words on your rack and play them horizontally or vertically on the board. Bonus points are scored for crossing certain points on the main path, going around corners, or building a sentence three spaces up or down. Like Scrabble, it is for two to four (though there are solitaire versions, also); unlike Scrabble, it doesn't work.

The game has several problems. The directions are printed on the bottom of the box—a less than inspired notion by itself—and partly because of the space limitations are more suggestions than rules. Some of the ambiguities and gaps *can*, as the designer has suggested, be worked out with common sense, but that doesn't make them any less annoying the first time you're trying to play a game. However, the problem of what constitutes a legal play—

what is a sentence—is hopelessly ambiguous: the designer allows "headline English" and includes (on the cover) the phrase, "Quick, Harry, the club!" Human nature being what it is (and common sense not being all that common), disputes are going to arise, and there is no objective authority to refer to. (Image, you recall, had the same difficulty.)

The real problem of Syntactics goes deeper than shoddy rules and questionable presentation; it is that the average set of ten tiles does not allow a sentence that is either humorous or sensible. There are twenty-six letters of the alphabet, and very few possible draws in Scrabble don't allow the formation of *something*. Unfortunately, there are tens of thousands of English words, and no one knows how many meaningless combinations. Facing a rack of *the, if, it, and, although, as, because, her, white,* and *quick,* without even a provision for trading in tiles for new ones, you may be tempted to throttle the idiot responsible for the self-serving "warning" on the cover ("Be prepared to find your fingers arranging words in ways that reveal more about your character than you may want people to know").

Syntactics might be salvaged by dividing the words into groups —say, nouns and pronouns, verbs, and others—and drawing tiles as needed from the appropriate box or pile (along with, perhaps, using Scrabble's trade-in rule). As it is, it's a good idea that didn't quite make it.

MONTAGE®

Montage (Gamut of Games) is perhaps the ultimate word game— an interesting combination of Scrabble, Password, and tic-tac-toe —played by four people in partnerships. The board is divided into nine areas, or zones, of twenty-five spaces apiece. At the start of the game, the board is "seeded" with a prechosen pattern of blanks (to delimit the lengths of possible words) and random letter chips. The chips come in five colors, each of which represents *any one* of a group of letters; a yellow chip, for example, can be an *A, B, C, D,* or *Z.* A chip might represent one letter in a horizontal word and a different letter in a crossing word.

In his turn, a player thinks of a word that fits into a given space, indicates the location and direction of the word, and gives the other players a clue concerning it. If, within the time limit, his partner can think of a suitable word (which need not be the one the first player was thinking of), their team plays and gets credit for the word. The original player may continue proposing words as long as they contain two or more previously played chips, and the partner keeps guessing correctly. If the partner fails and the opposing players come up with an appropriate word, *they* score, and the turn passes.

Once one side has a majority of the possible tiles in a zone, that zone is theirs, and play proceeds elsewhere. In a short game, the team which first "occupies" three zones in a row wins; in a longer game, play continues until all zones are filled. The team with the most zones wins, but there is an elaborate scoring system that can be used by those so inclined.

Among other virtues, the board in play takes on the appearance of a multicolored art form. It should be a treat for word-game fans.

CHAPTER 9

Abstract Games

In this chapter are some of the oldest games in the world; go and mancala, for example, go back not just centuries but millennia. Ancient or modern, these games share little in common save a high degree of abstraction; they are simple to learn (but often hard to master) and exceedingly narrow (but often deep). People who play no other board games are often devoted to one of these (witness the multitude of chess, checkers, and go fanatics). Yet, curiously, the casual gamer is easily bored by them, and the game nut, lacking the single-mindedness necessary to become a real expert (and being dissatisfied with mediocrity), shies away from them. Both prefer more diverse and exciting games: the former Monopoly and Clue; the latter, Diplomacy and Panzerblitz.

Abstract games are for those who like their strategy and tactics pure and unsullied by dice or chance cards, who find complicated directions unnecessary, a variety of equipment distracting, and realism irrelevant. If you have tried several of these games and disliked all of them, go ahead and skip the chapter; if several of your favorites are here, you should find some others to your taste.

These games are easy enough to sample, but don't expect to become an expert overnight—not here!

OH-WAH-REE®

Oh-wah-ree (3M) is a modernization of mancala, the old pebble-and-pit game played from Africa to the Philippines. Whereas most versions of the parent game feature two rows of six holes or pits (one per player), Oh-wah-ree arranges the twelve pits in a circle and provides for two, three, or four players. In all versions, the game begins with each pit filled ("sowed") with a certain number of pebbles, and a player's turn involves nothing more than picking up all the stones in one of his pits and sowing them one at a time in successive pits (usually, but not always, in a counterclockwise direction). If the final stone so played becomes the second or third stone in a pit, the stones in the pit are captured by the player; if the previous pit also contains two or three stones, those, too, are captured, and so on. Usually, the object is to capture more stones than any other player. In some versions, pits as well as their contents can be captured, and the winner may be the holder of the most pits at game's end.

When first played (regardless of the particular variation), Oh-wah-ree goes quickly. Later on, as players develop some smattering of tactics, they meticulously count the pebbles in each pit* and compare their various alternatives; play is slowed considerably, and the game often becomes dull. Variations like Grand Oh-wah-ree, in which pits *and* pebbles may be captured, add an element of surprise and variety which tends to keep the game more interesting.

Tactics vary a bit from version to version, depending on the number of players involved. Obviously you should try to keep track of the number of pebbles in each pit as far as possible, strike when the opportunity presents itself, and protect yourself when threatened. The latter may be done in three ways: move the threatened pebbles; add pebbles to the pits in question (since a pit with three

---

* Players are forbidden to touch the pebbles while counting them, but this rule does not prevent them from eyeballing piles of stones from an inch away, at every possible angle.

pebbles already in it is, in most versions, safe from capture), or add pebbles to the *threatening* pit, making it overshoot its target. Offensively, avoid playing from one or two of your pits for some time, in order to develop a long-range strike force.

On a serious, strategic level, this sort of thing is not one of my favorites. If pit-and-pebble games appeal to you, mancala sets are available in better game stores, but the elegantly produced Oh-wah-ree is probably a superior alternative.

QUBIC®

The children's game of tic-tac-toe has been made into a playable adult game by several modifications, of which the most notable is probably the introduction of the third dimension. The most representative and the most widely played of this sort is perhaps Parker Brothers' Qubic, which is played on a series of four parallel square panels, each divided into a four-by-four grid.* The object is to place four disks of your own color in a row in any direction or dimension. Unlike tic-tac-toe, which cannot be won (or lost) when played by two persons of minimal intelligence, I have never seen a game of Qubic played to a draw.

The keys to winning are threefold. The first and most obvious is paying attention. This seems elementary—and is—but it is not so simple as it sounds in advanced stages of the game, and nearly half the time a game is won because one player does not notice that his opponent has succeeded in placing three in a row and, consequently, does not block the vital open space.

The second is the basic tactics of position. Certain squares are more important than others, because there are more combinations of four-in-a-row that run through them; the key squares are the four corners of the top and bottom levels, and the inner four squares of the two middle levels.† Most of the initial maneuvering (as much as the first half-dozen moves by each player) goes on in

---

* Because of the importance of the middle square of the middle panel, three by three by three games are little better than plain tic-tac-toe.
† Each such square can be a part of seven different combinations of four-in-a-row; every other square can be in no more than four.

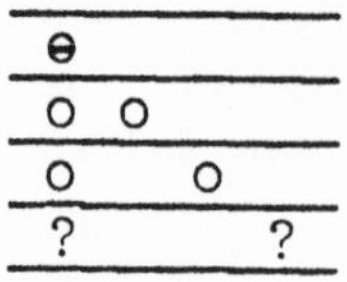

```
 ⊖
 O  O
 O     O
 ?        ?
```

Diagram 9-1

these squares. If one player can emerge from this initial maneuvering with a dominant position in the key squares, there is no reason short of carelessness that he should lose the game.

Finally there is the basic maneuver of the game. Since your opponent, if alert, will not allow you to get three in a row without occupying the fourth space in the line with one of his own pieces, you want to get him in a situation in which he cannot do so. This is done by playing a piece which simultaneously creates *two* different rows of three (a tactic which is something of a distant relative of the fork in chess). Being unable to play more than one piece, your opponent cannot stop you from completing one of the two rows. This two-in-one maneuver is illustrated in Diagram 9-1.

In a two-player game (assuming the two squares marked "?" are empty), if the player plays on the square marked "⊖", he will win the game on the next round (unless, of course, his opponent, *X*, also has three in a row and would then be making four in a row first). The intelligent reader may find such cautions as I keep inserting superfluous and possibly even insulting. Do not be too hasty in your judgment, however. The best laid plans of mice and men (and, I must relevantly add, the most elegant stratagems) are too often disrupted by total simplicity: the oblivious opponent, without the slightest artifice, places four in a row *this* turn while the master planner is busy gloating about what will happen *next* turn.

After a few games, the wary opponent will be on the alert for the two-in-one maneuver, and when such a situation arises will himself play in the crucial spot ("⊖" in the example above), thus frustrating two lines of play at once and defeating the maneuver before it can be brought to maturity. Such wariness, however, merely calls for more sophisticated preparation. This is illustrated

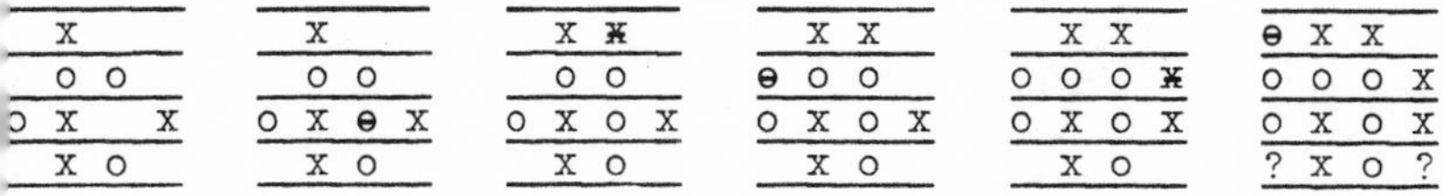

```
  X            X          X  ✳       X  X        X  X      ⊖  X  X
  O  O         O  O       O  O     ⊖  O  O      O  O  O  ✳  O  O  O  X
O X     X    O X ⊖ X    O X O X    O X O X      O X O X    O X O X
  X  O       X  O        X  O       X  O        X  O      ? X  O ?
```

Diagram 9-2

by the line of play shown in Diagram 9-2. (Please remember that only *one* of the four levels is shown. The use of four in the game not only vastly increases the possibilities for such maneuvers; it also means that the situation is much less apparent, even to the alert opponent.)

The lefthand position shows a seemingly innocuous situation that might occur during play. It is *O*'s turn. The middle positions show succeeding consecutive moves, including two moves by each player (for clarity, the move being made in each diagram is labeled "⊖" or "✳"). The righthand position illustrates the position after the *O* player has brought about the two-in-one maneuver and is, in fact, nothing more than a fleshed-out version of our earlier diagram of the maneuver. Note that each of *X*'s moves is forced by the continuing threat of *O*'s making four in a row.

The four-person partnership game is not essentially different from the two-person game, except for the difficulty of communicating strategies between partners. With a little experience, one partner should be able to pick up the other's tactics, especially in the later, crucial stages.

The game for three (or six, in partnerships), however, adds a further element of complexity, evidenced by the fact that in such a game the basic two-in-one maneuver can be defeated, since the two opponents between them can block both lines of potential victory. There is a way out of this problem; it might be termed, by analogy, the three-in-one maneuver. A simple, two-dimensional example is shown in Diagram 9-3.

In the diagram, "⊖" again represents the crucial play, which simultaneously threatens three lines of victory. Despite the far

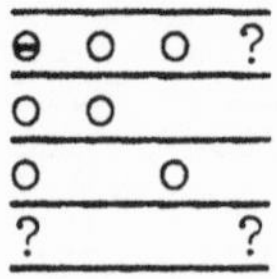

❺	○	○	?
○	○		
○		○	
?			?

Diagram 9-3

greater possibilities inherent in three-dimensional play, however, in practice this maneuver is extremely difficult to bring about; but while, logically, the problems of forcing a victory in the three-player game would seem to indicate a frequency of draws, this is not the case in practice.

Because the rules are short and simple, and the essential nature of the game is quickly grasped, Qubic can readily be played by those new to the game. Too, the nonenthusiast and the true game *aficionado* can compete on fairly even terms, with alertness and logical analysis going far to balance the scales against experience. It is not go, but it can be used as a lure toward more challenging and rewarding games.

GO-MOKU

Go-moku was originally played on a go board, but any rectangular grid can be used, and in the United States, at least, it is commonly played with pencil and graph paper. It is, in effect, an extended form of tic-tac-toe, the object being to get five in a row (rather than three) on a much larger board. The slight change in form results in a totally disproportionate difference in sophistication; the game takes only minutes but is as challenging as the players' wit and experience allow.

The basic solution is to get an open-ended four-in-a-row; the opponent blocks one end and you play on the other, making your five. While this situation can occur at any point in play as a result of luck or a complicated interaction, the basic maneuver to achieve such a solution is to form two open-ended intersecting threes, in the same way that the analogous maneuver was managed in Qubic. On a broader level, the essence of go-moku strategy is to remain on interior lines, while forcing your opponent to remain on exterior lines; keeping your own pieces in a compact mass gives rise to multiple possibilities, while an opponent whose pieces are scattered on the outside of your own force can seldom generate more than a single threat at a time.

FIVE STRAIGHT®

The most recent attempt to adapt go-moku into a contemporary board game is Five Straight (Skor-Mor), which employs a ten-by-ten array and three sets of colored pegs (allowing the participation of a third player). The chief difference is a deck of cards, one for each numbered square; you can place a peg only if you hold a card with the same number (or a lower one) as the square you wish to occupy. Each turn, you can play a card and a peg, or you can draw a card from the deck; in general, it is better to draw than to play in a useless square or in one which would be better occupied at a later move.

The lower numbers match the center squares, making them hardest to play but also hardest to block. Placement along the edge is easy, but an attempt at five straight there is also easily parried. Serious thrusts inevitably involve the center as well, but go-moku strategy is usually reversed: play is from the outside in. If you direct a thrust inward, your opponent will probably not have a low enough card to block the placement of your final, innermost peg.

The use of the cards tends to equalize play, allowing a poorer (or younger) player a chance against a superior strategist. On the other hand, you can always ignore the cards, if you wish, and play straight go-moku.

STRATO TAC-TICS®

Whatever else may be said about Strato Tac-tics (Strato-Various Products), it is the most visually striking game you are likely to come across. The board is a chessboard of clear and dark plastic, and if the two-player game looks, to the uninitiated, like a very mod chess set, a four-player game—with intricately interlocked pieces in four colors of translucent plastic—resembles an exotic free-form sculpture. As a conversation piece, it is without peer;

start a game at poolside or on the beach, and within five minutes you will have the attention of everyone within fifty yards.

Appearances to the contrary notwithstanding, Strato Tac-tics is less like chess than mill (an old game also known as nine-men's morris), though it resembles that game only in its method of capture. From a chesslike initial setup, the object is to maneuver three of your pieces into a row (horizontally, vertically, or diagonally, like Qubic), with the proviso that at least two of them must be within a gold band surrounding the center four squares of the board, where, unsurprisingly, most of the real action of the game takes place. When you succeed in doing so, those three pieces are frozen in place (unlike mill), and one of your opponents' kings is removed from the board. When a player loses all four of his kings, he is out of the game; play continues until only one player, the winner, is left.

The game's directions are something less than a model of clarity; many of the rules are awkwardly stated, and some seem irrelevant*; the concepts in the advanced rules are extremely confusing (e.g., "Peggability" and the special Spinner moves); and the sample games all have errors in them. Despite these drawbacks, you can, if you're careful, follow the sample games (and correct their mistakes), and after you've tried a game of your own, you will discover that the basic version of Strato Tac-tics is easier than the directions would lead you to believe. You will also find that once you understand the game, it's easier—and faster—to explain the rules to someone else than to have him plow through the directions himself.

Strato Tac-tics is one of the few abstract "strategy" (more properly, tactical) games that is not best for two. The basic two-player game is unsatisfying; the loser is inevitably only one move away from winning, a fact which is likely to give him the impression that the outcome was determined by something fairly trivial (and, indeed, unnoticed). There is no reason to stick with it any longer than it takes to grasp the basic concepts, but I do suggest that you add the advanced rules one or two at a time, not as a

---

* Rule 12, for example. In two-player games, it just doesn't matter whether you use a capture move to replace an opponent's king with one of your own; the "delayed vulnerability" is a factor only in multiplayer contests, and with the possible exception of the most advanced variants, the kings never get a chance to move.

package. You may find that some of them (like Peggability) are not worth the bother.

On the other hand, the basic game for four is fairly successful on its own terms and is diverting enough without additional rules. It is innately more complex, because of the greater number of levels and conflicting interests involved. Aggressive play is rewarded; replacing your kings forces opponents to eliminate the others first. However, the biggest flaw in the multiplayer game is that you cannot, with the best of play, guarantee a victory; the game, in effect, can be lost but not won. Within the limitations of the king replacement rule, the other players can remove whosesoever kings they please and if they all pick yours, you've had it. While this difficulty deprives the outcome of a certain level of meaningfulness, it eliminates neither enjoyment nor skill in play.

Although I am unconvinced of any great depth to the game (it is more on the level of go-moku than go), it is interesting, if peculiar. It looks intriguing enough to entice people into trying a game, and it's attractive enough to leave set up in your living room. Strato Tac-tics can be bought in a variety of versions: a two-color set for two players, a four-color set for four, and a Crescendo set for four, which includes special pieces for a final advanced variation. Although it is more expensive (and this is definitely not a cheap game to start with!), I have a clear preference for the four-player version; it is more colorful, more flexible, and more fun.

Strato-Various markets companion sets (with similarly stacking pieces) of Strato Checkers® and Strato Chess®. Since the board is the same for all three, you can add a second or third game merely by buying the pieces (which are available separately).

TWIXT®

Twixt (3M), in a sense, takes the trend we have been following to its extreme. Each player in turn places a peg in a vacant hole in the board; whenever two or more of his pegs are a knight's move apart (that is, are on the opposite corners of a two-by-three rectangle), he can link them together. The object is to form a continuous chain, however crooked, from one of your colored borders to the other on the opposite side. Since Black cannot play a peg in the

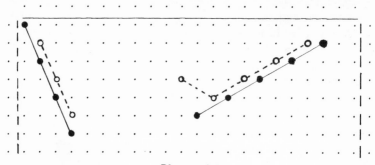

Diagram 9-4

row of holes behind the Red borders (and vice versa), a chain connected to the row in front of your own border cannot be kept from connecting to the row behind; in fact, experience will show that a peg in even the fourth row cannot be kept from connecting to the border without help (i.e., the presence of prior opposing pegs or the close proximity of a second border). Since links cannot be crossed, a victory for one side automatically means defeat for the other. Ties are possible but not common.

The normal game is for two, but Twixt can be played with four persons in two partnerships, like Qubic—with the same problems. In my discussion I assume the existence of only two players, but the application to the partnership version should be obvious. For the sake of clarity, in all the diagrams which follow, Black is assumed to be playing vertically (that is, to have the top and bottom borders) and Red, horizontally.

The first thing to notice about play in Twixt concerns what I term lines of development. Due to the nature of the basic linking move (the twix), there are only two such lines of parallel development: the sixty-degree line (two spaces up and one over—the more vertical) and the thirty-degree line (one up and two over—the more horizontal). While, in general, the former favors Black and the latter, Red (assuming the configuration we are using), the winner of such contested lines as are shown in Diagram 9-4 (that is, the player who can connect his extended chain to his own border, which often simultaneously prevents his opponent from doing so) depends on the exact space on the board from which the line developed. In both illustrated examples, Black cannot be prevented from connecting to his top border.

In developed form, such contested lines are common only in beginners' games, since it takes very little experience to determine *in advance* who will win at any point; just imagine a thirty- or sixty-degree angle extended from the hole you or your opponent is occupying and see whose border is intersected. *Potential* lines of development, on the other hand, are perhaps the most basic tactical consideration and are the subject of innumerable Twixt battles. If a favorable line presents itself, a player will reasonably take advantage of it; rather than continue the same line uselessly, his opponent will either counterattack the end of the line away from the nearest border (making the line useless to the first player), try to head off the line by playing several spaces ahead of his normal twix, or abandon the area and start a new offensive elsewhere on the board.

The basic maneuver of Twixt is the setup: two pegs placed in such a way that a third peg placed in either of two positions will link all three pegs. There are four such setups diagramed in the rules: *beam* (two pegs placed in a straight line with three holes between them), *mesh* (two pegs placed in a straight line with one hole between them, *tilt* (two pegs on a diagonal line with two holes between them), and *coign* (two pegs occupying the opposite corners of a two-by-four-holed rectangle). Setups are often desirable but not invincible; all but the mesh can be stopped if the opponent plays a twix across the path of both possible links. However, the originating player can counter such an attempt by changing the direction or the nature of his setup. An alternative defense against the setup is to make it useless by going around it or blocking it off from the desired border. Often a simple twix is preferable to a setup, and, indeed, the delicate balance between these two alternatives is responsible for much of Twixt's tactical depth.

These and other points are illustrated by Diagrams 9-5 and 9-6. In Diagram 9-5, Black responds to Red *1* by placing himself between the Red peg and his opponent's far border. Red re-

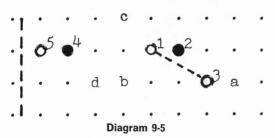

Diagram 9-5

plies with the simplest and most effective countermeasure, a twix from *1* to *3*. Rather than follow a losing line of development by playing at *a*, Black attempts to divert Red by playing the beam setup *4*. Although the *2-b* link is blocked by Red's *1-3* twix, Black can still double-link *2* and *4* by playing at *c*. If Red takes the time to block the *2-c* link, Black may be able to close off the near-side border; instead, Red plays *5*, a beam setup of his own. If Black now double-links *2-b-4*, Red can double-link *1-d-5* and connect with his near border.

In Diagram 9-6, Red places his peg between Black *1* and the Red border; this move threatens to block most of the setups directed toward the upper right-hand corner. The coign set up by Black *3* is a dubious move; while Red cannot prevent the eventual

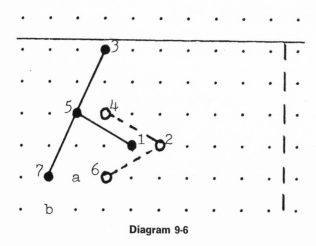

Diagram 9-6

linkage of *1* and *3*, he could counter it effectively by linking *2-6* immediately, a move which would threaten Black's connection to his *lower* border. Instead, Red links *2-4*, a mistake, and Black double-links safely *1-5-3* to his top border. Red's *2-6* twix is a move late; now Black can link *5-7*, which allows a favorable sixty-degree line of development even if Red links *6-b*. Note that Black did not link *1-a* instead of *5-7*, since the former would have resulted in an unfavorable thirty-degree line.

Diagrams 9-7 and 9-8 are alternatives to the events shown in Diagram 9-6. In Diagram 9-7, following Red *2*, Black plays the simple twix *1-3*. Red replies immediately with *2-4* to cut off Black from his lower border. Black tries to escape this with *5*, a coign setup with *3*; if the double-link could be completed, Red would be cut off from his near border, and Black would be solidly on his way to linking his chain with both his borders. Unfortunately for Black, he did not see the possibility of Red *2-6*, which severs both of Black's alternative double-links (*3-a-5* and *3-b-5*) and maroons both halves of Black's divided force.

Diagram 9-8 shows the proper line for Black: after Red 2-4, he links *3-5*, outflanking Red and cutting him off from the border. If Red attempts the simple twix *2-a* or the tilt setup at *c*, Black can frustrate either attempt by linking *5-b*. If Red himself plays *b*, for

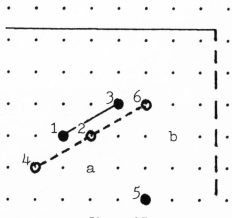

Diagram 9-7

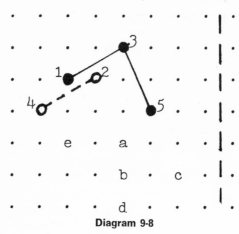

Diagram 9-8

a coign setup, Black can reply with a coign of his own at *d*; if Red then double-links *2-e-b*, Black double-links *5-c-d* and remains on top of the situation.

From the above examples it should be evident that a defense that opens by playing adjacent to the opponent has distinct weaknesses. Diagrams 9-9 and 9-10 explore the possibilities of a defense which starts two holes away.

Red opens play in Diagram 9-9 with a peg in the middle of the board. Black's reply, *2*, is two spaces away, directly between Red's first peg and one of the Red borders. Red plays *3* (beam setup), knowing that Black cannot block both of his double-link alternatives, *a* and *b*. Black's simple *2-4* twix, however, is an effective counter; if Red now played *1-a-3*, Black could continue *4-c*, separating Red from the lefthand border and making a strong bid to connect with the top along a favorable line of development. To prevent this, Red links *1-5*, and Black now blunders by linking *2-6*: not an unreasonable move, perhaps, but premature. Had he linked *4-d*, he could have forced a long continuation of the sixty-degree line (which Red could not have abandoned for fear of a play like *4-c*) that would ultimately have left Red in an untenable position. Black's *6* allows Red to link *5-7*, pushing toward his righthand border and threatening Black's lower connection. After

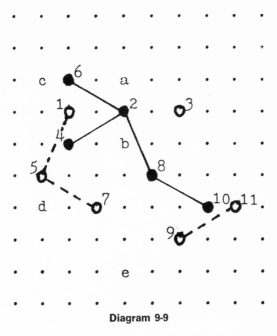

Diagram 9-9

Black 8, Red plays 9, a dual setup with 3 (beam) and 7 (coign). Black can prevent 7-e-9 only by playing e himself, a peg which would be stranded when Red played a twix from 7 toward 9 (or vice versa); instead, he defends against the beam by linking 8-10. Red follows with 9-11, protecting his flank and cutting off Black; 3 is by this time an abandoned but unnecessary peg in Red's development.

To prevent a counterattack like 2-4-d in 9-9, Red in Diagram 9-10 sets up a coign with 3. Unable to block both of Red's alternative double-links, Black makes a parallel move with 4, setting up a coign of his own. Red 5 is brilliant: a dual setup with 1 (beam) and 3 (tilt), with multiple threats to Black. If Black were to play 2-8-4 now, Red could double-link 1-a-5 and cut him off at the top; instead, Black chooses the oblique 2-6 (rather than 2-10, which at this point would leave him more vulnerable to a Red 1-b-5 thrust). Red meets Black's twix with one of his own, 5-7. Hav-

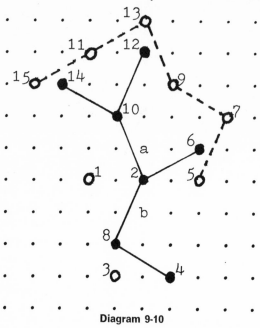

Diagram 9-10

ing severed the possible *1-a-5*, Black moves now to consolidate his lower position by double-linking *2-8-4*. Red's *1, 3*, and *5* pegs are now sundered, but his *7-9* twix threatens Black's connection with his upper border. In an attempt to head off this threat, Black plays *2-10*; however, Red *11*, another dual setup—with *9* (coign) and *1* (beam)—seals his fate. Black's futile *10-12* cannot prevent Red from double-linking *9-13-11*, and his second attempt to break out, at *10-14*, is easily countered by *11-15*. The order of these attempts could have been reversed without changing the situation: Black will be unable to connect his chain to his top border; nor, at this point, does he pose a threat to the successful completion of Red's chain.

These examples could be multiplied indefinitely, but they should be enough to give you a feel for Twixt tactics, for the delicate balance between twix and setup, and for the importance of lines of development. You could, I think, also draw the conclusion that it is better to initiate a defense from two or more spaces away from an opposing peg. I would go even further: the best defense, it seems to me, is a counteroffensive. Place your peg between an enemy peg and one of his borders—at least four spaces away from both—and start a chain of your own. Make your opponent come to you. Several Twixt players I know are convinced that anything but a strategic offensive is a waste of time, and there is much to be said for their view.

Offensively, the most daring move is the long-range double setup (illustrated in Diagram 9-11), the fastest way to extend a potential chain the greatest distance. Pegs *1* and *2* exemplify the most effective such setup, the beam-tilt: either *a* or *b* serves as a dual setup with *1* and *2;* the opponent cannot block both sets of connections. Pegs *1* and *c*, a beam-coign apart, are more vulnerable, since an opponent playing *b* and then linking to *e* severs all the more direct connections between the Black pegs. Note that a double-beam setup like *1* and *f* could easily be countered by an opposing peg at *b*. Further study may make even longer moves possible, but at this stage of Twixt theory, at least, pegs placed farther than a double setup apart seem hopelessly out of touch.

It is too soon to tell how good a game Twixt is. If I doubt that time will show a depth as great as go's, I believe it is at least the equal of checkers. The tactical potential seems as great, there is a

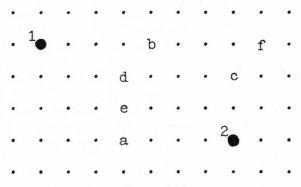

Diagram 9-11

wider range of openings, tediously drawn-out endings are impossible, and it is more fun. If the games in this chapter appeal to you at all, I recommend it highly.

GO

Go is a difficult game to deal with. On the one hand, most Westerners have never even heard of it; on the other, it has been studied in the Orient for centuries, and almost as much has been written about go as chess. Indeed, go is often called the oriental chess, a term not wholly unjust but certainly confusing, given the existence of shogi and hsiang ch'i, which are, respectively, the Japanese and Chinese versions of chess. The comparison with chess derives from similarities in depth, abstraction, and popularity, and the presence of high-level professionals, recognized theory, and abundant written commentary.

In form, go is less like chess than checkers, and more like Twixt than either. It is played on a board covered by a 19 by 19 rectangular grid resembling a piece of ordinary graph paper. There are two sets (one black and the other white) of playing pieces—round, flattened objects called "stones." Black always plays first; the two players take turns placing a stone on a vacant position on the board (one of the intersections of the lines, not the spaces between the lines). Once placed, the stones are never moved unless captured. The object is to arrange the stones so as to enclose the maximum amount of territory; at game's end (which occurs when neither player wishes to play further), the *vacant* points enclosed by each player's armies (his groups of connected stones) are added to the number of stones captured by each, and the player with the higher total wins.

Go is primarily a game of territory; in master play, the threat of capture may dictate many moves, but the actual removal of stones occurs infrequently. Because the process of capturing is easier to perceive than the subtle strategies of broad territorial occupation, beginners are often almost obsessed with taking prisoners.

Capturing is simple: like the occupation of territory, it involves

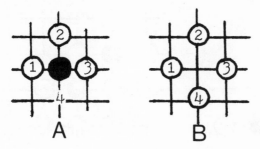

Diagram 9-12

the surrounding of an enemy stone or stones. When a stone's
adjacent horizontal and vertical intersections (its "liberties") are
all occupied by enemy stones, that stone is captured. Diagonal
"connections" or "liberties" do not exist. In Diagram 9-12A, if a
white stone were played at *4*, the black stone (which is therefore
said to be in *atari*) would be captured. Diagram 9-12B shows the
board after the fourth white stone has been played; the playing of
the white stone and the removal of the black one are both parts of
White's turn. Armies (groups of stones) can be captured the same
way; Diagrams 9-13A and 9-13B show a similar sequence involving the capture of a black three-stone army. Both sequences
are artificial, of course; usually Black would have taken measures
to save his stones. A black stone played at *4* in Diagram 9-12A
or *8* in Diagram 9-13A would have saved the black stones, at

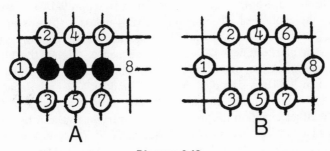

Diagram 9-13

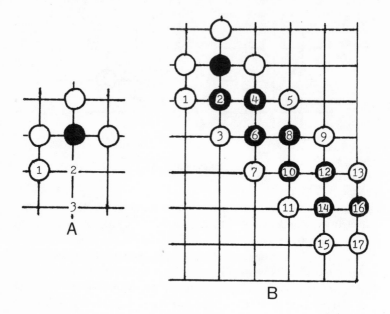

Diagram 9-14

least temporarily, since each black group would then have three liberties.

Diagram 9-14A is the same as 9-12A, except for the presence of an additional white stone at *1*. Note the difference this makes! If Black seeks to avoid *atari* by playing at *2*, White plays *3*, and the black group is back into *atari*. This sequence will continue all the way to the edge of the board, as shown in Diagram 9-14B—resulting in the capture of all the black stones—unless a stone is in the way. A white stone will end the sequence early, capturing the stones; a black stone will break the sequence, freeing the black ones and imperiling one or more of the white stones. The sequence shown in 9-14B is called a *shicho*, or "ladder." Since its conclusion is so predictable, Black would not ordinarily pursue it; he would either abandon the stone in *atari* or try to rescue it by some form of counterattack. (On the other hand, if White had mistakenly played *4* instead of *3*, Black could escape the ladder by playing *3* himself.)

Diagram 9-15A shows a situation like that in Diagram 9-12B. Ordinarily, a black stone played at *1* would be captured immediately, having no liberties, and indeed such a suicidal move is specifically forbidden in the rules. However, examine Diagram 9-15B. Now, if Black played at *1*, the marked white stone would be captured and removed from the board as part of Black's turn, leaving the situation of 9-15C; the black stone lives, having a liberty. If White were now to play at *2*, the black stone would be captured, and the situation would revert to Diagram 9-15B; the entire sequence could be repeated endlessly, leaving the game in a boring stalemate. Since in more complex situations, the lives of many stones might be at stake, the problem is significant. To avoid this, there is the *ko* rule: no player may play a stone which would duplicate exactly the situation on the board at the end of his previous move. Thus, in Diagram 9-15C, White cannot play *2* immediately; first he must make a move elsewhere on the board. Then, if Black has not played *2* himself (to prevent White's counterattack), White can play there on his *next* turn. This can lead to a *ko* fight: White makes a threat elsewhere on the board so urgent that Black must reply, allowing White to capture the black stone; by replying with a threat that demands an answer from White, Black manages to recapture. This may go on for as long as both sides can muster threats, but since, on each exchange, other moves have been made, the *total* board situation has changed, and progress is made.

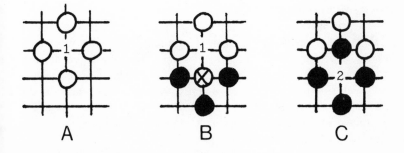

A   **B**   **C**

Diagram 9-15

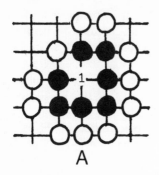

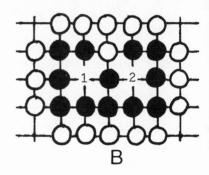

A   B

Diagram 9-16

In Diagram 9-16A, a group of black stones is surrounded by a group of white stones, but the black army has one liberty left, the internal point *1*. If Black played there, the army would be without liberties and would be captured; if White played there, the black army would again be without liberties and would be captured. Note that, because of the suicide rule, White could not play there until all of the black group's other liberties had been taken away; such an internal point, or "eye," must be the final point occupied by White for his attack to succeed. The situation in Diagram 9-16B is similar; however, the black army now has *two* eyes. Because of the suicide rule, White cannot play at either *1* or *2*, since the black army would have one more liberty but the white stone would itself be without liberties. Therefore, *any group of stones that has—or can make—two separate, unconnected eyes can never be captured.*

Theory has shown that any group of stones which encloses at least seven connected points can always make two eyes, regardless of the action taken by the other player. When fewer points are enclosed, the fate of the group depends on the shape of the stones or which side is first to move, or both. Aspiring go players should familiarize themselves with all the three-, four-, five-, and six-point positions, so that they know which groups are always alive, which dead, and which are dependent on the move.

The most basic concepts of go strategy in general and opening strategy in particular are illustrated in Diagrams 9-17 and 9-18.

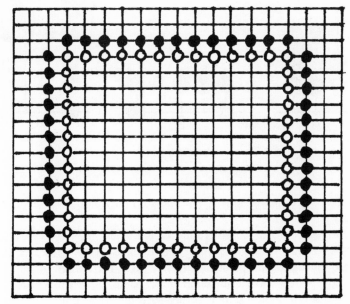

Diagram 9-17

Diagram 9-17 shows the entire go board: Black occupies the third line (counting from the outside) and controls all the territory on the first and second lines; White occupies the fourth line and surrounds the territory in the center. Although White's territory appears substantially larger, it is in fact slightly *smaller* than Black's (count it and see!). Push their positions out one line, so that Black occupies the second line and White the third, and Black's territory is now grossly inferior to White's; shift them in the other direction, so that Black is on the fourth and White on the fifth, and Black's superiority is even greater than it was to start with. However, White would logically try to make more territory by occupying portions of the empty third line. For these reasons, the third and fourth lines are the scene of most of the early action in the game; in anything but the artificial arrangement of Diagram 9-17, a position on the fourth line is generally regarded as equal to a holding on the third, because of the "influence" of the former

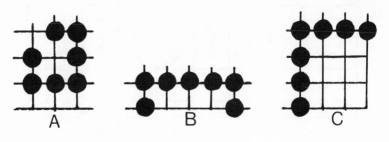

Diagram 9-18

on the center and on activity elsewhere on the board (e.g., a ladder coming toward it).

The other major consideration of early play is shown in Diagram 9-18. In Diagram 9-18A, seven stones in the center of the board surround one point of territory; in 9-18B, seven stones on the edge of the board surround three points of territory; and in 9-18C, seven stones at one corner surround nine points of territory. It is easier to occupy territory—or to capture enemy stones—with one or two edges doing part of the work. It should not be surprising, therefore, that go players generally occupy the corners first, the edges next, and the center last.

Diagram 9-19 shows an opening made by a beginner who took the lessons of Diagram 9-18 too literally. Taking "advantage" of a handicap stone (marked *X* in the diagram—about which more later), Black has decided to occupy a corner.* After six turns, he has succeeded in walling off a twenty-one-point area that is very likely safe from White's attack. Unfortunately, in the meantime Black has effectively surrendered the other several hundred spaces on the board to White's control! Obviously, White's grip on his territory is not so firm as Black's on *his*, but the effect remains. Barring catastrophic blunders, White will win the game handily.

Remember that the object of go is to occupy the maximum amount of territory with the minimum expenditure of stones. Un-

---

* Barring the presence of a handicap stone, Black usually plays *a* or *b* as an initial corner move; with the handicap stone, a likely move would be to *c* or *d*. A counterattack by White might start at any of the four points, or at one of the adjacent points on the third or fourth lines.

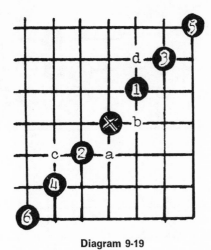

Diagram 9-19

less they are under attack, it is wasteful to place stones close together before the end game. Ideally, stones in the opening are scattered about at strategic points. Gradually, a chain (or chains) connecting them is sketched in; finally, they are actually joined in a firmly connected army.

At each stage of the game (as in Twixt), the security of a literal connection must be balanced by the expanded possibilities of a more distant—and therefore more tenuous—one. I have already suggested that, unless an attack is underway, placing stones horizontally or vertically adjacent is considered bad form. How close, then, is not too close? Especially on the third line, the answer is a two-skip extension, as shown in Diagram 9-20A.* As is shown by Diagram 9-20B, Black cannot successfully separate these two stones. The first several moves are obvious enough (had Black tried to play *3* at *6*, for example, White could play at *a*, putting the black stone in *atari*, from which, in this instance, it could not escape); after White *4* puts Black *1* in *atari*, Black must rescue it with *5*, giving White a chance to connect *2* directly with one of the original stones (via *6*). Black *7* is a futile attack on the other

---

* The relationship between *c* or *d* and the handicap stone in Diagram 9-19 is a variation of this two-skip extension.

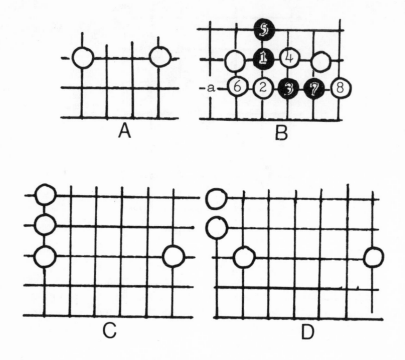

Diagram 9-20

stone, which is stopped by White *8*; Black's *3* and *7* stones are now lost, and White's connection is solid. Larger extensions are secure only when a vertical wall has been raised (usually because of the presence of enemy stones); in this case the extension can be one space longer for each additional stone in the wall, to a maximum of about five spaces in total (see Diagram 9-20C). Generally, this rule holds true even if the wall is a bit crooked (see Diagram 9-20D).

Whether or not go is deeper than chess is enormously debatable (and will not be settled here). One of go's unquestioned advantages, though, is its handicap system. Ordinarily, when two people of distinctly different levels of ability play chess, the game is not really a contest. The only way to give the poorer player a chance is to take away pawns or pieces from the better player. This not only alters the strategies of both players (to say nothing of tactics), it distorts the basic nature of the game—a major reason for the system's unpopularity. Playing without such a handicap, the game may well be educational for the lesser player, but it is apt to be unchallenging and dull for his opponent. Go neatly avoids this dilemma by giving the weaker player extra stones on the board at the beginning of the game; without altering the nature of the game, players of unequal skill can compete on even terms. This makes it easier to teach your wife/husband/child/friend the game and makes it much less frustrating for them; being annihilated the first couple of times a game is tried is enough to dim anyone's enthusiasm.

A further warning: as is the case with all games so extensively played and studied, it is not possible to become an "instant expert" in go. Playing regularly at a go club, one of the best ways to learn the game, you may play for a couple of years before becoming even moderately competent. This fact in itself will discourage most people from trying the game, but if you like deep, abstract games —if, indeed, you enjoy any of the games in this chapter—have a go at go.

FLIP & FLOP®

Flip & Flop (Gameophiles Unlimited) is a member of that large group of games (of which Chinese checkers is the best-known example) whose object is to get from one side of the board to the other before any of the opponents have done so. It is played on a board identical in configuration with a checkerboard except that its 64 squares are not alternately light and dark. Two, three, or four can play (with the usual difficulties for the man in the middle if three are playing); each has four pieces. The goal is to be the first to get two pieces to the farthest row and into the opponent's starting positions.

The pieces are flat, square pieces of wood, with the numbers 1, 2, 3, and 4 facing successive edges on top; on the bottom are the numbers 5 through 8, with the numbers so arranged that the numbers facing the same edge always add up to nine—as 1 and 8, 2

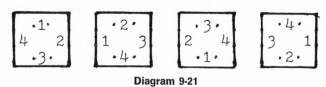

Diagram 9-21

and 7, etc. (much as the opposite numbers on a die always add up to seven). Diagram 9-21 shows each player's arrangement at the start of the game.

Pieces can move sideways or forward, never backward. They move by "flipping"—i.e., by being turned over so that, in a forward move, the number formerly on the bottom at the trailing edge becomes the forward facing number. When two pieces belonging to opposing players are adjacent, the piece with the higher number facing the other can take the other piece by flipping into the other's position. The losing piece is then removed from the board.

The first thing to know about Flip & Flop tactics is that a player's righthand pieces (the ones headed 3 and 4) can always defeat the pieces which start directly opposite them, regardless of the row on which the encounter takes place, so long as they are in their original columns (obviously, therefore, his lefthand pieces, headed 1 and 2, must similarly lose). The situation is reversed if the pieces are flipped into the adjacent columns to right or left but is brought back to the original relationship if they are flipped another column. And so on. There is no such easy relationship between pieces approaching each other at right angles, however.

You should also acquaint yourself with variations of the following "mousetrap" maneuver. Two of your pieces occupy the same rank but are separated by a column, which is occupied by an opposing piece one rank farther up. One of your pieces flips forward one space, moving adjacent to the enemy piece. In that position, the enemy cannot avoid combat with one of your two pieces. Generally—need I say?—you do this only when you have a numerical superiority in all possible positions, so that the enemy piece is captured whether he remains or moves. One such position is shown in Diagram 9-22.

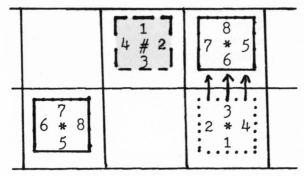

Diagram 9-22

Strategy is similar to parcheesi's. When two persons play with two sets, the righthand set of pieces is used for defense, the lefthand set for offense. In multiplayer games, the burden of defense falls on the 1 and 2 pieces. In all cases, the path of the offense (the 3 and 4 pieces) is the rightmost column(s).

Not a great game, to be sure, but easy to learn, quick, unpretentious, and—if you like this type of thing—enjoyable.

CHINESE CHECKERS

Chinese checkers comes in a variety of configurations, the most common board being in the shape of a six-pointed star, allowing play by two to six persons. The object in all cases is to be the first to move all of your pieces (usually ten marbles or pegs) from their starting position in one of the points of the star into the starting position directly opposite them. Movement is similar to checkers, except that movement in any direction is permitted: a piece can move into any vacant adjoining space, or it can jump over an adjacent man if the space beyond is empty. Any piece belonging to any player may be jumped but not captured (no piece is ever removed from the board); multiple jumps are permitted and, in fact, are usually desirable.

The key involves keeping your men together, maneuvering them to allow each other jumping moves (while—if opportunity permits —blocking opponents' jumping moves). Nonjumping moves should be minimized, and you should avoid stranding your men in positions that leave them several moves from the nearest jump. I prefer to concentrate on advancing my own pieces rather than worry overmuch after blocking the play of my opponents, but this may be a choice based on personal preference rather than clear strategic superiority.

For the rest, you'll have to play the game to get some feel for the tactics involved. It helps to have played it once or twice, but in the long run I think experience counts for less than a perception of the relationships involved and a talent for tactical maneuvering. A child can learn Chinese checkers in two minutes and can, with a bit of practice, play against adults without the game's becoming too one-sided. Though of only moderate depth, the game can be challenging when played by clever opponents.

HYPERCHECKERS®

If you like checkers, you'll enjoy Hypercheckers (Hypergames Co.); and if you don't, you won't. It's a variation of the parent game played on hexagons (six-sided "squares"), and it's definitely for checkers players looking for variety. The strategy is the same, and the tactics are similar, though it may take you a game or two to get used to the differences;* for example, the most common sacrifice move doesn't work in the same way.

The real advantage of Hypercheckers is that it allows play by three persons, a game which has the distinct flavor of a checkers/ Chinese checkers goulash. This version allows some interesting combinations by two players acting temporarily in concert; one can set the third player's checker up for the kill, allowing the other to apply the *coup de grace*. For example: Irene moves one of her kings directly between one of Joe's checkers and one of Karla's. In two-person checkers, such a maneuver (somewhat analogous to a fork in chess) would be devastating; the king could not be prevented from capturing one of the other pieces. In three-player Hypercheckers, however, Joe could move his checker out of the

---

* As is so often the case, the sample game provided has a flaw less than halfway through which invalidates the remaining moves. Do you suppose Somebody Up There has something against properly done examples of play?

way, simultaneously exposing Irene's king, which could then be jumped by Karla. Three-person Hyperchess (which we'll get to shortly) affords the same sorts of possibilities; in either game it is imperative to remember the order in which the other players move, so that *you* can set up—or complete—such maneuvers, rather than be their victim.

The only flaw I can see in Hypercheckers is the very real possibility of a stalemate (even a three-player stalemate), even with several checkers remaining on the board. Like bishops in chess, the checkers in Hypercheckers must remain on hexagons of their own color, except when capturing; so they cannot capture other checkers similarly "stranded" on the same color. Thus, several checkers which are quite free to move may nonetheless be unable to force a conclusion. I have not played the game often enough to know how often this occurs, but it can—and does—happen. This, however, is not a fatal flaw and seems strongly outweighed by the novelty of the game and the flexibility gained by allowing the option of three-person play.

PLOY®

Ploy (3M) bears something of the same relationship to chess that Twixt does to go. Like Twixt, though it can be played by four (either individually or in partnerships), Ploy seems to me basically a two-player game. The opening setup is similar to chess: only one piece can be moved per turn; capture is the same (by replacement), and the primary object is the capture of the enemy Commander.* Furthermore, Ploy seems to me to have the potential in the direction of chess that Twixt does in the direction of go. By this I mean that if Ploy were played and studied with a fraction of the intensity that chess has been, a similar pattern of standard openings, recognized gambits (accepted or declined), and well-known thrusts, combinations, attacks, and counterattacks would ensue. If such a fate is unlikely, it is not because of a lack of depth or virtue in the game; realistically, new board games do not

---

* You can also win by slaughtering all of the other player's pieces *except* his Commander, but this is not at all likely except in the four-player game, where it is not infrequent.

receive that kind of concentrated attention. This limits the kinds of things that can be said about Ploy tactics. Truly sophisticated play is the product of years of study, and my comments here may seem somewhat superficial.

But first things first. For my money, Ploy is one of 3M's most attractive "bookshelf" games. The pieces are comfortably sized, flattened hemispheres of hard, brightly colored plastic. On top of each piece are from one to four raised lines (radii), which control the direction of movement of the piece. The board is also of plastic, inlaid with circles in a nine-by-nine array, along with lines connecting the circles horizontally, vertically, and diagonally. Both circles and lines are slightly recessed, but if the circular recesses were deeper, the pieces would rest more securely in them.

Movement of pieces is along the lines from circle to circle. Pieces can move only in the direction their radii are pointing; in general, the number of spaces they can move in each direction (as well as the number of directions) is determined by the number of radii on them. That is, Lances (with three radii) can move up to three spaces in any one of three different directions; Probes (with two radii) can move up to two spaces in either of two directions, and Shields (with a single radius) can move one space in the direction of their radii. The exception is each side's Commander, which has four radii in a simple X-pattern, but which can move no more than one space at a time. In a player's turn, a piece can either be moved *or* rotated in place (preparing for a future move in a new direction); the Shields alone can be moved and then rotated after their arrival as part of a single turn.

The board and the starting positions for the pieces in the two-player version are shown in Diagram 9-23: Shields are in the front row, with Probes in the middle, and Lances in the back row, flanking the Commander. I confess to being underwhelmed by 3M's terminology, particularly in the case of the Shields, which are often the first pieces moved (inevitably so in the four-player individual version); they are used to scout or probe the center and the enemy more than to shield anything. At the risk of confusing you with an idiosyncratic nomenclature (since 3M also does not differentiate among the three kinds of Lances and Probes), I find it useful to call the Lances starting at B1, C1, and D1, respectively, T-Lances, Y-

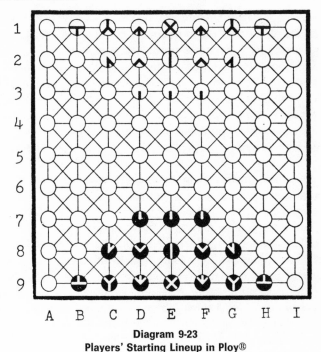

Diagram 9-23
Players' Starting Lineup in Ploy®

Lances, and W-Lances, and to term Probes of the sort at C2, D2, and E2, respectively, V-Probes, L-Probes, and I-Probes.

Based on my own experience, it appears that the W-Lance, with its closely spaced radii, is the most potent offensive weapon in a player's arsenal—and therefore the most valuable piece; however, it is also the most vulnerable of the Lances. Consider the plight of such a Lance if it were rotated 180 degrees in its starting position (a position analogous to one which would occur if it advanced all the way across the board). In this position, the Lance threatens no one and has no move available until it regains its mobility through a turn spent rotating. For a turn, therefore, it is helpless, an easy prey even for an enemy Shield or Commander. On the other hand, the Y-Lance, perhaps the least helpful offensively, is the hardest to trap; the T-Lance seems to me somewhere in between.

There is a similar offense-to-defense spectrum among the Probes: the V-Probe is the most deadly but again the most helpless on the edge; the L-Probe is harder to trap but not as efficient offensively, and the I-Probe is almost worthless on offense but can retreat easily. Determining how much superior any particular Lance is compared to a certain Probe is difficult at best; at this stage an absolute answer is probably not possible.

A first-time Ploy player complained that Probes were even weaker than pawns in chess. He was right—among other limitations, Probes cannot be promoted—but the real point is that *all* Ploy pieces are weaker than their chess counterparts. This has profound effects both on strategy and tactics.

Strategically, the limited mobility of Ploy pieces tends to slow down advances, forcing players to move up their pieces in a group rather than send out single raiders. On the other hand, this is sound chess strategy as well. Since attacks take longer to develop, a player at times may telegraph his punches, but this is partially mitigated by the corresponding delays encountered by the defender and—more important, I think—by the degree to which a situation can be changed by the simple rotation of a powerful piece. Certainly it is more difficult to "transpose" lines of attack. The occupation of the middle and the general tempo of the game are no slower than chess, however, because of the pyramidal arrangement of the pieces, which allows the more mobile (and powerful) pieces in the rear direct access to the rest of the board.

Tactically, the differences in the two games are more significant. Both the pin and the fork are used in Ploy, but because of the limited mobility, only Lances, in practice, can make much use of the pin; usually it occurs only when the Commander is threatened.* The fork, on the other hand, is as much a staple of Ploy tactics as it is of chess. Examples in actual play abound, but for the sake of illustration, imagine the lance at D1 in Diagram 9-23 to be a member of the opposing force: in its position, it would be

---

* For the benefit of those who do not play chess, a pin occurs when a lesser piece is caught in the line of fire in front of a greater one; if the lesser piece moves, the greater one behind it is subject to capture by the attacking piece, so the lesser piece is "pinned down" in military terms, and immobilized. A fork occurs when a piece simultaneously threatens two or more enemy pieces; generally, since the opposing player has but a single move, he cannot avoid losing one of the two threatened pieces.

forking the three Probes at C2, D2, and E2. For an example of a pin, take the same W-Lance (now restored to its own side) and slide it along the diagonal to A4 (after moving the V-Probe out of the way, of course), then forward along the column until it stops at A6, where it now pins the V-Probe at C8 (because of the threat to the W-Lance at D9, but note the caveat in the next paragraph).

Pieces on the edge of the board (especially the far edge) are much weaker in Ploy than in chess, and are, in fact, direct invitations to attack. Be wary of capturing on the edge of the board, however, unless your mobility is not drastically impaired; the waving red flag may hide the matador's rapier. When you rush up to gore the sacrificed Shield or Probe, an enemy Lance may come forward and, before you can disentangle yourself, deliver a *coup de grace* of its own. Remember, too, that pieces are vulnerable anywhere on the board if attacked from their "blind side," even by a less powerful piece.

Don't be too quick to retreat when threatened; it is usually better to bring up a defending piece, instead, which continues your development and preserves the initiative. The lack of mobility in Ploy (compared to chess) means that a really long-range attack is not possible, which in turn implies that capturing is more common than in chess, but don't exchange unless there is some real end in view. Exchanges can be used to strip a Commander's defenses or to destroy the momentum of an attack. Make sure you are the one profiting from any exchange.

A few words should be said about the opening; after that, you're on your own. (Remember that, unlike chess, Ploy is horizontally *and* vertically symmetrical, so comments made about one side—in either sense of the word—apply to the other as well.) The immediate destination of the Shields at D3-F3 is the next rank, followed by control of the central rank either by actual occupation or by the threat of attack. One possibility is to have one flank Shield (or both) move ahead one space and rotate to point to the central circle, E5, then move the E3 Shield up to E5. The V-Probes are usually moved forward one space—to threaten or guard the center or to guard the nearest Shield—or two spaces—to attack the enemy's advancing Shield. Alternatively, the L-Probe at D2 might advance on its open diagonal one space, to similarly guard/ threaten the center, though this is often better done after advancing the V-Probe. A second possibility involves moving the central Shield forward one space and then taking advantage of the now-open diagonal to advance the D2 L-Probe to F4, where it paves the way for the Shield's further advance.

If the L-Probe is moved, the W-Lance may occupy the Probe's starting position at D2; if the V-Probe is moved, the W-Lance may, instead, advance along the diagonal to C2 or B3. The Y-Lance is best positioned at B2 or A3; if the former, it is preferable to allow the T-Lance to move first, since it inevitably moves forward along its own column (usually two or three spaces). The Commander remains where he is well into the game, but it is often a good idea to rotate him to face any adjacent open space that becomes available.

There are several considerations unique to the four-player game. For one thing, any player can go down to quick defeat if attacked by all three others, and even the presence of a single piece from one player can spoil an otherwise brilliant attack on another. Gambits are dangerous for that reason. One of the two major ways to win involves an all-out attack on one player (since you take over his pieces when you capture his Commander), but watch your back! Exchanges should also be avoided, generally, since an exchange benefits the two players not involved. The easiest path to victory, in fact—at least for the first couple of games, until everyone else catches on—is to avoid involvement; let the other three players slaughter each other, and they will be no match for your own delayed attack. This policy won't work, of course, against a determined attack, but it is often possible to subtly turn attackers against another target: for example, you might counterattack an advanced enemy piece, leaving him an escape route which takes him away from you and into contact with another player. This stratagem is called "divide and conquer," and it works in Ploy as well as anywhere else.

Ploy is easier to learn than chess, since it lacks the older game's more peculiar rules (castling, *en passant* captures, etc.), and since the possibilities for movement are, in effect, emblazoned on each piece. In either two- or four-player form, it is enjoyable and challenging; the very lack of established lines of play allows you to develop your own and, in keeping the game novel, ensures that it

will be won by wit and tactical maneuver, not by a superior
memory.

SMESS®

Despite its unintellectual facade, Smess: The Ninny's Chess
(Parker Brothers) is not just a game for dummies. Five minutes
into an average game, the two players involved will be wearing the
same intense frown of concentration found on the face of the
average chess player—and may not be moving any more rapidly.
Smess is, by design, considerably easier to learn than chess, and in
fact anyone remotely familiar with the latter game can learn all he
needs to know about the former just from looking at the board.
The Ploy technique has been taken one step further: the direction
of movement of all pieces is controlled by arrows printed on the
board spaces themselves. The pieces have been simplified and
streamlined: each player's Brain (king/commander) and his seven
Ninnies (pawns) can move one space at a time; his four Numskulls
(bishops/rooks/queens) can move any number of spaces in a
straight line. Limitations and variations of movement have all been
transferred to the board, where they are readily visible. As far as
the *rules* go, there is nothing to remember.

This means that even the rankest novice can concentrate on
strategy and tactics from the beginning of his first game—a delightful feature in any game. Tactics are a combination of chess
and Ploy; the pin and the fork are common, though obviously only
Numskulls can make use of the former. All pieces are vulnerable
to attack from squares to which they are not pointing, and the
value of a square is largely determined by the squares it commands. Those squares which point in only a single direction are
not just worthless but dangerous; a Numskull resting on one will
be lucky to escape with its life.

Unlike chess, which is vertically symmetrical, the Smess board
is *diagonally* symmetrical (like a crossword puzzle). Because of
the pattern of the arrows, the natural development of the game
tends to be—for both players—like an S: to the right, first, then
across the center, angling to the left corner, then back across to the
right, toward the opponent's Brain. The middle is explosive, and

control there—so important in chess—is vital in Smess; since the board is one column narrower, the "center" is really two squares instead of four, and those two squares are the only two on the board with arrows pointing in every direction.

D4 (in Diagram 9-24) is thus the most obvious initial target, and C3 and E3 are not only the most direct ways to get there but also act as D4's closest defenders. The most common opening for both sides involves advancing the C2 and E2 Ninnies to C3 and E3, followed by a move from either square to D4. In his articles in *Games & Puzzles*, Leonard Barden refers to this as the "Symmetrical Ninnypush." At this point there is considerable divergence. The pure Ninny opening continues with a Ninny from B2, D2, or F2 replacing the advanced Ninny at C3 or E3. This takes two turns, whichever Ninny is used. Another continuation advances the Numskull from C1 to C3, in one move (this can be done with the Numskull on the other side, at E1, but this seems to me an inferior line).

From this point much depends on the action of your opponent and your own taste. A Numskull at C3 can move to the opponent's G4, putting the Brain in check ("Brainthreat," in Barden's terminology) or pinning a Ninny, but it is easily driven off by Ninnies at F3 (to protect the Brain) and G3 or an obstructed Numskull at G1; so this move is probably best saved for later in the game or else used as a feint in combination with action elsewhere on the board. The symmetrical point—your own G4—is less vulnerable to attack (because farther away from enemy Ninnies) and is a good place to station a Numskull, though it will take several turns to get one there. One way is to move the G2 Ninny to G3 and then out of the way at F3, followed by the F1 Numskull to G1 and then G4; a slower but more aggressive play involves moving the G2 Ninny to G4 and then across into enemy territory at B4, followed by the F1 Numskull as before. A third alternative stems from a variation of the Double-Ninny opening: the righthand Ninny takes over the center, and the E1 Numskull advances to the vacated E3, moves up diagonally to the enemy A4, and then retreats a step to G4. This can work, even if the enemy Ninny at B3 is enticed out to B4 to threaten the Numskull at A4; when the Numskull retreats, the tables are turned. Admittedly, the Ninny can always move to A4, threatening your Numskull again, but your E4 and his C3

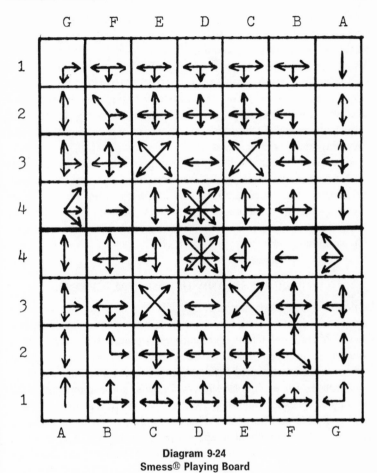

Diagram 9-24
Smess® Playing Board

spaces will be open for your Numskull, and your opponent may
well have lost control of the center.

Be careful of allowing chess habits to carry over too strongly
into Smess. I have seen players advance their G-column Numskull
all the way down to the opponent's A1, attempting to take advantage of an "exposed" Brain, only to discover that the A1 arrow
allows only a retreat! On the other hand, the Brain can be vulnerable to attacks from any other point in the last row if the Ninny at

D2 remains there; unlike the king in chess, the Brain has no diagonal escape move available and may well be trapped. Also, moves are not, often, reversible: just because you went from point A to point B doesn't mean you can go back to point A again, and the unthinking assumption to the contrary has lost more than one piece. Finally, because of the sparsity of diagonal arrows, such lines are more important in Smess than in chess: aside from the center square at D4, the most important squares in general are the three diagonals—C3, E3, and G4.

Smess can be played by quite young people, though not with much success against older, more experienced players. It's a pleasantly sneaky way to entrap reluctant friends who are put off by the confusing elements of chess; but besides serving as an indirect introduction to the parent game, Smess is a challenging and enjoyable game in its own right.

HYPERCHESS® AND HEXAGONAL CHESS®

Hyperchess (Hypergames Co.) is not the only hexagonal chess game; there is at least one other, called, simply enough, Hexagonal Chess (Hexagonal Chess Publications), invented by W. Glinski. There are a number of similarities between the two: the boards in each case are made up of hexagons in three colors, there are three bishops (one for each color) in both games, and the movements of the major pieces are identical (and are all fairly logical analogs of their orthodox counterparts). Hexagonal Chess has its virtues: for one thing, the hexagonal shape of the board—which consists of ninety-one small hexagons, six on a side—seems esthetically appropriate, regardless of how well it actually works. The layout is peculiar: each side's pieces are centered in one of the points of the hexagon, rather than on a side, and the bulk of the pieces are arranged in a five-by-five rhombus. This allows some of the major pieces instant access to the center, gives all of them maneuvering room, and ensures that a single central pawn move brings the pawns into contact with each other—all facets at considerable variance with the parent game. On the other hand, these "defects" could be lessened if the front sides of the rhombus were collapsed, retreating the central three (or five) pawns one space apiece. The real virtue of Glinski's arrangement is that it allows each pawn to advance straight up a column, allowing it the straight move and diagonal capture of pawns in regular chess.

The greatest weakness of William Groman's Hyperchess is the pawn. Groman's board is less straightforward; it allows a more compact, sensible setup, but it enables pawns to hop straight forward (an effective move of two spaces, which allows them to cross the board in four turns), move or capture diagonally forward, or even capture sideways. The slight gain in power afforded the rook (with six directions to move instead of four) and the corresponding loss in power of the bishop (since the board is now divided among three bishops, not two) and the knight (since the board is larger) are nothing compared to the distortion of the game wrought by the pawns: in Hyperchess, a pawn line becomes the Great Wall of China. I find this concentration of power in the normally lowly pawn unnecessary and excessive, and recommend stripping the pawn of its sideways capture, at least in the two-player game.

On the other hand, there are some significant practical advantages to Hyperchess: the other game is not readily available in the United States; Hexagonal Chess requires an extra pawn and bishop per side, necessitating two ordinary sets, while Hyperchess can be played with a regular set (by capping a pawn to represent the third bishop), and Hyperchess boasts the flexibility of a three-player option. Like Hypercheckers, Hyperchess comes with two handsomely done boards (one for each version) of heavy vinyl, which come rolled but flatten out nicely for play; like both other hexagonal games, it does not include playing pieces.

Newcomers to Hyperchess will find themselves making the sort of silly errors beginners make in chess: moving a piece onto a "square" from which it can easily be captured (without even noticing the threat), and so on. This wears off, however, as you become familiar with the board.* Beginners' games, at least, tend to involve many captures and exchanges, rather than more elegant checkmates; this, too, is typical of chess novices, and may similarly decline as you gain experience. On the other hand, the increased mobility of the king would logically make it harder for him

---

* The Hyperchess sample game contains no errors, but Black's play—at least—cannot, even in charity, be described as inspired.

to be mated, which in turn suggests that the overall quality of play may be somewhat less "elegant" (in the mathematical sense) than regular chess.

As was the case with Hypercheckers, much of the fun inheres in the three-player version; it adds complexity, of course: you now have to worry about two other adverse interests and twice as many opposing pieces. On the other hand, what could be more thrilling than putting two kings in check with a single move? Further, it opens up all sorts of crafty two-player combinations: for example, in the course of play, one of your men is shielding Donna's piece; you move your man, exposing the piece, and Elvin (whose turn is after yours) captures it. Double-checks (involving pieces belonging to two different players) are possible, too, which is probably a good thing, since three-player Hyperchess, at least in beginners' games, often has all the elegance of a free-for-all.

In either version, Hyperchess allows the realization of every chess player's dream: to develop new openings and combinations that have not been tried, exhausted, and discarded by a grand master fifty years ago. The strategy and tactics of regular chess prevail, but every move—every line of play—is necessarily new and different. Besides its obvious market of chess players looking for variety, Hyperchess should appeal to the sort of serious game-ster who would rather *play* games than memorize them.

CHAPTER 10

Semiabstract Battle Games
(*War Games I*)

STRATEGO®

Stratego (Milton Bradley) may remind some of you of the outdoor game, capture the flag, but it is more directly descended from an old board game called the jungle game. Each of the two players involved has a set of forty pieces, consisting of a Flag, some Bombs, and an army of men ranking from a Marshall down to a Spy. The pieces are upright and shielded so that their identifying face is visible only to their owner; since the initial setup is left to the players' discretion, they have no way of knowing the identity of any of the opposing pieces until contact has been made.

Most pieces move one square orthogonally in any direction; in a turn, a player either moves a piece or, if one of his pieces is adjacent to an opposing piece, he may "strike" or "challenge" that enemy piece. At this point, the identities of the two men are revealed, and the "combat" is resolved simply: a higher-ranking piece removes a lesser-ranking piece (e.g., a Major captures a Captain; a Captain captures a Lieutenant) and takes its place; if both are of equal rank, both pieces are destroyed. There are two exceptions: a Bomb (which cannot move) destroys everything but a Miner, and the lowly Spy can assassinate the mighty Marshall *if he strikes first*. Quite often, the Spy is recognizable as the fellow tagging along behind his Marshall, being protected and awaiting his chance to strike; against a player familiar with this habit, the substitution of, say, a Scout for the Spy can provide a ruse whereby an unsuspecting Marshall can be exposed to a Spy lying in wait elsewhere.

The object is to find and capture the other player's Flag; this, however, inevitably follows a long period of mutual slaughter. If, at any time, one player can gain a one-man superiority in any of the higher-ranking pieces, he can usually force a victory by exchanging the other equal- and higher-ranking men. Since the only remaining threat is a Bomb, which cannot move, all he has to do is destroy those pieces which *do* move, one at a time, until nothing but Bombs and the Flag are left; at that point, a Miner takes over, and the game is won. In such an instance, of course, the opposing player should long since have surrendered.

While there are more interesting other-service and mixed-service versions (notably Tri-Tactics®) available in England, in its American incarnation Stratego suffers from a slow pace (the game can last hours) and limited scope for strategy and maneuver alike. It has its adherents, but I find it dull.

BATTLESHIP®

Battleship (Milton Bradley) is simply a board game version of the old pencil-and-paper classic of the same name and is preferable only for those who desire something more presentable than a piece of graph paper, or who are simply too lazy to draw their own grids.

BROADSIDE®

Broadside (also by Milton Bradley), on the other hand, is an excellent game—fast-moving, challenging, and enjoyable. It differs from the previous pair in several respects, not least of which is the fact that the two sides have different forces and different aims. The Red player's object is to sink the four unarmed and motionless merchant ships at anchor in the harbor; the Blue player's object is to prevent this from happening. The Red fleet is more powerful, but Blue has some compensating advantages. There are only two entrances to the harbor: each is three spaces wide, is flanked by a pair of invulnerable shore batteries, and is protected by a row of mines. However, half of the six mines are duds, and two of the guns don't fire; only Blue knows which is which (forcing the Red player into a form of Russian roulette). Since all three "real" mines are not permitted on the same side, and since the working guns have a two-space range, the most common arrangement is to split the good guns (one per entrance) and block each "exposed" space with a real mine. The "extra" mine is usually placed in the nearer entrance. A good alternative is to place both working guns at the near entrance and two working mines at the other; this forces Red to concentrate his attack on the far entrance and gives Blue time to set up his ships in solid defensive formation there.

Movement in Broadside is simple: each turn, a player may move any *one* of his warships, regardless of its initial facing, any number of spaces in a straight line, orthogonally, though it may not move into or through a space occupied by another ship. Ships may neither turn in place without moving nor turn *after* moving.

From the space on which it stops, the ship that has just moved may fire a "broadside" at any adjacent enemy ships to which its guns are pointing. If the opposing ship's guns face the attacking ship, there is an exchange of broadsides; on the other hand, if the moving ship stops so that its side faces the stern or bow of an enemy ship, it can deliver a broadside without receiving a hit in return (this key maneuver is called "crossing the T"—a standard feature of naval warfare since the invention of gunpowder). Similarly, a ship which blunderingly stopped with its bow exposed to an enemy broadside would receive a hit as the concluding part of its move.*

Every time a ship is hit—either by a broadside or a shore battery—it loses a mast; when its last mast falls, the ship is "sunk" and out of the game. A single-masted cutter's broadside is thus the equal of a three-masted frigate's, but the smaller ship won't last as long in battle. This combination of strength and weakness can

---

* Although only implied by the rules, this is a reasonable interpretation and is certainly in keeping with the spirit of the game and the facts of naval warfare.

often be exploited *kamikaze* fashion: a cutter (or any other ship reduced through combat to a single mast) moved between two enemy ships can loose *two* broadsides (one for each side), inflicting one hit on each ship. It receives two hits in turn, of course, but one of those is obviously superfluous—and therefore wasted.

Red can make a similar use of a single-masted ship to probe Blue's defenses. The novice's inclination is to send a Red ship into one side of one of the harbor entrances, thus risking at most a single hit. However, more information can be obtained by boldly sailing a cutter into the *middle* of the entrance: the ship, of course, will almost certainly be sunk, but the inexpensive gambit forces Blue to reveal the nature of *both* cannons guarding the entrance (for this purpose, a cutter should be stationed in the front rank of the Red fleet, in line with its intended path). If both are working, Red will immediately shift operations to the other entrance; if not, the safe passage will be revealed. It should, I trust, be similarly obvious that Red should never essay an unknown mine buoy with anything larger than a single-masted vessel.

A final word on tactics: two ships (of either side) can provide strong mutual support if they are *diagonally* adjacent: i.e., one rank and one file apart. In that position, no enemy ship can attack one without leaving itself open to a counterattack from the other. Conversely, a ship which does not have another friendly ship somewhere on either the adjacent rank or file is much too inviting —and helpless—a target.

Although it is easy to learn and takes only an hour or so to play, Broadside may be too competitive for some "family" game fans (i.e., those who are lost without dice to move their tokens) and will probably be slighted by Avalon Hill purists who sneer at anything less involved than the simulations of Chapter 12. The game would be a particularly appropriate gift for an intelligent young person (of, say, ten to fifteen), but can be played enjoyably by gamers of all ages.

FEUDAL®

In designing Conquest (Donald Benge), it was Benge's avowed intent to create a "chess on a map." The description could apply with equal validity (or the lack of it) to Feudal (3M). Unfortunately, neither game is chess—on or off a map—and, though neither is without interest, neither one is entirely successful, either.

Feudal's board is more stylized and abstract, resembling Twixt's with the addition of colored and patterned spaces representing, respectively, mountains and rough terrain. In the two-person version, each player commands a force of thirteen medieval warriors (plastic figures with pegs on the bottom to fit into the holes in the board), including a King, a Prince, and a Duke. The object is to capture the opponent's castle or all three members of his royalty. While the players initially deploy their men as they please, capturing is the same as in chess, and the movements of the pieces are somewhat akin to those of chessmen but are restricted by range (only the mounted men can move more than twelve spaces in a single turn) and terrain (mounted men can't cross rough terrain, and no one can cross mountains).

Most of the pieces are too powerful and too hard to trap. The powers of the weaker pieces (the Squire, the King, and, to a lesser extent, the somewhat useful Archer, which can capture without moving—by "shooting") are not on the same order of magnitude. They cannot possibly keep up in movement; so they are useful only as defenders of the castle. Feudal's biggest problem, however, is that a player may move every one of his pieces in a single turn; this sabotages gambits and replaces the elegant advanced planning of chess with a great deal of inconsequential skulking (something like the "Panzerbush" syndrome described in Chapter 12) and impromptu skirmishing.

Three to six players may play, either as two teams or (with four players) in four separate factions, but with six armies involved, the game opens up with a short period of enormous mutual destruction and then reverts to the problems of the two-player game. The two-player (or -team), four-army version may well be the best compromise between indiscriminate slaughter and tedious stalemate. A more radical—but probably more satisfying—solution is to change the movement rule: allowing a player to move only *half* his men each turn will probably add more challenge and interest to the game than any variation suggested in the rules.

Regardless of the version played, there are a few tips to keep in mind. First of all, the castle should be placed so as to minimize the possible entrances to the green. All four quarters of the board have positions which allow the castle green to be entered from *three* squares, one of which is usually rough terrain; however, the quarter with *five* rough terrain squares (instead of four) allows castle placement in such a way that the green can be entered only from *two* spaces. In all cases, the castles fit into similar slots in the mountains, with the green facing in for maximum protection and minimal exposure. Second, since the King is good for nothing else, he should be stationed in the castle itself; that way, the opponent must, in effect, fulfill *both* criteria of victory. Third, since an attacker must stop on the green before entering the castle, it is probably pointless to station a defender there (he would simply be killed in the first attack). Finally, the pictures and setups on the game box and in the brochure are usually wrong and should be ignored.

CONQUEST®

Conquest's board more nearly resembles a map but is scarcely less stylized than Feudal's; it represents several land masses surrounded by water, and the whole is covered with circles (on which the pieces may rest) and the connecting lines which delineate the allowable paths between them. Each of the two players commands a force of knights, chariots, elephants, and ships—a total of twenty-six units on a side. These are represented by heavy cardboard pieces (something like the standard Avalon Hill/SPI units, but larger and twice as thick), each of which begins from a specified position, as in chess.

The ostensible object is the capture of all five spaces of the enemy capital, but in practice this inevitably means the destruction of the opposing forces. Capturing is again as in chess, but movement is a compromise between that of chess and that of Feudal (and much resembles a regularized version of Campaign's); each player has an allowance of twenty moves (spaces) per turn, which he can distribute among his pieces as he wishes, subject to the particular move limitations of each unit (e.g., a foot soldier can only move two spaces in one turn; a chariot can go eight spaces). Ships, elephants, and chariots can carry pieces on top of them at no additional movement cost.

Capturing, however, complicates matters; a capturing piece can, in effect, start over. A knight, for example, might move five spaces, capture an enemy piece, move six more spaces, capture another, and move again, up to the overall twenty-space limitation of his side. From the standpoint of realism, this is obviously absurd; pitched battles are not fought to speed soldiers on their way!* (And let's not hear the copout, "It's only a game.") One man or ship can in this way in a single turn destroy an enormous chunk of the enemy force, if the pieces are properly separated.

A second rule somewhat mitigates this effect, but only in close formations: if there is an available defender within two spaces of the capture, he can capture the attacking piece, following which the other player finishes his turn as usual. The effect of these two rules is to encourage movement in large, defensible masses, which of course slows down the game and leads to stalemates of the old John Foster Dulles school of massive retaliation: two huge masses facing each other, each of which is afraid to move because of the escalating response any such move would engender. Calculating the precise results of such exchanges is often complicated (not to say tedious) but it is, in fact, only in such involuted situations that the game bears any resemblance to chess.

For a change, the game does include tactical tips, in the form of a series of problems. Once you have grasped the tactics involved (which may take a while), you will, indeed, be able to play the game successfully, and Conquest is sufficiently peculiar that someone who has played it before has an enormous advantage over a newcomer to the game, regardless of their overall gaming experience or skill.

While neither Conquest nor Feudal is really a *bad* game, their virtues are not sufficient, in my opinion, to attract the attention of anyone except those with a particular interest in games of this general sort. Most gamers, I think, could more profitably spend their time and money elsewhere.

---

* And *this* from a man who criticized Risk for the absence of fleets to transport the armies from Kamchatka to Alaska!

THE MAJOR BATTLES AND CAMPAIGNS
OF GENERAL GEORGE S. PATTON®

Like "science fiction" written by non-science-fiction writers, war games designed by people outside the war-gaming fraternity often leave much to be desired; so I confess to an initial prejudice against The Major Battles and Campaigns of General George S. Patton* (RGI/Athol). Down to the cheap cardboard counters, it looks like a poor imitation of an Avalon Hill/SPI simulation, and purists will undoubtedly shun it for lacking the high degree of verisimilitude to which they have become accustomed.

For all that, it's as good a way as any to prepare your girl or boy friend for more complex war games, and it's not even that bad a game in its own right. A typical game lasts an hour or two, but it can be learned in ten minutes, and the mechanics are simple enough so that you can play without constant recourse to the rules (which is, at least, a welcome relief from standard SPI procedure). Its movement system—something of a cross between Conquest's and Campaign's—is unique: by employing *pairs* of "movement cards," one of which is altered each turn, the two players' per-turn allotments are randomized but somewhat predictable and, in the long run, equal. As in the two aforementioned games, each player is free to expend his movement points among his units as he wishes; movement is purely on roads, from city (intersection) to city, the point cost varying inversely with the quality of the road traveled.

Combat in Patton is relatively bloodless and also unusual. It is a direct dice system (as in Risk or Emperor of China); one die is rolled for each armored unit or pair of infantry units on each side. For each double rolled (or 6, when only one die is used) by one side, one infantry unit is lost to the other ("triples" cause two losses, "quadruples" three, etc.). The side with the higher dice total (regardless of casualties, unless one side is wiped out) captures (or retains control of) the town for which the battle is being fought; the other side must retreat to an adjacent town. From this several tactical points can be drawn. One die has as good a chance

---

* Patton's chief designer, Sid Sackson, has a considerable reputation in the gaming field, but war games are not his usual metier.

of inflicting casualties as two, though it is less likely to take the city. To have a reasonable chance of inflicting casualties, you must roll at least *three* dice—preferably more. Finally, really decisive combat occurs only when you can completely surround a group of enemy units; without a path of retreat, units with a lesser dice roll must "surrender" and are thereby eliminated. (This last is also an important tactic in more involved war games which include a retreat—e.g., "D Back 2"—in their Combat Results Tables.)

The game includes three distinct mapboards and scenarios. The Sicily Campaign is similar in theme and strategy to D-Day and other copyrighted invasion games. Despite the theoretically infinite (but in practice slow and irregular in appearance) Axis reserves, the Allies seem to have the edge because of the mass defections caused by one or two Allied units loose on the island. Because they are so hard to annihilate, such units, even when they "lose" a battle, simply get pushed from town to town, which can be disastrous for the Axis. Breakout at Normandy seems to be biased in the other direction: if the Allies cannot *immediately* seize and hold the unnamed crossroad city between Avranches and Fougeres, they haven't a prayer, and even if they do manage, their chances are only mediocre, since they can be delayed so easily at the important crossroads of Fougeres, Utre, and Mortain. The third scenario is The Bulge, a battle long popular with war game enthusiasts; whether it will remain so in this incarnation remains to be seen.

QUEBEC 1759®

Quebec 1759 (Gamma Two Games, Ltd.) is a re-creation of the epic struggle between Montcalm and Wolfe, which decided the fate of a good deal of North America. It demonstrates that a game can be strategic without sacrificing tactics, that it can be deep without being complicated, and that it can recapture with considerable accuracy the flavor of a real battle without recourse to thirty pages of rules. Movement is like that in Diplomacy—simultaneous but simple.

In brief, Wolfe has a limited time to take Quebec (actually, in the game, the Plains of Abraham) without falling below a required minimum strength; if he fails, Montcalm wins. The French (that's

Montcalm and company, for those of you who are shamefully remiss in your knowledge of Canadian history) have more troops, but the English forces are individually more powerful.

The pieces are tiles or blocks with a series of descending numbers, representing the unit's current strength, facing successive edges à la Flip & Flop; but, as in Stratego, the identification is on one side only, so you can't tell the exact disposition of the other player's forces until battle is joined. While there is provision for deployment in columns, reserves, retreats, and other appropriate tactical details, the basic combat system is like Patton's but simpler: in battle, a player is allowed one die roll per turn for each of his troops' remaining strength points. Every 6 reduces the enemy's strength by one point. This is recorded by rotating the stricken square piece so that the next lower number is forward (or up). When a piece's last point is gone, it is removed from the board. A fight continues until one side is annihilated or decides to retreat and try another battlefield.

Easy to learn, challenging, not too long (an hour or less), fun—what more could you ask?

## CHAPTER 11

Multiplayer Conflict Games (*War Games II*)

4000 A.D.®

If the setting of 4000 A.D. (House of Games)—a simulated three-dimensional "universe" of forty-eight star-systems—is unique, the theme is familiar: conquest of the world (or, in this case, of the universe). This is generally accomplished in stages: first, the occupation of resource stars, to allow the development of huge fleets;* second, the gradual decimation of enemy ships, and finally, the conquest of enemy home stars.

The charm and fascination of the game are based on two factors: movement and combat. The movement system uses a variation of a common science-fiction device: the space warp, or hyperspace. Each player has two warps at his command. Any number of ships can be taken from a star, placed inside a warp, and entered on one of the warp paths which surround the board. Each turn, the warp—and its cargo of ships—is advanced one space, after which

---

* As in Diplomacy, the number of new ships—built every other turn—depends on the number of resource stars a player controls.

it may remain on the path or exit to deposit its ships on the board. Each block on the path represents one turn and one sector of distance; *it does not indicate direction*. No player (including, possibly, the player who sent the ships on their journey) knows the destination of the ships—only the range of possible destinations. After five turns in the warp, ships can land on any star that lies five sectors away from their starting point. The tension, excitement, and fluidity generated by this gimmick are equalled in no other game I have ever seen.

Credit goes to the combat resolution system as well, of course, which is even simpler than Diplomacy's: the larger force destroys the smaller. In a sense, this is a game devoid of tactics: in 4000 A.D. a force of twenty-one ships annihilates a force of five ships or twenty ships with equal speed and ease—and at no damage to itself. Little wonder the presence in warp of a large fleet causes such consternation among players!

The combat system has several important implications for play. Initially, advance outposts on resource stars are very large, to preclude the possibility of counterattacks. Soon, however, such garrisons are reduced to two or three ships. The reason is simple enough: the loss of a resource star and a few ships is certainly annoying, but the loss of the same star and ten or twenty ships can be disastrous. In the long run, increased size brings increased vulnerability. No system except the home star is worth the risk; there are too many others available.

It is a fairly simple matter to maintain a garrison which, in conjunction with the new ships being built every other turn, will be large enough to deal with any single force in warp by the time it can arrive. To overcome this, however, the offense uses the basic "tactical" maneuver of the game: the use of *two* forces in warp coming from two different stars, scheduled to arrive at their target simultaneously. Separately, either would be destroyed; joined together, however, they are enough to overcome the garrison. A particularly devilish form of this maneuver involves forces so placed and timed that they can arrive at either of *two* enemy home stars on the same turn; if that does not cause catalepsy among your opponents, nothing will. Needless to say, midgame strategy concerns itself largely with setting up such one-two punches.

Like Campaign or Origins of World War II, 4000 A.D. allows

alliances (and the mind-boggling possibilities of three or four fleets arriving simultaneously over a target star) but emphasizes individual action more than Diplomacy. The two-, three-, and four-player games are all attractive, although, as usual, in the three-player version the man in the middle (i.e., on Mira) is at something of a disadvantage. When two play, each uses two home stars and two pairs of warps; although large forces can be accumulated quickly, the game lasts as long as the other versions, since a fallen home star can be recovered. In multiplayer games, it is not usually worthwhile eliminating someone at the outset; the effort involved reaps fewer rewards than gaining unoccupied resource stars. The advantage of such attacks grows quickly, however, since a defeated player's ships can be "converted" to the use of the other players. This is one of several reasons that the home star closest to you is the most reasonable initial target.

4000 A.D. also lends itself to play by mail, although as of this writing few such games are in progress. One aspect of such play, however, has universal application. Veteran players who find themselves easily countering the thrusts of their opponents may add spice to their games by introducing a Diplomacy-style version of simultaneous movement; this would, in effect, cause a one-turn delay in reaction time and would also eliminate the slight advantage of the player(s) going first in the regular versions.

While 4000 A.D. is not nearly so complicated (i.e., "wide") as some of the space war games in the following chapter (e.g., Lensman) and takes less time to learn, it is no more intended for the casual gamer than Diplomacy. It is a deep game for the person who likes real strategy. As such, it is superb. My single complaint is presentational: the board and the pieces are attractively done, but whoever decided to color two of the sets of ships red and red-orange—which, under most lighting, are nearly impossible to tell apart—should be strung up by his thumbs next to the creators of The Game of Life and Anti-Monopoly.

CAMPAIGN

Campaign (House of Games) is something of an anomaly. With its emphasis on the tactics of maneuver and capture, it recalls the games of the previous chapter, while its multipersonal nature (two can play, but the game is better for three or four), the importance of key cities for reinforcements, and the possibilities of alliances all relate Campaign to Risk, Diplomacy, and the others of this chapter.

The scene is Europe of the Napoleonic Wars. The board represents six countries: France, Prussia, Spain, Italy, Russia, and Austria. Each player begins with the country of his choice and an army of handsome plastic pieces representing four infantry units, four cavalry units, and a general (each with different movement capabilities). The goal is ostensibly the conquest of Europe; in practice, the occupation of eight foreign towns wins the game. There are other ways to win, but they are much less likely to occur.

Each country has four towns, two of which are tied to extra units. If, for example, the Spanish general occupies Milan for one turn, Spain receives a new cavalry piece adjacent to the city; Turin similarly yields an infantry unit. When Milan is recaptured (not *if;* such cities change hands as fast as a dollar bill)—by say, Austria —Spain *loses* the closest cavalry unit and Austria *gains* one. Because this is almost the only way lost units can be replaced, the occupation of these cities is vital; since the strength of opposing forces can change so drastically when one or two cities change hands, the situation is always explosive.

Note that the above system of rewards applies only to the standard game; without it, the *basic* game becomes almost completely a war of attrition—a game of tactics, not strategy. I strongly suggest that if you play the basic (i.e., introductory) version first— and I'm not convinced that it's necessary to do so, if you have much game experience—you include the provision discussed in the previous paragraph.

Movement and capture are unique to Campaign. Movement involves dice—something like the backgammon/parcheesi method carried to extremes. A roll of 7, for example, allows you to move one infantry unit seven spaces, seven pieces one move, or anything in between. Obviously, the luck of the dice can be important. On the other hand, for Campaign it seems to work; a more regularized movement system leads quickly to static situations in which two armies face each other across a gap, each being unwilling to risk moving forward (as in Conquest). The capture method is still more idiosyncratic—something of a cross between Diplomacy and go. It's definitely awkward and means that at any time, half your force (more or less) is useless for attack. Especially in the standard game, when a defending piece can be "reinforced" by adjacent friendly units (again like a combination of Diplomacy and go), the General, which has a defensive strength of two ordinary pieces, is almost impossible to pin down.

The game's biggest shortcomings, in fact, involve the Generals. Unlike the other pieces (which are eliminated when captured), old Generals neither die nor fade away; they just keep coming back. If you stick around long enough to exterminate the last of the General's troops (which puts the player—and his General—out of the game), you find that the rest of your key cities have been invaded by everyone else on the board, and if you leave to defend your homeland, the pesky General starts hopping around retaking cities and raising a new army. This may well be what Napoleonic warfare was like, but it's a pain in the neck, nonetheless. Since only Generals can capture (or recapture) cities, and since you only have one (even if practically immortal) General, there is no viable way to defend against two or more widely separated threats. The result is a seesaw contest that fluctuates as wildly as hemlines, and with as little sense.

Furthermore, while alliances are allowed, the mechanical details are lacking, and I am not at all sure how (or how well) two allies could act together to effect a single capture. There may be more potential than my limited experience with the game has allowed me to exploit, but I'm dubious.

I also have a minor packaging quibble. The game board folds neatly into thirds, making it almost two inches narrower than the box. Why? The board would fit nicely into the smaller Ratrace (made by the same company) box. Summit (with an even larger box) is another example of gross overpackaging. Why do game manufacturers insist on wasting customers' valuable shelf space? Are they still stuck on that bigger-is-better nonsense? (Is anyone out there listening?)

Campaign has its moments, but there are better games of this sort available, even if most of them are in big boxes.

RISK®

Risk (Parker Brothers) is perhaps the simplest of the strategic games; it is the only one in which no provision is made for alliances among players, and it is the only one, I think, that can be played satisfactorily by a single person. It is played on a simplified map of the world consisting of forty-two territories grouped into six continents: North America, South America, Europe, Africa, Asia, and Australia (more properly Melanesia). The object, simply enough, is to conquer the world—to occupy every territory on the board with one or more armies.

The means by which this is accomplished are armies represented by small wooden blocks; these come in sets of six different colors, one for each possible player. Each turn a player receives a certain number of armies as "income"—basically one army for every three territories held by the player, with a three-army minimum. Additionally, a player gets a bonus for holding an entire continent; this varies from two (for South America or Australia) to nine (for Asia), depending on the size of the continent. Finally—and, at least toward the end of the game, most importantly—armies are obtained by turning in sets of cards. There are forty-two regular cards—on each of which is depicted one of the territories and either an infantryman, a cavalryman, or artillery piece—and two jokers. If, in his turn, a player conquers a minimum of one territory, he gets a card; when he has collected enough to have a rummylike set of three (e.g., three infantrymen, or one of each figure), he can turn the threesome in for extra armies. (The exact number increases, as the game progresses, as fast as the cost of living. Or almost.)

Having distributed his "income" among his territories as he sees fit, the player is now free to attack as many adjacent enemy territories as he wishes. If an attack succeeds, he must move into the conquered province, from which he can attack farther provinces. As long as he has the armies and the inclination, there is no limit to the number of attacks he can mount. Once his bloodlust has been sated, our warring Walter Mitty gets a move to adjust his defenses and allows the Attila next to him *his* chance to rape and pillage.

The combat resolution system of Risk is dealt with in considerable detail in the rules; so I need not repeat it here. It involves dice and is the bugaboo of chess players seeking to broaden their game horizons. I am not the world's number one fan of dice games, but I am not convinced that Risk's methods are any less reasonable—to say nothing of being less realistic—than the replacement capture of chess, Feudal, or Conquest. Dice are simply a mechanism used to generate excitement by exploiting the short-term statistical variations in what are, in the long run, mathematically predictable events. Since there *are* statistical variations ("luck," if you will), a player will occasionally win or lose because of a "lucky" run of the dice or draw of the cards, but such fluctuations significantly affect the outcome of the game only rarely and, in any event, balance out in the long run. Luck alone won't allow a bad player to survive very often. In a well-designed game, such chance elements, by adding variety, keep the game from becoming totally predictable, and, in turn, require a greater flexibility than chess does; no attack goes quite the way it was planned, and a good player must be quick to adapt to constantly changing conditions. The fact that things, in Burns's phrase, "gang agley" now and then is no reason to pick up your tinkertoys and go home.

There are two ways to begin the game. Under the original French rules, the territories—as represented by the cards—are dealt out at random, and then each is occupied by a single appropriately colored army. The cards are returned and reshuffled; the first player takes his three armies (as income); and the game is on. This method has obvious drawbacks, especially for the purist. For one thing, it is slow. (How much can you do with three armies?) For another, most of the initial placement is wasted. Of each player's original armies, two or three will survive the first half-dozen turns; the others, scattered out of reach of each other, fall quick victim to the consolidation efforts of the opposing players. Finally, it emphasizes the element of luck in the game, not just in the matter of initial placement (itself significant) but also more subtly, at a later stage of the game; by delaying the occupation of entire continents, it reduces the importance of the continent bonuses (which are the result of strategy) in comparison to the number of armies acquired by turning in sets of cards (which are more a matter of luck).

With so many objections, then, the alternative would seem more desirable. And so it is, sometimes. In the "American" version, each player is given a block of armies to distribute as he sees fit, first in the vacant territories, then, when all are occupied, as strategic reinforcements. Placement becomes a matter of strategy rather than luck, things get rolling immediately, and the influence of the sets is at least matched by the bonus armies given for holding entire continents. So what's the problem?

Simply this: the average Risk game is played by a mixture of newcomers and veterans (an unfortunate practical difficulty Risk shares with the other games in this chapter). The typical novice tries to occupy a continent impossible to hold, like Europe or Asia, or drops his armies on such vital areas as Madagascar, Japan, or Alberta. Around about the third turn, as his last four armies are swept away by the onrushing hordes, the poor clod decides Risk is a lousy game and who suggested it, anyway? *He* did, probably, but his complaint is not entirely unjustified. Insofar as luck is blind, the randomized beginning is more palatable to the newcomer and more frequently employed; the American version is usually saved for those rarer occasions when a bunch of old hands get together to have a good time driving each other into the sea.

There are two major aspects of Risk strategy: placement and timing—*where* and *when*. There is a brief answer to the first part —Australia—but it deserves some amplification. The most important aspect of a continent is not the number of its territories or the size of its bonus, but its defensibility. If it cannot be held, the largest bonus in the game is meaningless. Asia, which sprawls over twelve territories and borders on four continents, is too huge to be conquered—much less held—in the early and middle stages of the game. Europe's four border countries (out of a total of only seven) face six territories in three continents. Two of Africa's three border provinces separate three continents and can be attacked from four territories. Like Europe, Africa lies at the crossroads of the board and is an attractive spot from which to lose the game. North America's three border provinces are accessible only to three other territories—a fact which makes the second-largest continent very attractive, indeed, especially in the American version (which makes more armies available at the beginning of the game). The fewer the players, the better it looks. Its problem in the French version is its size; it takes time to conquer. South

America has two borders, only two access routes, and can be conquered, with luck, in a single turn—even under the French rules. The mutual problem of the Americas is that the logical target for expansion lies on the other side of the Panama Canal. Whichever player wins the struggle will meet the holder of Australia for the showdown.

There is only one invasion route to Australia—from Siam to Indonesia—and, consequently, only one province to fortify. Since fearsome invaders do not *originate* in Asia, the huge continent provides both a natural barrier to would-be conquerors and a logical area for Australian forces to expand. The small continent provides a secure base and a steady income from which to manage the slow job of enveloping Asia. Eventually, the game's Maginot Line —the Ukraine-Middle East—seals off all approaches from the West, and a fortified Kamchatka forbids access from the East (and North America). The sequence is slow and requires patience, but it is usually irresistible.

This brings us to the matter of timing. When should you attack and when stand pat? Should you gain a continent at the cost of leaving your territories defenseless, or should you put it off until you have more armies to defend your borders?

Taking the second question first, you should go all out to conquer a small continent; it is not usually worth the trouble of the other players to break it up. The larger the continent, the trickier the problem. Taking North America, Asia, or Europe before you can fortify them adequately usually results in a lot of unwelcome (and sometimes fatal) attention; on the other hand, there may be no organized opposition close enough to do you harm, or your opponents may have more pressing concerns. You have to make your own decisions.

Risk is a game of the strategic offensive; the combat-resolution system, which, in general, favors the attacker, sees to that, even if there were no bonuses for sets or continents. Obviously, there are turns in which the benefits of a *major* attack are outweighed by the advantages of consolidating and securing previous gains; however, while fortification is at times a desirable—even a necessary— tactic, it is not a winning *policy*.

When to strike, then? When the estimated benefits exceed the estimated costs ("costs" here including foregone alternatives—a cost of all human activities). Before you get frustrated, let me say that there *are* ways to estimate at least some of these factors. Say you are considering invading Africa from South America; you will need one army for each of the six territories involved, just to occupy the conquered provinces. Second, you must allow for your losses. In a large attack, in which you can (and should) roll three dice, the odds are nearly two to one in your favor; so your losses will be equal to about half the number of the opposing armies. Finally, you will probably want some "surplus" to fortify your new holdings. How much? The risk of counterattack—either against Africa or South America (especially if you have denuded South America of its defenses to add to the invading army), or both—is something only experience and good judgment will allow you to estimate. If Europe or Asia are wholly occupied, you can certainly expect a determined effort to damage your bloc. If the resulting total of armies, whatever it is, is more than you have available, you will have to decide whether to risk an inadequate defense, settle for a partial conquest, or postpone your attack another turn.

The standard go-for-broke situation occurs when you have a chance to wipe out another player, take his cards, combine them with your own, and turn in one or more sets immediately for additional armies. This is the one time that you can get armies in the middle of a turn, and this will allow you not only to fortify but also to continue attacking. If the sets involve a large number of armies, you may very well repeat your feat, crushing player after player, and sweep to victory, even if (as is usually the case) the original victim was the weakest of your opponents.

There are two questions involved: (1) can you eliminate every one of the opposing player's armies? and (2) will his cards and yours make a set? The mathematics involved in both is uncomplicated. The first question was answered, at least in part, two paragraphs ago. However, since you must often figure the situation to the last army, more details are required. Rolling two dice to one, the odds in your favor are only four to three (which means your losses are three-fourths those of the enemy); at two dice to two, the odds are *against* you by about the same amount (and your losses will now average about four-thirds those of the enemy). At one to one, the odds against you are seven to five.

The odds of making one or two sets depend on the total number of cards in your and your opponent's hands, not on the particular ones you happen to be holding.* Because of the presence of two jokers in the deck (which raise the odds slightly in your favor), there is slightly greater than a one-third chance that any three cards will make a set and a probability of just over seven-ninths that four cards will do so. A group of five cards will always produce a set. The odds for getting *two* sets out of six, seven, or eight cards are roughly the same as those for getting one set from, respectively, three, four, and five cards.

Risk's simplicity has proven fertile ground for a number of unofficial variations (allowing alliances, adjusting bonuses, etc.), but the most common—what I call the Colyer variant—often arises from a misconception of the "final move" rule. In this version, as his final move, a player may *completely* rearrange his defenses— moving armies from Siam to the Ukraine and from Yakutsk to the Middle East—provided only that there be an uninterrupted path of controlled territory between the new and old locations. This variation allows a player to correct past mistakes (stranding a large force far from his front lines, for example, where ordinarily it would do him no good) and emphasizes all-out offense.

Regardless of the version played, Risk will be popular with those who enjoy the complications of multipersonal conflict and don't mind the fact that luck can affect the outcome. Those who can't stand the presence of dice had best push on to Diplomacy or go back to 4000 A.D.

SUMMIT®

Summit (Milton Bradley) is a flawed but not uninteresting game. Like the others in this chapter, it concerns itself with power and conflict (and powers in conflict), but it eschews actual warfare (while allowing military threats). The designer's grasp of economics is ludicrous (raising the minimum wage, for example, increases unemployment, not productivity), and in an era of Viet-

---

* This is not entirely true. If you have a joker, any two other cards will make a set, and any five other cards will make two sets. On the other hand, if you hold three cards which do not in themselves make a set, the odds that a single card in your opponent's hand will, combined with yours, make a set, is only two-thirds.

nam and the Pentagon Papers (remember them?), the summary seems naive and the game dated and lacking in the realistic parallels it so grandly claims. Further, Summit is one of those games that take less time to play than to wade through the rules.

Like Risk, the game is played on a simplified map of the world. Unlike Risk, all countries but a home country for each of the three to six players start empty. In keeping with its de-emphasis on combat, the game is won not by conquest, *per se*, but by achieving the highest score. Each country has a point value from two to ten which goes to the player occupying it at the end of the game; to this number is added "popular votes" which derive from factories every time one of the game's five Censuses occurs. Players "colonize" unoccupied countries anywhere on the board by placing one or more military bases there; the bases protect the mills and factories which can then be built there. Each base, mill, and factory is built from two I-beams; home mills produce one I-beam every turn, while foreign mills produce *two* per turn. Hence the impetus to imperialism.

The other "income" is power chips, given each turn for every three bases (which yield a red, "military" chip), mills (a black, "economic" chip), or factories (a white, "popular" chip). The chips are the game's combat mechanism. If I "attack" your holdings in Eastern Europe with a red chip, you must match my red chip (whereupon both are discarded) or lose a base there; when all bases are gone, whatever factories and mills are there must also be dismantled. It's not a total loss—you get back one I-beam for each dismantled unit—but it is a losing proposition. As in Risk, you can attack as often as you have the ability (the chips) and the inclination; unlike Risk, you don't have to occupy countries you have "conquered."

Alliances allow two players to support each other either in defense or attack (by sharing chips) and to build mills and factories in countries protected by each other's bases. This last can be particularly helpful, but it is quite risky, since alliances can be ended at any time, unilaterally.

One of the game's biggest problems is the presence of the chance cards, also known as the Current Events deck. As part of his turn, each player draws a card; the entire deck is gone through once, after which there is a final round, and the game ends. This has the virtue of preventing the six-hour marathons Diplomacy players regularly contend with, but the cure is worse than the disease. When six people play, most of them get only three turns before the final "summit round." There's not a whole lot you can do in this game in three turns. Furthermore, the importance of the Current Events cards overwhelms all other considerations. Over time, the good and bad outcomes of the random events generated by such chance devices as dice or cards cancel out, but three turns is *not* over time! If you get hit with a General Strike (losing two I-beams and a power chip of each color) on one turn and draw an Economic Cooperation or Military Assistance Pact card (both of which cause you to give I-beams to other players)—or something equally unhelpful—on another, neither superb strategy nor a solid alliance will keep you from a miserable finish.

With fewer players, each gets more turns, but the flavor of the game is very different. With three it's pretty much every man for himself, since a two-against-one alliance will quickly prove fatal to the third party. When four play, the game soon degenerates into a war between two solid alliances. Only when five or six play is there the possibility of the shifting alliance structure that can make multiperson games so challenging. Perhaps going through the deck twice would help.

There are a variety of tips I could give you to improve your performance in the game, but I will give you the simplest and best: try another game, instead. Summit *seems* like a game with considerable promise; the first few times you play, you are convinced that if you could just get organized, some minor adjustments would allow the *real* Summit—an interesting game with vast strategic potential—to emerge from the fog of its current flawed presentation. I may be pessimistic, but I'm beginning to think it really *is* just "swamp gas."

EMPEROR OF CHINA®

Though it has its problems, Emperor of China (Dynamic Design) has saving graces as well. For one thing, it has character; though it possesses clear relations to the other games in this chapter—notably Risk, Summit, and Diplomacy—it is unquestionably oriental in flavor. Besides the obvious—that the setting is China and the object the uniting of the provinces under a single ruler—the strategy and tactics involved, the bits of advice in the instructions, the "alliance" system (actually mergers with junior and senior partners), the disasters which are an everpresent part of the game, and the language throughout are all distinctly Chinese. There is a hint of go in the occupation of provinces by "inference," and the instruction booklet includes a pronunciation guide, historical background, and a bibliography.

There are chance cards in the game, but these are beautifully in character and are handled better than in any other game I have seen. There are *two* sets of cards: Yang and Yin. Yang cards bestow symbols of agricultural, commercial, or mineral wealth (which yield an extra population marker or two per turn for the province in which they lie), protect against disasters, or enable attacking armies to cross geographical barriers—rivers, mountains, the Great Wall—into adjacent, defended provinces (e.g., "Bribe guards on Great Wall"). Yin cards cause nothing but disasters: e.g., "Sparse rainfall brings drought: Lose one marker" or "Crop failure causes famine: Lose two markers." At the end of his turn, each player draws one card from *each pile*, so that, while luck is present, it is automatically balanced—to a degree, at least. Further, the player can choose which of his provinces will be affected by each card, allowing him to absorb his losses where he can best afford them and to gain benefits where they will be most secure.

At the beginning of the game, like Summit (and unlike Risk), each player occupies only a single province, but little advice is given in the rules about initial placement—a decision which may well be critical. I have not played the game enough to make definitive judgments, but I suggest picking a province on or near the edge of the board—one which is provided with some geographical barriers. Szechwan in the west is protected by mountains but allows expansion in three directions; Fukien enjoys a similar position in the southeast. In the north, Inner Mongolia has a secure position behind the Great Wall, but several adjacent provinces—Shansi, Hopei, and Liaoning—have barriers of their own and seem like reasonable alternatives. The provinces of the eastern plain between the Yellow and Yangtze rivers strike me as being the most vulnerable and least likely prospects for a good base of operations.

Individual provinces have a potentially greater strategic significance than any in Risk, in part because of the greater influence of geographical features and in part because of the presence of the economic chips (which remain in a province regardless of who occupies it). Similarly, the Yin and Yang cards cannot determine the winner of the game, but the Yang Special Advantage cards do affect foreign policy. For such reasons, it would not be too misleading to think of Emperor of China as a conceptually improved Risk in an oriental setting. Each turn each player gets three population markers (or armies) to distribute among the provinces he occupies—as well as any extras granted by the economic symbols. He can then colonize any vacant adjacent provinces to which he can transfer three markers. After he has shifted whatever other markers among his provinces he wishes, he may attempt to expand into adjacent, occupied provinces—first by attempting to persuade the opponent to withdraw or to merge, and, if that fails, by direct attack. Combat is resolved with dice in a manner similar to (but different from) Risk's.

This, unfortunately, brings us to an area in which Emperor of China is *too* "oriental": all too often, the rules are totally inscrutable. Line by line, they are by turns contradictory, vague, and ambiguous. For example, there is a clear contradiction between the second line of Rule No. 3 and the second sentence of Rule No. 5: the former states that new markers (i.e., the turn's income) must be secured and placed *before* colonization; the latter seems to imply that new markers can be used to colonize simply by dropping them into a new province, without the intermediate step of being placed in occupied territory. The difference may seem immaterial, but it has profound implications for a significant later ambiguity. In Risk, armies can attack a series of provinces in succession, moving from one to the next indefinitely. I don't think this is allowable in Emperor of China, but I'm not certain. The first sentence of Rule No. 6 prohibits moving any marker more than once (i.e., from one province to an adjoining one) per turn; however, in the context, it is not clear whether this refers only to preconflict movement or to *all* movement. If the latter, can armies moved in the turn engage in combat but not occupy the province, if it falls? Or are they prohibited from combat altogether? If Rule No. 5 is taken literally, *new* markers that directly colonized a new province would be free to engage in combat and to move into the defeated province. Having tried several different interpretations of the rules, I have found that the freer movement permitted by a narrow view of Rule No. 6 results in a game that is too fluid. My own suggestion is to apply Rule No. 6 to *all* movement: markers which have colonized new territory *or* moved from one friendly province to another may not *in that turn* either attack adjacent enemy markers or move into the enemy province if it is vacated. I similarly discount the problem phase of Rule No. 5 in favor of Rule No. 3.

Regrettably, there are further difficulties. At one point it is suggested that you try to induce an opponent to withdraw from a province you desire by persuading him you have the appropriate Special Advantage card and can attack him, anyway. This is meaningless. He can withdraw even after you show the card and announce your attack (Rule No. 10), forcing you to use (and then discard) the card in question (Rule No. 4). Since he can call your bluff without penalty to himself, there is never any reason to do otherwise.

If you defeat an opponent with the dice, you can occupy the fallen province with as few or as many markers as you wish (of those available, of course)—including, apparently, fewer than the three markers normally required to colonize a new province. But what if, under the imminent threat of attack (the situation discussed in the previous paragraph), the opponent withdraws? Can you *in that turn* put markers into the vacated province? If so, is it subject to the three-marker colonization minimum? I don't have definitive answers to these questions, I'm sorry to say. Unless it succeeded in delaying the enemy advance for a turn, there doesn't seem to be much of an advantage to withdrawing your markers from a threatened province, but the other interpretation seems, perhaps, slightly more consistent with the hints in Rule No. 9.

I have assumed that the defender may withdraw in the middle of an attack (that is, after several rolls) if things are going badly for him. As long as this is not done while the attacker is in the act of rolling the dice, this does not contradict anything in the rules. Now, by Rule No. 9, if a White force in Honan annihilates a group of Yellow markers in Shansi, White can advance and occupy Shansi. If, in the middle of a losing battle, Yellow breaks off combat and withdraws the remnants of his army, it seems only reasonable to allow White the same privilege of advancement (the offense has, in effect, been victorious). By the same logic, a withdrawal in the face of an announced attack—a retreat from combat, in other words, before losses are sustained—is probably intended to bring about the same result for the victorious offense. If this is correct, the three-marker minimum would not be in effect in either case.* I freely confess this is no more than a guess as to how the game is supposed to work; if you're not happy with my interpretations, you're welcome to your own. Try a few games using different possibilities and see how you like them, but decide on the rules you're using *before* the start of play, or you'll spend the whole game arguing.

Although those of you who have slogged through the preceding paragraphs may have decided it's just too much trouble, I believe that, despite the weaknesses of the rules, which are in obvious need of rewriting, Emperor of China is (unlike Summit) definitely worth making the effort to salvage. It is less affected by luck than Risk and shorter than Diplomacy; not only does the Mandate of Heaven card (which automatically ends the game) at the bottom of the Yang deck impose an automatic time limit, but the game simply moves faster. The aims of the game—the occupation of provinces with economic symbols, the control of territory, the elimination of your opponents' markers—are clear enough, and the lessons of Risk and Diplomacy can be put to good use. The advice in the booklet is generally sound and encourages not only a well-played but also an *enjoyable* game. Getting into the spirit of things is half the fun, but most people seem to grasp this almost at once. Players who would fight to the last army in Diplomacy will, in Emperor of China, cheerfully merge into a stronger state as soon as their own chances for victory dwindle significantly. The game can be played by two to five people, but, as is usual with this sort of game, the more the merrier.

As of this writing, Dynamic Design plans to discontinue the game. I sincerely hope there will be enough interest in Emperor of China to persuade the publishers to change their minds and issue a new, revised edition, instead.

---

* On the other hand, would the same standards apply if the withdrawal was made before any attack was announced?

DIPLOMACY®

Games & Puzzles called Diplomacy (Games Research) "the greatest indoor board game invented this century." If there is a likelier candidate for the title, I haven't seen it.

The basic idea has the simple elegance of a knifeblade: you put seven people around a mapboard of pre-World War I Europe, explain that only one player can survive, and turn them loose. Thereafter, they are free to maneuver, negotiate, make alliances, break alliances, deal, double-deal, double-cross, triple-cross, lie, betray, plot, and eavesdrop—to behave, in short, just like their political counterparts in real life. There are just enough rules to lend the game some semblance of order: players can break promises but not the rules.

Each of the players takes the part of one of the seven major countries in the Europe of the time: Austria, England, France, Germany, Italy, Russia, and Turkey. This is usually done by drawing lots, or some such method, and is the only element of chance in the game. The counters, or pieces, are colored wooden blocks that resemble oversized **Risk** pieces and represent fleets and armies. Russia begins the game with two armies and two fleets; England starts with two fleets and an army; and each of the other countries starts with two armies and a fleet.

Movement is simple. The board is divided into a number of seas and provinces (see Diagram 11-1), each of which can be occupied by a single unit. In a turn, a fleet can move from a sea or coastal province to an adjacent one; an army can move from one land province to another next to it, or it can be convoyed by a friendly naval piece over bodies of water. Each country can move all its units each turn, and all movement is effectively simultaneous; orders for each piece are written in secret and exposed at the same time.

There is a simple method for having combat and resolving conflicts (as, for example, when the British fleet in London and the French fleet at Brest are both ordered to the English Channel): the majority rules. This is not exactly a democratic process; nor are votes involved. Instead of the chaos that would ensue if four different units were ordered to the same province (which would, not unreasonably, result in none of them being allowed in), any

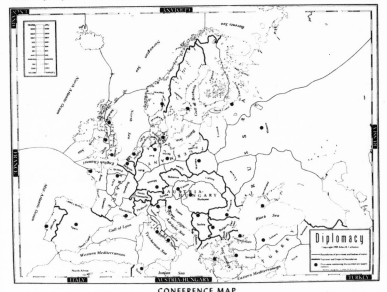

CONFERENCE MAP

Diagram 11-1
Conference Map Used in Diplomacy®

such unit which *could* move can instead lend its support to a
similar move on the part of another unit; the moving unit thus
attacks with a force equal to two units. A two-against-one attack
always succeeds, as does a three-to-two move. Ties are stalemates.
The rules are considerably more explicit, but this is the general
idea.

Turns are assumed to take place in the spring and fall of successive years, starting with 1901. At the end of each fall turn, the
status of each player-country is re-evaluated. If he controls more
Supply Centers (strategic provinces marked on the map with a
black circle—something like the key cities in Campaign or provinces with economic symbols in Emperor of China) than he has
units, he can build additional units in the Supply Centers of his
home country; conversely, if he holds fewer Centers than units, he
forfeits enough units to bring the situation back into balance. In
this way, the strength and fortunes of each country rise and fall.

The game is won when one country controls eighteen of the board's thirty-four Supply Centers.

Despite the importance of tactical maneuver, coordination of movement, and the proper disposition of units, the key to the game is in its title: in order to win (or, indeed, in order just to survive the first couple of rounds), players must negotiate with the others in the game. No country is strong enough to go it alone, and beginners who fail to realize this can (and do) get wiped out in almost unbelievably short order. Alliances, nonaggression pacts, defensive agreements—the possibilities are limited only by the players' imaginations (and their scruples). How much to trust an ally and how honest to be with another player are questions left entirely to each person's discretion. The essence of Diplomacy strategy lies in the paradox that cooperation is essential to survival and development, but the winner must ultimately oppose everyone, including his closest allies.

It may be obvious that Diplomacy is not a game for everyone. It is definitely a gamer's game. The *aficionado* finds in its freedom of action, lack of luck, and multiplicity of minds working at cross-purposes the ultimate challenge. Nonfans don't care for its subject matter and deplore the deceit and double-dealing the game necessitates. Of the people I know, half of them couldn't be pried away from a Diplomacy game with a crowbar, and the other half couldn't be forced into one with a sawed-off shotgun.

Strategy in Diplomacy depends largely on the country you are playing, but there are certain facets common to all. A long-term goal of all countries is to achieve as narrow a front as possible: that is, to attain an "end" position on the board, such that all possible enemies are on fewer than three sides of you. Obviously, some countries—e.g., Turkey and England—begin this way, which is one of the major reasons they have an excellent chance of winning. Such an advantage can be thrown away by improper development which allows other countries to envelop you (e.g., a drive by Turkey through Austria-Hungary toward the center of the board, if it thereby enables Russia and Italy to outflank it), just as central countries can gain it (e.g., an Austrian conquest of Turkey, or Italian participation in the dismemberment of France).

Only in the late stages of the game might it be wise—or, indeed, possible—to fight an opposing country single-handed. Such a battle is usually a stalemate and, in any event, takes far too long; it gives the uninvolved countries too much time to develop and too free a hand elsewhere. A two-against-one alliance is very common, *usually* doesn't take too long, and promises the victors rich rewards (at least two Supply Centers apiece). However, a dual alliance is often subject to counterattack by another country, resulting in a long, indecisive campaign. A three-way alliance is often the best answer: the campaign is brief, and if the immediate spoils seem small, there are compensations—particularly if you have made arrangements with one ally to dispose of the other when the first battle is over.

Perhaps the biggest policy decision you must make is deciding how honest you are going to be. I prefer to make one solid alliance that I will preserve for the duration of the game, or at least until it gets down to essentially a two-country contest. Other, temporary alliances will of course be necessary, but at least one relationship is sacrosanct. Other successful Diplomacy players display a more cavalier attitude toward *all* pacts and allies. This, too, seems a matter of taste; choose the policy you feel comfortable with.

Though the game is as well balanced as one might reasonably expect of anything involving seven players, the countries do differ in power and popularity. If countries are chosen or assigned deliberately, England is the best place for the cautious, conservative player, the nondiplomat, and the newcomer; England naturally develops slowly, giving the first-time player a chance to learn the nuances of play gradually, and it is one of the few countries on the board in which early mistakes may not be fatal. Germany and Austria are no place for novices; both demand the utmost in diplomatic skill and should be played by experienced (and devious) players. Turkey and Italy are easier to play, requiring only the most obvious and elementary grasp of diplomacy; a good tactician can do well in Turkey. France and Russia are strong enough initially not to fear immediate annihilation (which might be discouraging to someone just being introduced to the game) and allow ample scope for a variety of strategies; they are good spots for newcomers with promise (i.e., these with a good grasp of the game's essentials and the proper blend of cunning and deceit).

Austria-Hungary

Barring immediate aggressive action against an opponent (or an immediate, concerted attack on the part of your neighbors), each country has access in the first year to some of the board's twelve unoccupied Supply Centers. Austria-Hungary's traditional share consists of Serbia and Greece, which are usually occupied by sending the Fleet in Trieste to Albania, the Budapest Army to Serbia, and the Vienna Army to Trieste (to guard against Italian treachery) in the spring, followed by Fleet Albania, supported by Army Serbia, to Greece, while the Army in Trieste holds, in the fall. There are various alternatives, but that is the safest sequence. If you want to build a fleet in Trieste in the re-evaluation turn which follows each fall move—a period termed the "winter" move in postal Diplomacy—presumably for use against Italy, you can move the Army in Trieste back out during the fall of 1901—but this, of course, has its risks.

Austria and Germany have no business fighting each other, at least in the early and middle game. If they do not enter into an active alliance against Russia, a nonaggression pact providing for the neutrality of Tyrolia and Bohemia is *de rigueur*. This is so obviously in the best interests of both countries that a failure to come to terms is a clear indication that one or both of you is definitely in the wrong game.

Germany aside, Austria has three potential foes at the beginning of the game: Italy to the west, Turkey to the southeast, and Russia to the northeast. Italy is the most obvious opponent, because its home Supply Center of Venice is directly adjacent to Austria's Center, Trieste. If either Supply Center is left open, a sneak attack by the other country can be a fatal blow. An Austro-Italian war is often the result, not of design, but of a failure of diplomacy; neither country trusts the other, and the result is a bloody combat. In itself, this is not undesirable to Austria. With a bit of help from France (which usually has some to spare), Austria can defeat Italy, add a couple of Supply Centers (Venice and Naples are the most likely choices when the spoils are divided), improve its access to the Mediterranean, and get a chance to develop its sea power.

The problem with this otherwise favorable development is Turkey, which has a regrettably narrow range of choices: fight Austria or fight Russia (or fight both and get eliminated—but that's not a *voluntary* choice). Regardless of the target (and Turkey cannot afford to be picky), Turkey wants an ally; if Austria won't help it fight Russia, then Turkey will try to talk Russia into an alliance against Austria. Because of her self-supporting position, the wealth of Supply Centers in the Balkans, and the advantages of interior lines and superior coordination, Austria can probably last longer against the resulting triple alliance (don't forget Italy!) than any other country on the board, but the end is inevitable extinction.

An alliance against Russia will keep Turkey off Austria's neck temporarily, but with or without German help, Turkey will gain the most from the alliance's victory against Russia—notably a solid defensive position around the Black Sea. Division of the spoils in the Balkans leads to arguments, and the resulting situation leaves Turkey with only one reasonable direction to expand: right through Austria. In the Austria-Turkey conflict that inevitably ensues, Turkey has all the advantages; prying it loose from the Black Sea is like trying to steal food from the mouth of a crocodile. Turkey cannot be assailed from the rear and can devote itself 100 percent to the fight. Not so Austria, which has to worry about Italy and perhaps whoever took over northern Russia.

All things considered, the best bet looks like an alliance with Russia against Turkey—possibly with Italian help as well, if Italy favors the so-called Lepanto Opening. In the standard situation, Austria gains increased access to the sea and a favorable corner position, and Russia eliminates its chief troublemaker; both are free to expand separately—Austria in the south and Russia in the north and east. To keep Italy occupied (for Italy is definitely Austria's next target), Austria should encourage a joint German-Italian invasion of France. England has a potentially crucial swing role; with English help, the conquest of France may be too rapid, allowing Italy to turn east before Austria is ready. An English-Russian squabble in Scandinavia might harm the Russian effort against Turkey but is probably preferable. The delicate balance involved will require Austria's full diplomatic talents. If the Lepanto Opening is used, Austria must pick the right moment to turn against Italy: too soon, and the war with Turkey collapses into an Italo-Turkish alliance; too late, and Russia and Italy can crush Austria in the middle.

No one ever claimed Austria-Hungary was an easy country to play.

England

England has the best defensive position on the board; it is entirely surrounded by seas and starts the game with a clear naval superiority. Unfortunately, its early offensive potential is like Italy's— i.e., terrible. Its single "neutral" acquisition, Norway, is far away and hard to take, at least if Russia is being ornery. Standard spring moves are Fleet London to North Sea, Fleet Edinburgh to Norwegian Sea, and Army Liverpool (probably) to Edinburgh. In the fall, one fleet can move into Norway (with the support of the other, if necessary) or the army can be convoyed into Norway by one and, again, supported by the other. The first new build will probably be a fleet, but all these choices depend on England's first opponent.

Due to its offensive limitations, England should probably have two allies in its first attack. Before a target is picked, therefore, England must consider the second-stage consequences: after the first victim, what happens? Consider an attack on France, for example. England needs the firm cooperation of Germany and probably Italy for such a campaign to succeed; England and Italy lack the manpower to do it alone, and Italian help is needed to put pressure on the French rear. In such a war, Germany develops a strong position in central Europe (taking, probably, Belgium and Paris); Italy gets Spain and Marseilles, develops her navy and (possibly) Atlantic aspirations. In short, England gets less, overall, than either and cannot readily turn its two erstwhile allies against each other; its best course after the fall of France is an alliance with Russia against Germany or vice versa. If England is going to attack France in the early going, it should be initiated *at once*, as France gains far more in the first year than England. If an attack on France is not in the works, a neutrality pact is called for; the English Channel, Irish Sea, and North Atlantic should be kept vacant, and some agreement might be made regarding the building of fleets in Brest and London.

A three-way alliance against Germany (with France and Russia) has much to recommend it: it gives England a foothold in Europe, strengthens its holdings in Scandinavia, and allows it time to develop. Even if Russia is uninterested, France and England can usually manage to handle Germany if Italian pressure is not too great. The problem, again, is afterward: a German campaign tends to leave England between France and Russia—and a security risk to both. Only some fast talking will prevent an immediate invasion of England.

An attack on Russia offers minimal material gains (St. Petersburg and Sweden, at best) but more solid strategic ends. Particularly if Germany can be persuaded to allow English possession of Sweden (in return for Warsaw and Moscow), England emerges supreme in the north, with an unassailable line of fleets and a firm grip on Scandinavia. After Russia falls, Germany is next; Turkish or Austrian help can be bought with the promise of Germany's Russian holdings, and, with French armies attacking from the west, England should be able to pick up Denmark, Kiel, and Berlin. After that, it may be France's turn. Throughout this sequence, a long-term alliance with Turkey is a very low-risk, medium-to-high-return investment good for the whole game. Keep it in mind.

I must emphasize that none of England's major choices are obviously bad. Picking the opponent is not as essential as being on the winning side, and short-term improvement is less important than the promise of a firm alliance in the early midgame.

France

France's defensive position is, perhaps, second only to England's, but Gallic offensive potential is much greater. No other country is more flexible. France can send fleets north against England or south against Italy or build armies to fight Germany in the center; no country boasts a superior balance of land and sea power. Much of its early strength is due to what is effectively a Gallic franchise of the Iberian peninsula and its two supply centers. Since the Army at Paris has a good shot at the Belgian Supply Center, with luck

France can manage three builds in the first year. Usually, Fleet Brest moves to the Mid-Atlantic and thence to Portugal, and the Marseilles Army moves immediately to Spain; should an Italian threat develop in the form of an army in the Piedmont, the Army based in Spain can keep it out of Marseilles in the fall. Army Paris to Burgundy is a strong move but will undoubtedly annoy Germany; unless German deceit is feared, moving the army to Picardy is more tactful. In the fall, the army there has as good a chance at Belgium as anyone; at worst, there may be a standoff in that region.

The impassability of Switzerland—a formidable barrier against any invasion of France—channels any French land offensive into two directions; when France moves, its intentions are obvious. Fortunately, France's first year can be spent acquiring unoccupied Supply Centers before it must commit itself to a more specific course of action. Facing a triple alliance of England, Germany, and Italy, France has no more chance than any other country, but it can face a two-pronged attack better than most. France can keep Italy out of the south almost indefinitely, and neither England nor Germany, acting alone, will make quick inroads onto French soil.

An attack on Italy with Austrian help is not a hard campaign, but there are only two supply centers to be gained (Rome and Tunis), and the French position does not gain enormously thereby. The best reasons for postponing an Italian offensive are geographical: the stronger foes are in the north, the Franco-Italian border is easily neutralized, and a double-cross in the south is far less dangerous than one in the north. Being crushed by its powerful neighbors is Italy's major fear, and it will usually welcome a non-aggression pact that declares the line Piedmont/Gulf of Lyon/Western Mediterranean/North Africa *verboten* to either country.

England is no more rewarding a target than Italy, and it takes more effort. If England is to be attacked, France should not reveal its true designs until the second year, when its position vis-à-vis England should be considerably improved by its first-year builds.

An Anglo-French alliance, even without active participation by Russia, should be able to handle Germany, which cannot resist the combination of English fleets and French armies. Adding Russia to the alliance means a smaller share of the spoils for the others (especially for France, which might have to settle for Munich alone), but it is a good idea if a long-term Franco-Russian pact can be arranged.

Unless England can be relied on for the entire length of the game (an unusual but not completely impossible situation), England must be destroyed before France turns its attentions south. The best time for this is after the fall of Germany: Russia takes over all of Scandinavia and consolidates its grip on most of Germany proper, while to France falls the burden of invading England itself. It is far better to cede Holland, too, if Russia must be further placated, than to allow a dangerous Russian presence in England and the seas around it.

Provided these precautions are taken, however, the Franco-Russian alliance can be durable and fruitful; after England falls, the powerful pair can turn south and crush the survivors there between them.

Germany

Germany has all the positional difficulties of Austria-Hungary, compounded: it is even harder for Germany to attain an "edge" or "corner" position, and its natural enemies are stronger. The sole advantage of its central position is that it does allow temporizing moves in the first year—usually Fleet Kiel to Denmark, Army Berlin to Kiel, and Army Munich to the Ruhr in the spring, with the Army in Kiel taking Holland (with support of the Army in the Ruhr, if an English fleet is threatening) in the fall. Barring an immediate concerted attack by its neighbors, such moves virtually guarantee Germany two builds the first year.

However, Germany cannot afford a longer delay; nor can it afford indecision. If Germany is to survive, it must throw its full weight against a single foe—a policy which necessitates a network of nonaggression pacts to guard its back. Again, such a neutrality pact with Austria is obvious and easy. Others are possible but depend, obviously, on which country Germany is attacking.

In *Games & Puzzles*, Don Turnbull has urged an attack on England in conjunction with France; other writers have disparaged such a move. The problem with an English offensive—assuming Russia does not immediately advance into Prussia or Silesia—is that, even if it "succeeds," it leaves Germany stretched out between two powerful foes, France and Russia. (Such a policy, after all, relieves all pressure on Russia's northern front, allowing it to delay even an Austro-Turkish offensive almost indefinitely.) I think such an attack can be better timed.

A triple offensive against France has merit (if, again, the neutrality of Prussia and Silesia can be assured): if no attempt is being made to conceal its intentions, Germany can move Fleet Kiel to Holland, Army Berlin to Kiel, and Army Munich to Burgundy or the Ruhr in the spring. In the fall, a variety of moves are possible: moving Army Kiel to Denmark and Army Ruhr to Belgium (with support from Fleet Holland) can lead to three builds in the winter, unless the French Army Paris went to Burgundy in the spring and Munich in the fall. Ordering Army Munich to Burgundy—even if it bounces off a similar French move from Paris—and leaving one of the Supply Centers open (or allowing it to fall to England) might be safer and more effective, offensively. Unless France is caught completely unaware, the campaign will be helped enormously by Italian pressure on Marseilles. The problem with all this is that it leaves Germany flanked on three sides by England, Russia, and an expanding Italy; Anglo-German alliances have survived the duration of the game (e.g., if England, building only fleets, controls the coasts from St. Petersburg to Smyrna, while German armies occupy the center of the board), but they require unusual confidence and cooperation.

It is safer if England is eliminated—but only after a possible Franco-Russian coalition has been prevented. My own choice for Germany's first victim is Russia, provided that an agreement with France has been reached to destroy England immediately afterward. The Russian offensive should be executed with the help of England and at least one of the southern powers (preferably Turkey, which is less likely to confront Germany in the near future). The key move for Germany's first year is advancing the Fleet in Kiel to Denmark in the spring and then thrusting Fleet Denmark to Sweden in the fall; this prevents Russia from occupying Sweden and deprives it of a needed build. Army Berlin can be moved directly to Prussia (or Silesia) or, if Germany wishes to conceal its intentions, can hold or move to Kiel in the spring. A German Baltic fleet (built in Berlin or Kiel in the winter of 1901) can support the German conquest of Sweden in 1902 and, with the help of a German (or Austrian or Turkish, if necessary) army in Moscow can take St. Petersburg in 1903. If Germany can persuade England to deploy its forces in the far north for an attack on St. Petersburg and to vacate the North Sea (as a precaution against an English double-cross), London will be open to French conquest in 1902. If Germany is properly innocent when the French move Fleet Brest to the English Channel in the spring, it should have no trouble taking Sweden in the fall—and England might even take St. Petersburg (to keep from losing a unit), eliminating the last of the Russian threat.

France will take the three English Supply Centers, but Germany will have ample compensation in its complete control of Scandinavia and northern Russia—and the much-desired corner position. There is no reason why the Franco-German alliance cannot then turn south—the French by sea, around Iberia and into the Mediterranean, and the Germans overland through Austria-Hungary and Russia.

Italy

Unsurprisingly, Italy is everyone's unfavorite. It survives the early years purely on the suffrage of its neighbors, its peninsular armies have nowhere to go, and its only assured extra Supply Center, Tunis, is out of the way and hard to defend.

Italy has two traditional courses of action: fight France or fight Austria-Hungary. Doing both at once is quick suicide unless a Russian-Turkish coalition attacks Austria from behind, but this only postpones the crunch.

If fighting France, Italy will usually move Army Venice to the Piedmont and Fleet Naples to the Tyrrhenian Sea; Army Rome can be sent to Venice (as protection against Austrian treachery) or Tuscany. In the fall, the fleet can move to Tunis or convoy Army Tuscany there; if Germany has managed to take Burgundy and is willing to support the Italian army, Army Piedmont might grab Marseilles for an extra build. Because of its limited mobility, Italy will be hard put to equal the gains of its allies (and it *must* have allies). If Germany is headed east, an alliance with England alone against France can be fruitful (it is difficult for France to protect both flanks), provided that a clash over Iberia can be prevented and if England can then be persuaded to turn its attentions northeast and away from the Mediterranean.

One of Italy's biggest problems is the proximity of Trieste and Venice; any course of action that leaves Venice open risks complete disaster if Austria moves in. France, at least, is a more trustworthy neighbor. If Italy has reason to suspect conflict on the eastern front, it usually moves Fleet Naples to the Ionian Sea, from which it can move to Tunis directly or convoy an army. If Austria is not expecting an Italian attack (particularly if it is beginning an active campaign against Russia or Turkey), the direct Army Venice to Trieste and Army Rome to Venice can work. Otherwise, moving Army Venice to Tyrolia, which threatens Trieste and Vienna (and, for that matter, Munich) and guards Venice, can cause Austria enormous problems. While such an offensive may be the most direct way of dealing with the most persistent thorn in Italy's side, care must be taken that Italy does not fall victim to an expanding Turkey. The best way to deal with this is to ally with Russia—first against Austria (with Turkish help); then, when Austria and the Balkans have been dismembered, against Turkey. This course of action leaves Italy master of the Mediterranean and is not at all against the interests of Russia. During this time, of course, France must be kept busy in the North, but this, too, is not against French interests.

The only significant alternative to these two traditional courses of action is to ally with Austria-Hungary against Turkey. This is the Lepanto Opening so much in vogue in theory, if still rarely practiced. After the usual first year moves (the Ionian Fleet convoying an army to Tunis and the Army in Venice remaining there as a permanent guard against Austrian deceit), Italy builds a fleet in Naples, moves the two fleets to the Eastern Mediterranean and the Ionian Sea and, in the fall of 1902, convoys Army Tunis to Syria. The immediate success of this is largely dependent on Turkish ignorance, but if it works, Turkey will be crushed in 1903. Austria gains far more than Italy, however, and even with the guardian army in Venice, Italy is extended in hopelessly indefensible exterior lines; if Russia can be diverted northwestward (which requires no great effort of persuasion), Italy is not strong enough to resist an Austrian offensive which would leave Austria-

Hungary the absolute master of the Balkans and the Mediterranean Sea.

Russia

Russia has four supply centers and can usually take two more in the first year, but it is the only country on the board which must face a reasonable possibility of a four-way attack. Such a terrifying prospect must obviously be avoided, even if it means that Russia is committed to fighting a two-front war in cooperation with dubious allies. Given a choice, it is best to neutralize the central front, for three reasons: (1) there are natural buffer zones there that can be kept vacant (i.e., the Baltic Sea, Prussia, Silesia, and Galicia), (2) a central Russian offensive leaves Russia too exposed to a pincer movement from countries on its flanks, and (3) Russia's traditional share of the unoccupied Supply Centers lies in the south and north. Unfortunately, the way in which Sweden and Rumania are occupied reveals more about Russian intent than is often desirable.

In the north, Fleet St. Petersburg (south coast) inevitably moves into the Gulf of Bothnia; if a squabble with England over Scandinavia is anticipated, Army Moscow moves to St. Petersburg in the spring and on to Finland in the fall (leaving St. Petersburg, north coast, open for building a fleet). If the south is secure, Army Warsaw can move to Livonia and be convoyed to Sweden; usually, however, that army is required elsewhere, and the fleet in the Gulf proceeds itself to take Sweden in the fall.

In the south, the situation is even more complicated. Fleet Sevastopol can move immediately to take Rumania unopposed, but if Turkey is hostile this surrenders control of the Black Sea to Fleet Ankara, which, in cooperation with Turkish armies moving to Bulgaria and Armenia, threatens Rumania *and* Sevastopol. For this reason, Army Warsaw is usually brought down to Ukrainia (or Galicia, if Austria is a problem); Fleet Sevastopol to Black Sea will bounce a similar Turkish move, and in the fall one of the Russian units can support the other into Rumania. If three units can be spared for the south, Army Moscow can be moved to Ukrainia (with Army Warsaw going to Galicia) or Sevastopol (with Army Warsaw going, probably, to Ukrainia and Fleet Sevastopol going at once to Rumania or to the Black Sea).

All this is much simpler if Russia can ensure that it faces only *one* hostile presence in the south. Austria is a better ally (against Turkey), particularly if an agreement with Italy is reached to eliminate Austria after Turkey has fallen. Under such circumstances, the Lepanto Opening is very much in Russian interests, particularly if a full-blown war with England is developing in the north. If Austria refuses to join a Russian fight with Turkey, then Turkey should be persuaded to join with Russia in an attack on Austria. Again, Italian help should be sought, and a long-term pact with Italy to dispose of Turkey has many advantages. Any agreement with Turkey should probably include the neutrality of the Black Sea, however much it may slow down the advance on Austria.

In the north, control of Scandinavia and the security of St. Petersburg seems to me a more desirable short-term goal than an attack on Germany. More important than either immediate objective, however, is a long-term agreement with France to destroy both England *and* Germany, in either order. Since these two countries are also France's major worries, a Franco-Russian alliance is not at all implausible.

Turkey

Turkey's problem is simplicity itself: it is in the interests of both Russia and Austria-Hungary to annihilate Turkey immediately. Turkey will not survive the first few years against such an anti-Turkish coalition unless it receives immediate help from Italy, Germany, and England . . . and even that may not be enough. The first requirement, therefore, is to talk Russia into attacking Austria or vice versa. Turkey can't afford to be choosy; midgame shortcomings are less important than the fact that without an ally, Turkey will *have no middle game*.

Given a choice, Turkey's best policy probably is to take part in a general dismemberment of Russia: it is potentially the more dangerous antagonist, and not only does Turkey thereby solidify its grip on the Black Sea and secure its position in the corner, but it opens the way for an alliance with England that should have valuable end game uses. Turkey typically opens a Russian offensive by ordering Army Constantinople to Bulgaria, Fleet Ankara to the Black Sea, and Army Smyrna to Armenia. This puts tremendous pressure on Russia's southern flank, even should the fleet be kept out of the Black Sea by a similar launching from Sevastopol. In the fall, with Bulgaria putting pressure on (or taking, with Austrian help) Rumania, Armenia on Sevastopol, and Ankara on the Black Sea, Russia will be hard put either to gain a Supply Center or to empty Sevastopol for a much-needed build in the winter. Most of the Russian centers will fall by the end of 1902. Rather than encourage an Italian drive on France, it is probably in Turkey's interests to encourage an Austro-Italian squabble; while not enough to damage the Russian offensive, this should allow Turkey better leverage around the Black Sea and is a logical precursor to a full-fledged alliance against Austria, which is clearly Turkey's next target.

A triple alliance with Russia and Italy against Austria offers quick gains—access to the Mediterranean and a good chunk of the Balkans (usually Bulgaria, Serbia, and Greece)—but presents midgame problems. If Russia is neutral to or allied with Turkey, the fleet in Ankara is moved to Constantinople in the wake of the standard Army Constantinople to Bulgaria. In the fall, the fleet will move into the Aegean unless the allies are attempting to deny Greece to Austria, in which case Army Bulgaria is ordered to Greece, and the fleet follows it into Bulgaria; this may not succeed even in standing off the Austrian unit (if it is supported from Serbia), but if Austria is under considerable pressure in Trieste, Turkey may manage two builds right away (probably a fleet in Smyrna and an army or another fleet in Constantinople).

Italy and Turkey can tackle Austria by themselves if Russia is occupied in the north and wishes to preserve its neutrality in the south. Such a campaign is only marginally different from a three-way attack, both in the gains afforded Turkey and in the method of conquest. The Lepanto Opening is opposed to Turkish interests not so much because of any immediate danger (it can be countered with a fleet built in Smyrna) as because it blocks the formation of a Turkish-Italian alliance against Austria; it should not be too difficult, however, to persuade Italy to shift allegiance.

The real problem with an initial conquest of Austria is that it leaves Turkey between Italy and Russia—and a logical target of an alliance between the two. Italy might be shunted toward France while Turkey occupied southern Russia, but it is probably better to negotiate a temporary neutrality pact with Russia and go after Italy. After Turkey has conquered the Mediterranean, it can move west against France or northeast against Russia, or both, in conjunction with similar moves on the part of England.

If Turkey can avoid being wiped out initially, it has an excellent chance to win the entire game.

Diplomacy has only two problems: it is often difficult to find seven people who are willing and able to play at the same time, and the game lasts inconveniently long (six to eight hours is not atypical). While there are variations for fewer than seven persons, I find that playing with less than a full complement detracts considerably from the challenge and appeal of the game. Much as I like Diplomacy, I think four or five people would do better to play Emperor of China or 4000 A.D.

One partial solution is postal Diplomacy, which requires the presence of an eighth player, the gamesmaster, to adjudicate the moves and publish the results. At any time, there are dozens of amateur Diplomacy journals and perhaps hundreds of games in progress therein. One highlight of such activity is the "press release," in which a player creates an involved and imaginary background for his country, replete with court gossip, political scandals, popular unrest, denunciations of opponents, and outrageous (and often irrelevant) humor.

Playing Diplomacy by mail does not appeal to all gamers, but if it is not a panacea, the prognosis for across-the-board play is not hopeless, either. The causes of the malaise are obvious: with too long a time period for negotiations, everyone has a chance to talk to everyone else; doubters are swayed, minds are changed, and strategies are struck down before reaching maturity. The novice's commonest affliction, a tendency to "stab" a turn too early, reaches epidemic proportions, and if a few ailing countries are thereby revived, the real victim is the game itself—an all but unnoticed fatality. The cure is harsh but simple: enforce the time limit on diplomacy sessions between moves. This remedies much of the time problem and breathes new life into the game by allowing the development of intelligent, long-range plans.

In its prime, there is no finer specimen of the board game family.

ORIGINS OF WORLD WAR II®

Although the rules, which are a masterpiece of redundancy, obscure the issue, Origins of World War II (Avalon Hill) is basically a fairly simple game and can be played in an hour. As in Diplomacy, each of the five players takes the part of a country: the United States, France, Britain, Russia, or Germany. Though the board is of pre-World War II Europe, the aim is not direct conquest but, as in Summit, the accumulation of points. Unlike Summit, however, the principle of differential valuation has been introduced: points are awarded according to a National Objectives Chart which differs from country to country. Control of the Baltic states, for example, is worth five points to Russia and two points to Germany, but if neither can manage the task, the United States gets four points. Conflict is not just inevitable; it is the crux of the game and is clearly intended to induce the frenzied negotiation and double-dealing that make Diplomacy so fascinating. In this, however, it is only partly successful. The Political Factors, the countries' income and their combat mechanism, are more reminiscent of Summit's power chips than of anything in Diplomacy; and conflicts are resolved according to the standard methodology of the "pure" war games—a fact that tends to emphasize individual action at the expense of diplomacy.

Unlike Summit, the game's real flaws stem not from the importance of the luck of the draw; *au contraire,* the problem is a stacked deck. Like various other Jim Dunnigan-designed games (e.g., France, 1940), Origins is not at all balanced. Germany is the overwhelming favorite, not only because it has nearly twice as many Political Factors as the next most powerful country, Britain (and *four times* the PFs of the United States!), but also because it plays last; it can pick up cheap Controls in places the other players have missed, and it can frustrate an attack by the placement of a single PF.* The United States is so weak it might as well not be in the game, and France is little better off. Germany *can* be stopped by a strong coalition of the other players, especially if Russia joins.

---

* Changing a combat ratio from 10:5 to 10:6 alters the simplified odds (according to standard AH/SPI computation) from 2:1 to 1:1, the difference between a reasonable attack and a suicidal one. See the next chapter for a more detailed explanation of the system.

The best technique seems to involve everyone's piling up PFs in Germany itself, which prevents German attacks elsewhere until it removes the PFs—and destroys the Understandings—at home. If Germany is kept from victory, Russia has the best chance to grab it; the advantage of playing fourth seems more important than Britain's slightly greater PF allocation.

The four alternative versions seem neither realistic nor, often, any more balanced. Dr. John Boardman has criticized the absence of a Collective Security variant, which would have been a more reasonable idea than, say, the Aggressive French Policy, which, however, at least gives France a chance. The Aggressive French-British Policy helps neither France nor Britain, and the chart involved is most peculiar, indeed: the United States becomes a tacit ally of the autocratic powers, since it gains NU (No Understanding) points in countries Russia or Germany control. The Aggressive British/U.S. Alliance, which increases the PFs of Britain and the United States, gives the latter a shot at victory, though English chances are much better.

The easiest way to eliminate a large chunk of Germany's advantage is to use the play-by-mail rules: have each country write down secretly the placement of PFs for the turn and then reveal the orders simultaneously (as in Diplomacy). This is only a little more work and improves the game enormously. It's still not Diplomacy, though.

CHAPTER 12

"Pure" War Games (*War Games III*)

Early war games used models—"toy soldiers," if you will—made to scale and maneuvered over appropriate miniature terrain, often in elaborately constructed, giant-sized sandboxes. In contemporary military establishments, sophisticated computer simulations have replaced the model figurines used by Napoleon and the Prussian officer corps, but miniatures survive as a private hobby clearly akin to model railroading. While they probably represent the ultimate in realism available to anyone outside a Pentagon think tank, miniatures are self-limiting in scale (they cannot, for example, simulate a campaign or an entire war), and the cost of the equipment involved and the ultraspecialized nature of the hobby limit its access to general gamers, thus putting it clearly outside the scope of this book.

Nearly all serious commercial war games are based on an approach pioneered by the Avalon Hill Company in the early 1960s, in which the sandbox was replaced by a mapboard on which a grid—originally rectangular but now generally hexagonal—was superimposed to facilitate movement; trees and slopes became colored spaces and contour splashes, and the troops themselves took the form of thick cardboard counters or pieces, on which were printed identifying symbols as well as "factors"—numbers which represented their combat strength and movement ability (i.e., speed).

With suitable modifications of terrain, factors, and such, the system can be—and has been—adapted to battles from Cannae to Waterloo, from the sinking of the *Bismarck* to the saturation bombing of Europe. If, in the minds of many, war games remain synonymous with Avalon Hill, quantitative leadership (at least) in the field has passed to Simulations Publications, Inc. (SPI), publishers of the magazines *Strategy & Tactics* and *Moves*, and at least a dozen new games per year. Indeed, the output of these two giants and their various lesser-known competitors has been so prodigious in less than a decade and a half that there are now literally hundreds of such war games on the market.

War games of this sort are most definitely intended only for game nuts, and often for a very particular species of game nut. The time required is forbidding: learning and preparation may take an hour or more, and a typical game lasts several hours—though some go on literally for *days*. If he does not bog down in the morass of the rules folder, the average gamer will boggle completely at the sheer magnitude of a game in which hundreds of pieces may be moved *every turn*.

REALISM vs. PLAYABILITY IN WAR GAMES

For all this specialization, there is by no means a unanimity of accord as to what the purpose of a war game is or how the field should be evolving. The most widely recognized and hotly debated issue is the difference between a simulation and a game—often expressed as the conflict of realism *vs.* playability. Jim Dunnigan and his staff at SPI are avowedly intent on producing *simulations* —reproductions, in short, of battles and campaigns that are not only historically accurate in location, terrain, orders of battle (i.e., the troops involved), and general mechanics, but are also faithful to the tactics, limitations, problems, and "feel" of the combat of the era involved. (Whether they *succeed* in this is something else again.) If, in their opinion, a valid simulation of a certain situation

requires thirty pages of rules, thousands of counters, and a game
that takes twenty or thirty hours of solid playing time, that's what
they'll publish.* The "gamers" (who include, to some extent, most
of the other designers and publishers and many players who *don't*
subscribe to *S & T*), on the other hand, tend to feel that the *game's*
the thing. Besides acknowledging greater practical limitations on
realism, they are far more concerned with play balance; they see a
war game primarily as a *contest* between two players within the
framework of the war game format.

A variety of researchers have convinced me that any claims to
historical fidelity on the part of Waterloo® (Avalon Hill) are dubious; aside from errors in the composition, placement, and arrival
times of the troops involved, the terrain of the mapboard is almost
entirely imaginary. *Nonetheless,* as a *game,* it succeeds quite well:
it is not too complicated, not too long, fairly balanced, and both
interesting and challenging.

France, 1940® (Avalon Hill—but Dunnigan-designed and originally published in *S & T*), on the other hand, is a poor game
defended as a good simulation. In fact, it falls on its face on both
counts. Its subject is the German blitzkrieg across France at the
start of World War II, and the game does, on a simple level, re-
create the swift advance and stunning victory of the Nazis. The
game's victory criteria, however, are silly and *not* historical: Paris,
for example, is not important enough; the only way for the French
to have a chance to "win" is to retreat without losing units, even if
it means abandoning Paris—historically, an absurdity.

More importantly, the reasons for the German success (or at
least its magnitude) lay in the fact that the French, in 1940, were
completely unprepared for the plans and capabilities of the German war machine. There is no way to simulate complete ignorance; a contemporary war gamer would no more rely on Hitler's
peaceful intentions or the invincibility of the Maginot Line than a
modern Priam would be taken in—*again*—by the Trojan horse.

But Dunnigan wanted a repeat of the German victory and he got
it by grossly, and grotesquely, unbalancing the game. To give him

---

* This is not an exaggeration, as any number of veteran gamers will attest.

credit, the bias is as subtle as it is telling, until you've played it or been suitably warned. Most of the trick involves the Combat Results Table. First, the German units are one point stronger than the French units; if a German unit attacks a French unit—at 1:1— a likely result is a forced counterattack by the French, which, because fractions are always rounded in favor of the defender, would be made at the suicidal odds of 1:2. The CRT is also prejudiced against the defense: for the defender, negative results apply to all units in the hex/space, but on the other side similar setbacks apply only to those units actually attacking. When you realize that in the game (and historically) the French are committed to a strategic *defensive*, you begin to get an idea of the odds against them.

Only a sadist or a masochist would enjoy playing the "historical" version of France, 1940, while other scenarios with alternative orders of battle are equally unrealistic and, at best, manage only to "balance" a series of wildly unbalanced factors. By playing around with the variables long enough, you can manage to come up with something you can live with, but what's the point? With one or two hundred alternatives, who needs a bad game and an inaccurate simulation?

Interestingly, *S & T* has criticized 1776® (Avalon Hill), one of those multiday marathons, on much the same grounds: specifically, for unbalancing the game in favor of the British by not including some sort of "idiocy factor" which would simulate the historical lack of British control and coordination of their forces.

"Command Control" Rules

This, in turn, brings us to a major battleground in the simulation *vs.* game war: "command control" rules. Simulators argue that the knowledge and control the modern game player possesses over the situation and his forces is unrealistic, that no general ever had complete knowledge of the enemy or complete control over his army, that orders frequently were ignored if they were not intercepted or lost, that troops habitually failed to do what was desired or expected of them, either from malice, cowardice, confusion, overenthusiasm, panic, or ignorance, and that such considerations should somehow be taken into account in designing a war game. SPI's answer is what they call "command control" rules.*

In one form or another, they have been around for some time. In certain scenarios of Centurion® (SPI), for example, a particular die roll meant that some units immediately defected to the enemy and began fighting against their former comrades. Most of the medieval and Renaissance games included provisions for panic among the troops in battle, though it might be restricted by losses suffered by units or their leaders. Command Control came into full bloom, though, with Battles of Bull Run® (SPI); in that game (which also employed simultaneous movement), units not in Command Control (that is, troops not close to a stationary leader) were subject to scattering. A first die roll, cross-referenced to the last digit of the hex number occupied by each unit, determined which troops would disregard their orders (their plotted movements); subsequent die rolls determined how far and in what direction they would move, instead. Variations on this theme have recurred frequently in subsequent SPI games.

No matter how "authentic" such rules may be, the uncertain aftereffects of such an injection of luck into the body of a game of skill can only detract from player satisfaction. Someone who loses a closely contested game of Centurion because of the "traitor" rule may legitimately feel victimized; the fact that Marius and Sulla (or Caesar and Pompey) had to worry about such treachery doesn't make the rule any less annoying. It may be argued that such surprises do no harm to solitaire play, and that is quite true; if you are playing alone (as is regrettably often the case, due to a paucity of people with the necessary interest, skill, and time to be suitable opponents), you *want* variables that keep your left hand from knowing exactly what your right hand is doing. Nonetheless, I don't believe even historian/gamers, in general (regardless of how S & T chooses to interpret its feedback), would rather play by themselves than against a compatible opponent, and the randomization resulting from Command Control (and other) rules cannot

---

* This is not the *only* possible approach to the situation short of ignoring its existence. Diplomacy and 4000 A.D. deal with the problems of faulty communications, miswritten orders, ignorance of enemy dispositions and intentions, and the like, in ways that do not involve dice or other randomizing elements.

help but reduce the meaningfulness of any *contest* between skilled opponents. The justification of chance elements in "family" games cannot be extended to pure war games, which, by design, make such heavy demands on time and mental effort. I have said repeatedly that "luck" balances out in the long run, but what is "the long run"? You can play five rounds of Clue in an evening, but you may not manage five games of Bull Run (particularly against the same opponent) in five years.

Perhaps the answer for nonsolitaire gamers is to avoid games with Command Control rules; perhaps it is to ignore such rules where they occur, though often this may damage the balance or the character of the game. It seems more likely, though, that a new design approach is needed.

Depth vs. Width

While there are many facets to the game/simulation dispute (as well as the more general problem of the purpose, use, and future of war games), it seems to me that one commonly overlooked underlying factor is a general failure either to distinguish complexity of concept or content—what I call "depth"—from complexity of form or format—what I call "width"—or to realize the lack of correlation between the two. In Chapter 9, I pointed out that chess and go, for example, were comparatively narrow but certainly deep; many "family" games are at least as wide but obviously shallower. It strikes me that the confusion between these two qualities is an albatross around the neck of the entire war gaming field: desiring depth, SPI insists on width—and the result is too often a mind-boggler like War in the East. Objecting to SPI's often excessive width, Simulations Design Corporation (publisher of *Conflict* magazine) is at times guilty of reducing *both* dimensions (as in Norad®, a short and otherwise quite playable little game); the resulting loss of depth draws equally valid criticism from many gamers. This is not to say that games at either extreme lack either fans or a place in the general scheme of things; only that the *real* fans of either type are few and far between, and the potential market for games which feature real depth without resorting to unworkable width is far greater than SPI, in particular, dreams.

Too many of the people with the necessary intellectual capacity are too busy to yield to the unreasonable demands on their time characteristically made by games in the field. Nonsimulation gamers are kept out of the genre—and even veterans are kept away from any number of specific games—because of what appears to be (and often is) a *comparatively* low return on their temporal investment.* It is entirely possible that the growth potential inherent in a radically new format may soon make the old familiar one as obsolete as a 5 percent savings account; 4000 A.D. and Quebec 1759 are examples of very different—and successful—approaches to the war game concept that may well prove, in the long run, more profitable for everyone concerned.

D-DAY®

Leaving any resolution of such speculation to the future, I think it would be well to turn our attention to a detailed examination of the most common type of war game, the strategic land game. Originally published in 1961, D-Day (Avalon Hill) was revised in 1965 and separated into a basic and an advanced ("tournament") version. In all cases, the setting is the same: Western Europe, just prior to the Normandy invasion. One player, commanding all the forces available to the Allies at the time, wins if he successfully invades Europe—specifically, if he can establish a beachhead at one of seven possible invasion areas from the North Sea to the south coast of France and, from there, march his troops inland and across the Rhine before the fifty-turn limit. The "German" player wins if he can prevent the "Allied" player from accomplishing his objectives. (Although it is possible to have any number of "subordinate commanders" or kibitzers, D-Day, like nearly all the other games in this chapter, is essentially a two-player game.)

The game mechanics are somewhat similar to Feudal or The Major Battles and Campaigns of General George S. Patton (and

---

* If the metaphor is unclear, allow me to elaborate: a $50 profit on a $75 investment, for example, is a good return in anyone's books; a $75 profit on an investment of $5000, on the other hand, is nothing to cheer about whether you're a starving student or the president of GM.

unlike chess): in his turn, each player can move every one of his units; how far each can move depends on its movement factor.* Basically, each unit can move one space per factor per turn, although terrain features can affect this adversely; for example, units moving through the mountains can move only one space per turn.†

Generally, combat occurs when one or more units move adjacent to an enemy unit. After he has moved as many units as he wishes, combat is resolved as the final portion of the attacking player's turn. This is done by comparing, in each case (for there may be a multitude of battles), the total number of the attackers' offensive factors and the total of the defenders' defensive factors, reducing this fraction, and finding the appropriate odds in the Combat Results Table (see Diagram 12-1). This sounds complicated, but it isn't, really. Say two Allied infantry units (4-4-4s) are attacking a pair of static infantry units (1-2-2s). The appropriate factors are, respectively, 8 and 4, which, expressed as a comparison (or fraction), reduces to 2/1. Having managed this far, you then roll a die and cross-reference the number with the proper column to get the outcome of the battle. Obviously, the greater the odds on the side of the attacker, the better the chance that he will eliminate the defending unit(s) at the least cost to his own.

It should be noted that terrain can affect not only the necessity for combat but also its resolution. For example, units in a city, in the mountains, or across a river, have their defensive factors doubled; had the static infantry divisions in the aforementioned attack been in a city, the Allies would only have managed odds of 1:1. (In other games, the attacker's factors might be similarly affected —positively or negatively—depending on terrain and circumstances.)

D-Day is not a particularly highly rated game, and it does have its weaknesses. The game is inherently slow-paced: the defensive nature of the struggle (the delaying tactics of the Germans, the defense-biased CRT, and the fortifications and terrain) combines

---

* A 5-5-4 armored unit, for example, has an offensive factor of 5, a defensive factor of 5, and a movement factor of 4; a German static infantry division is worth 1 on offense, 2 on defense, and can move 2 spaces per turn.

† In Tactics II (Avalon Hill), as another example, it requires *two* factors to cross a river, but travel on roads is done at three times the normal rate: a unit with a movement factor of 4 could move twelve spaces on a road.

COMBAT RESULTS TABLE

DIE ROLL / ODDS	1—6	1—5	1—4	1—3	1—2	1—1	2—1	3—1	4—1	5—1	6—1	ODDS / DIE ROLL
1	A elim	A elim	A back 2	A back 2	D back 2	D elim	D elim	D elim	D elim	D elim	D elim	1
2	A elim	A elim	A elim	A back 2	Exchange	Exchange	Exchange	Exchange	Exchange	D back 2	D back 2	2
3	A back 2	A back 2	A back 2	A back 2	A back 2	D back 2	D back 2	D back 2	D elim	D elim	D elim	3
4	A elim	A back 2	A back 2	A back 2	A back 2	A back 2	A back 2	D back 2	D back 2	D back 2	D elim	4
5	A elim	A elim	A elim	A elim	A elim	A elim	Exchange	Exchange	D back 2	D elim	D elim	5
6	A elim	A elim	A elim	A elim	A elim	A elim	A elim	D elim	D elim	D elim	D elim	6

Diagram 12-1
D-Day Combat Results Table—Courtesy Avalon Hill

with the low movement factors to hinder a quick Allied march to the Rhine; further, because of the number of units involved, each turn takes time, and if the Germans hold out, the game may take days to finish. Unfortunately, remedying these problems would require a completely new design, so players looking for a quick game had best look elsewhere.

Additionally, the 1965 revision created as many problems as it corrected. It took note of the Allied air superiority, but the seventeen-space Allied supply length limitation it inserted (by way of compensation) was arbitrary and unrealistic and effectively eliminated southern France as a viable Allied invasion target. For all this, I think the strategic scope of the game makes it worth salvaging, and I think the game *can* be balanced without eliminating what was, historically, the Allies' second invasion area.

I propose three revisions of the tournament game. First, adjust the supply rule so that a beach supply factor of 4 can supply four units within ten spaces of the supply hex, two units between eleven and twenty spaces away, or one unit up to thirty hexes distant. This change reflects the difficulties of supply more accurately than the original rule and simultaneously restores southern France to the game.

Second, deprive the Allies of the false advantage of complete intelligence (caused by requiring the German to place all his units on the board, in plain view, before the Allied player decides where to attack) by allowing the German player to deploy his units *face down*. A unit must be turned face up whenever an Allied unit moves adjacent to it, and *all* German counters must be revealed after the eighth turn. Restrictions on the placement of certain units remain in force; half a dozen or so dummy counters (blanks) may be used as an option.

Third, to balance things, give the Germans a historically accurate taste of uncertainty by revising the invasion rule. The Allies may make a second invasion *whenever they wish,* but troops may be moved into only *one area* per turn until the eighth turn, after which troops can be moved onto the continent through both areas. No more than two areas can be invaded, and all other invasion restrictions must be followed.*

---

* E.g., if the Allies land first at Normandy, attack Pas de Calais on the second turn, and return to Normandy on the third turn, they are still under the latter area's *second* turn restrictions (because it is only the second turn they have attacked it) and can bring ashore only two armored and four infantry units.

The latter change allows Allied feints, and the entire suggested revision package makes D-Day a better simulation and brings out its potential as an enjoyable and challenging game (even if it's still not for the impatient).

Kriegspiel (AH), Tactics II (AH), Blitzkrieg (AH), and Strategy I (SPI) have certain things in common: uniquely (at least among land games), none of them have specific historical referents, and none of them are very good. I think the two facts are related. You can't identify with the causes, personalities, issues, or nationalities involved, and the struggle becomes meaningless. Anyone who attends sports events regularly knows the importance of an emotional commitment to one team or the other; without it, even the most well-played game lacks appeal.

Politicians who try to be all things to all people tend to be as slippery and hard to pin down as Proteus, and games similarly designed give me that old Wizard of Oz feeling—that beneath the shifting facade is nothing of substance. There is nothing wrong with optional rules, *per se*, but—to indulge in another metaphor— a Chevrolet festooned with options is not a Mercedes-Benz.

BLITZKRIEG®

Blitzkrieg is probably the best of the lot, and fans of its width-for-the-sake-of-width approach—with its extralarge board; land, sea, and air movement, and hundreds of counters of a dozen types—will probably appreciate the Blitzkrieg Module System® (SPI), which adds armies to the neutral countries and still *more* options to the rules. But most people will find better ways to spend their time.

STRATEGY I®

Strategy I represents a modular approach to strategic games—a package of components designed to simulate the warfare of any era from the ancient past to the near future. Unfortunately, all but the most hardend fanatics will lose themselves in the jungle of completely optional rules long before they have managed to hack out a playable scenario.

KRIEGSPIEL® AND TACTICS II®

Kriegspiel and Tactics II are both intended as introductory games, but while the basic versions of each are not very complicated, they are not very rewarding, either. Both suffer from an excess of inertia and entropy (i.e., they don't go anywhere). There are not enough units or movement factors in Kriegspiel to risk anything more daring or decisive than a cautious advance, and the combination of roads behind the lines and bottlenecks (mountains, forests, etc.) at the front leads Tactics II into a nearly inevitable stalemate along the middle of the board. Far from adding skill, Kriegspiel's matrix system of combat resolution is chancier than the standard CRT, and Tactics II (which still uses the outmoded system of squares, rather than hexagons) is playable only with its full complement of options (atomic weapons, hidden movement, and all) —and even they are not always enough.

NINETEENTH-CENTURY WARFARE GAMES

Gettysburg® (Avalon Hill), another "introductory" game, is not very good, either, and it, too, is stuck with a rectangular grid. If you want to start with a land game, you are better off with Napoleon at Waterloo® (SPI), especially if you get the Napoleon at Waterloo Expansion Kit® (SPI) at the same time, which, by using more (smaller-sized) units and additional rules, allows you an easy step up. Slightly more complicated, but still better, is Borodino® (SPI), yet another game of Napoleonic warfare.

WORLD WAR II NORTH AFRICAN CAMPAIGN GAMES

Despite its narrow scope, the campaign in North Africa in World War II is a popular one with many gamers. Of the four leading contenders, Panzer Armée Africa® (SPI) and Desert War® (SPI) are, overall, distinctly better than El Alamein® (SPI) and Afrika Korps® (AH). The first is a strategic and the second a tactical treatment of the subject; the last is the oldest (by a decade) and the simplest.

WAR IN THE EAST®

Frustrated Genghis Khans will be happy to know that the Mongol Horde is alive and well in War in the East (SPI). The culmination of a seemingly unending succession of games on the Eastern Front war between Hitler's Germany and Stalin's Russia, War in the East has four "short" scenarios which replace various of the company's earlier efforts, but Blitzkrieg fans will doubtless be content with nothing less than the full, 200-turn campaign version which involves 2,000 units on a 17-square-foot mapboard. (And you thought the brontosaurus was extinct!)

WORLD WAR II®

Even larger in scope—if on a slightly more manageable scale—is World War II (SPI), a simulation of the whole shooting match. One of its more interesting aspects is that it can be played by either two or three players; however, if only two play, Germany can pretty much run rampant over Europe as long as it does not violate Russian neutrality (which would allow the Allied player to bring in Russian forces on *his* side). In the three-player version, Russia's only feasible option is to attack Germany sooner or later—an act which, if properly timed, should be enough to steal the "game" victory from the Third Reich. Though lesser minds may cringe at the thought, both these games have been extraordinarily well received by "hard core" war gamers.

GAMES ON CONTEMPORARY AND HYPOTHETICAL SUBJECTS

Concurrent with a notable rise in SPI's game quality following a pronounced depression from late 1972 to mid-1973 are two trends, the first of which is an emphasis on contemporary and hypothetical subjects. Sinai® (SPI) is an excellent strategic simulation of the various Arab-Israeli wars, but even more interesting and possibly better are Red Star/White Star® (SPI) and NATO® (SPI), which are, respectively, tactical and strategic versions of a possible NATO-Warsaw Pact confrontation in Germany in the 1970s. The East is Red® (SPI), which covers a hypothetical Sino-Soviet war in Manchuria in the same period, Seelowe® (SPI), Hitler's projected invasion of England, Operation Olympic® (SPI), a solitaire game which avoids most of the problems of Fall of Rome® (SPI) and which involves the planned but historically unnecessary Allied invasion of Japan in 1945, and Starforce: Alpha Centauri®, SPI's first science fiction war game, all look promising. The last should appeal particularly to the many science fiction fans who are also gamers.

PANZERBLITZ® AND ITS IMITATIONS

The second apparent trend is a renewed focus on tactical games, the most famous of which is the most popular war game ever designed, Panzerblitz (AH). Tactical games differ from strategic ones not just in scale but in mechanics: range of weapons becomes an important factor (since combatants no longer need be in adjacent hexes), and the combat resolution system changes; a firing unit cannot be negatively affected by its attack. A quantum jump closer to miniatures, tactical games project more of the color and feel of combat than their strategic cousins and for that reason to many people seem both more realistic and more comprehensible.

This quality was accentuated in Panzerblitz by the use of extra-large counters depicting the actual silhouettes of the tanks and vehicles represented. Combine all this with the popularity of the subject matter (the Eastern Front, again) and the flexibility of geomorphic mapboards (i.e., three small boards which can be combined in a variety of ways) and a dozen scenarios (some of which, initially unbalanced, were revised in subsequent printings), and the game's success is not hard to understand. Panzerblitz *is* complex; it's got a lot of rules and is definitely not the first war game a novice should tackle. But it's challenging and a whole lot of fun, and that's what games are all about, isn't it?

Panzerblitz is not without weaknesses. For one thing, many games exhibit the so-called Panzerbush syndrome: units skulk from woods hex to woods hex, from ravine to protecting slope, without incurring the enemy fire which, in reality, they would have drawn when they exposed themselves on open ground. Since, in the game, this exposure occurs in the middle of the movement portion of *their* turn, they are safe, and, often, so are their eventual "hiding places," even though, again, properly positioned enemy units would have seen them "disappear."

Furthermore, the smaller the scale of the game, the more obviously unrealistic is the familiar method of alternating turns, and most recent SPI tactical games employ various simultaneous movement (simov) systems, in which both players write their units' orders secretly and reveal them at the same time, *à la* Diplomacy. The bookkeeping involved, however, prohibits the use of such a system in games with very many counters, and even in smaller games whether the added complication, tedium, and the time required in writing orders and adjudicating disputes is worthwhile or not remains solely a matter of taste.

Nitpicking aside, I think it's clear that the upsurge of tactical games has been due in large part to Panzerblitz's success, and there has been no lack of subsequent imitations. Avalon Hill promised a Western Front version of the game some time ago, but as of this writing it has still not appeared, and Combat Command® (SPI), a similar idea, failed to live up to expectations (and is scheduled for revision).* On the other hand, Red Star/White Star, the aforementioned "contemporary" Panzerblitz, has equalled the high ratings (if not yet the popularity) of the first game, and fans of one are sure to be fans of the other. Without using simov, Red Star/White Star retains something of the flavor of Panzerblitz, while some unique rules have eliminated the Panzerbush syndrome.

Using essentially the same game system (with simov) as Desert War, Kampfpanzer® (SPI) covers the pre-Panzerblitz period (mid-1930s to the early 1940s). A decent enough effort, Kampfpanzer's biggest problem is that its scenarios and units seem inherently dull compared to the superweapons of the more "modern" games. Tank!® (SPI) is an even smaller-scale game (i.e., one counter represents a single tank instead of a platoon or company of them) that includes scenarios representing armored warfare during the periods covered by all of the others in this group.

---

* After this was written, Avalon Hill released Panzer Leader®, the long awaited West Front Panzerblitz, and SPI brought out the Combat Command revision, Panzer '44®.

SNIPER!®

One of SPI's hottest new items is Sniper!, an ultra-small-scale (one counter equals one man) simulation of intracity warfare. The scale, in fact, is very much the thing in this game: to some enthusiasts, ordering each man to stand up, lie down, fire a machine gun down an alley, reload, jump out a window, or whatnot represents the real nitty-gritty of combat. While it is probably easiest for a person to relate to events on this scale, my own feeling is that— to judge by the present example—it just takes too many rules to simulate action on such a level; ultimately, the trouble of learning so many directions and the tedium of order-writing will overcome most players' interest in the subject matter. Patrol® (SPI), an outdoor Sniper!, should appeal to those who disagree.

OUTDOOR SURVIVAL®

Outdoor Survival (Avalon Hill/Stackpole) is a similarly small-scale simulation of a *non*-war game subject and could as readily fit in Chapter 6 as here. "Combat" is strictly man *vs.* nature, and the interpersonal conflict in multiplayer scenarios is largely in the nature of a race—to get off the board, to find a "lost" camper, or a combination of both. The game may be played by as many as four or as few as one; each player faces essentially the same problems of terrain, a scarcity of food and water (a lack of which "weakens" and limits the movement of a player's counter), and a "scattering" rule (Command Control in disguise) that can send a man wandering about haphazardly according to the dictates of the die. If I'm not sure of its audience (purists will give it no more attention than Scrimmage), it's an intriguing idea with a variety of scenarios, and if the basic game is childishly simple (and so boring that it should be ignored), the regular versions are much easier to swallow than the standard SPI war game.

NAVAL GAMES

Scale is a perennial problem in naval games, and Midway® (AH), Bismarck® (AH), and Jutland® (AH) all use a combination of "strategic" *and* "tactical" boards. An undistinguished game of the Pacific Theater in World War II, Midway concentrates tactically on carrier warfare (i.e., aircraft *vs.* ship) rather than ship-to-ship combat. Bismarck is a simulation of the hunt for the famous German battleship; despite its one-sidedness (it's essentially one ship vs. the entire British Navy), it is easy to grasp and is, for a war game, quite short—an hour or two, at most. It is even possible for the German player to win, occasionally, if the *Bismarck* can elude its pursuers for a while and can catch one or two of the British ships alone *at night.* Jutland is just about the closest thing to miniatures you'll find in a war game: the counters are nearly two inches long, and the "battle board" is not a board at all, but any large level surface available (a basketball court is perfect, but thirty square feet of living room floor will do in a pinch), on which the ships—representing the British and German battleships in World War I—are maneuvered via a special rulerlike gauge. While the basic game is simple and playable, the advanced version is clearly preferable. It is not a short game. You may object to crawling around on the floor, and the carefully plotted formations are particularly vulnerable to dogs, cats, children, and other natural hazards; but for all that, even the advanced rules are logical and easy to understand, and it's *fun.* Distressingly, both Bismarck and Jutland are currently out of print, but unofficial sources report plans to republish them shortly in "bookshelf" form.*

CA® (SPI) is a fairly successful attempt to do a game similar to Jutland within the confines of a standard game board. It has a variety of scenarios centering on cruiser action in World War II, and, for an SPI game, the rules are relatively clear and uncomplicated. Frigate® (SPI), which seems to be a similar effort inspired by the Age of Sail in the eighteenth and nineteenth centuries, includes scenarios that vary from battles between individual ships to entire fleet actions.

RICHTHOFEN'S WAR®

My views on war games are somewhat heretical. Here they are: first, the best and easiest way to get into (or introduce a friend to) AH/SPI-type war games is *not* by land games at all, but by tactically oriented sea or air games—specifically, Bismarck and

---

* Jutland has, indeed, now been reprinted.

Richthofen's War (AH). Second, Richthofen's War is very likely the best war game on the market.

Since I do not expect you to take these two statements on faith, I will explain. There are three things most likely to discourage people from tackling a war game or from repeating the experience: the length and complexity of the rules, the time required both to learn and to play the game, and the large number of pieces (units) generally involved. These three contribute to and are aggravated by a fourth factor—a confused, "what's-going-on-here?" feeling. I have already observed that people seem able to comprehend and identify with tactical games more readily than those of a strategic variety (perhaps because the former are less abstract); without terrain rules—a major headache in games like Panzerblitz—the "cleaner" media of sea and air simplify both movement and combat. Bismarck and Richthofen's War (in its basic version) are not only less complicated than their land counterparts; they are also far shorter and employ fewer units than land games of *any* sort. The simplest scenarios of Richthofen's War involve only a single plane per player, and a game can be played in less than half an hour! Even the British player in Bismarck will rarely have more than two ships in battle at any time, and movement on the "search board" is easy.

Although it is excelled in certain respects by other games, Richthofen's War seems to me the best *overall* war game. It is as good a *simulation* as any I have seen, but that is the least of its virtues. I suppose some people will not care for the period (World War I), the tactical nature, or the air environment of the game, but this is true of all periods and types. I will concede that Panzerblitz has an edge in width *and* depth, but the difference is slight and may not even be significant. Richthofen's War has as great a variety of units, scenarios, and options, but the rules are much easier to remember, because most of the important considerations—speed; altitude; turning, diving, and climbing ability; damage; etc.—are right in front of you on the Aircraft Status Pad. As noted, it requires less time to learn, set up, and play than any other likely candidate, and it is easy to add options gradually, from game to game, as you become increasingly familiar with play.

The greatest advantage of the game is its flexibility: its scenarios offer an unparalleled choice of missions and aircraft (both type and number), and, though I would suggest that the individual characteristics (e.g., turning ability) of the chosen aircraft be used as soon as possible (in the second game, if not the first), the game is quite enjoyable with or without any of the other optional rules. The Deflection rule, for instance, will restore to maneuverable planes like the Fokker Triplane a measure of advantage they historically enjoyed, but the option is no more necessary to a good game than the Critical Hit Table. Limiting—and gradually decreasing—the time allotted to a player's turn adds realism and prevents even a trace of tedium. There is a campaign version that not only allows options like Aces and includes all the problems and complexities of a long game but also boasts the unique advantage that the campaign can be fought a sortie at a time, whenever you and your opponent have a few minutes—and the board and all the equipment *can be kept in the box between battles.* There is even provision for meaningful and realistic participation by up to six players.

In short, if I were limited to a single war game, it would be Richthofen's War.

The defense rests.

FOXBAT & PHANTOM®

If you like tactical air games enough to buy a second one, your best bet is Foxbat & Phantom (SPI), a simulation of the kinds of air combat that might take place in the 1970s. Though it lacks the variety, flexibility, and initial simplicity of Richthofen's War, the incredible aircraft involved have an appeal of their own. Spitfire® (SPI), the World War II alternative, is less successful, and Flying Circus®, SPI's World War I game, is decent enough but just not in the same league as Richthofen's War.

BATTLE OF BRITAIN® AND LUFTWAFFE®

Just about the only one interested in designing strategic air games is Lou Zocchi, whose efforts have appeared under a variety of titles and publishers in the last several years. All of them bear an obvious family resemblance, and their biggest common problem—

if it is that—is their creator's penchant for long games. Battle of Britain (now available from the designer), whose subject is obvious, has been revised several times and at last count was currently available in no fewer than six versions, the shortest of which could be played, according to Zocchi, in "less than three hours." Luftwaffe (AH), a game about the Allied bombing of Europe in the late stages of World War II, also has several campaign scenarios that last not quite forever. If I have a preference for the latter game over the former, it is probably because the basic version of Luftwaffe is a better and more challenging game in its own right and can be played in an hour or two.

The Allies have an advantage even in the short version of Luftwaffe, and to stop them the Germans must hit the bomber formations hard and often. Like the bombers, Allied fighters must be attacked early, forcing them to drop their tanks and abandon escort duty. ME 410s and ME 110s should get in the air at the first sign of trouble and stay there. They are most useful in the East and South, where large distances are involved and airfields are scarce. The Focke-Wulfs, the best German fighters, should be kept together for maximum effectiveness and along with the ME 109s —the bulk of the defense—should be deployed at the front, in the West, where most of the action is. The Allies will inevitably "sneak raid" in the far north, but it's not worth committing the necessary fighters to stop them.

The restrictions on refueling and tank-dropping are unrealistic and mildly annoying, but they minimize bookkeeping and are another good reason for keeping planes of one type together. A more serious difficulty is the Combat Results Table, which is too unpredictable; while the extreme variations represented are possible, they are not equally *likely*. Rather than dropping the extremes, as some players do, a better revision is to use *two* dice instead and substitute dice roll numbers as follows:

1 becomes 2 and 3	2 becomes 7	3 becomes 5 and 6
4 becomes 8 and 9	5 becomes 4 and 10	6 becomes 11 and 12

This will yield an approximation of the familiar bell-shaped curve, so that the middle outcomes are far more probable than the more extreme possibilities.

FLYING TIGERS®

A third Zocchi game, Flying Tigers (Third Millennia), is a simulation of the Japanese encroachment upon mainland China in the early years of World War II. While it is generally a less involved game, Flying Tigers does include an admixture of air tactics lacking in the other two games.

SPACE WAR GAMES

There are only a handful of space war games on the market, and the "strategic" games I have seen—Lensman® (Spartan International) and Empire I® (Third Millennia)—are only for science fiction fans who are also game fanatics. Both are in some sense "wider" versions of 4000 A.D., and both are involved—especially Lensman. Lou Zocchi's pair of tactical games, Alien Space® and Star Trek®, cross the line into miniatures and require even more floor space than Jutland. The only difference in the two games is that, with some name changes, Star Trek includes only three of Alien Space's eight ships. In both cases, each player maneuvers a single starship according to a compass-and-ruler system built into the huge (20 square inches) counters; depending on his judgment and the unique weaponry of his ship, he might fire such secret weapons as phasers/blazers or photon/proton torpedoes, lay cosmic mines, let loose an expanding beam of destruction that lasts for several turns (growing and annihilating vessels all the while), raise defensive screens, or retreat into invisibility. Good fun for frustrated starship captains everywhere.

WAR GAME MAGAZINES

Newcomers interested in war games are advised to consult any of the odd-numbered issues of *Strategy & Tactics* for ratings of SPI and Avalon Hill war games, along with some others of related interest. Approach with caution, however; in addition to the inherent problems of "complexity" ratings which do not distinguish between basic and advanced versions of a game, the people who rate the games for the magazine are, in general, exceedingly narrow-minded, and you will probably find their tastes peculiar. Diplomacy, for example, was rated *below* France, 1940—which is about like saying Anti-Monopoly is a better game than Monopoly. The less frequent ratings by Martin Campion and his staff that appear from time to time in *S & T*'s companion magazine, *Moves*, are more useful, in part because they try to differentiate the views of the various sorts of people who play war games (e.g., novice, gamer, historian).

Although each bimonthly issue of *Strategy & Tactics* includes a new game, its main emphasis is historical, with a pair of long articles on the background data behind SPI simulations. *Moves*, on the other hand, focuses more on the games themselves—corrections, variations, and playing tips. In this regard, it is still outdone by the Avalon Hill *General*, which, however, confines itself solely to AH games. *Conflict* (SDC) is the West Coast "answer" to *S & T*, but its publishing schedule is considerably more erratic.

Discussing winning tactics for every war game available is like navigating a ship along a stretch of savage coastline: even with an occasional lighthouse like *Moves* or the *General*, we run a considerable risk of foundering on the shoals of ignorance and error, running aground on the sandbar of tedium, or simply being overwhelmed by the unceasing waves of new entrants and drowned in the vast gaming sea. We might reasonably ask if it would be easier and faster to go by air; while many of the details might be blurred or submerged altogether, a certain distance might lead to the perception of some significant patterns not apparent close up. It is my opinion that an overall perspective is possible, and that certain general systems or principles which apply to *all* games are indeed evident in such a view.

GAME THEORY

Game theory is a mathematical discipline first described in the second quarter of this century by John von Neumann. I encountered it in college, a decade ago, in the form of a delightfully droll but nonetheless informative book called *The Compleat Strategyst* (Random House), by J. D. Williams—still, so far as I know, the most accessible book on the subject for nonmathematicians. Game theory is essentially conservative: it is concerned less with the greatest return than with the *safest* return. Assuming (perhaps pessimistically) competent and determined opposition, it seeks to make the worst that can happen as bearable as possible (in more technical terms, it maximizes the average minimum return or minimizes the average loss—depending on which side of the contest you're on). Those of you who want to know more about the subject (including the math—heh, heh) than the tantalizing glimpses afforded in this volume are entrusted to Mr. Williams's care.

Game theory's most obvious use for war gamers is to solve questions of strategy or tactics, even when those terms are allowed to encompass all questions of choice likely to arise in a game. This can be illustrated by a simplified model of the sorts of problems facing two people playing D-Day; to keep things manageable, the seven invasion areas have been abstracted into two large zones, the North and the South.

The first example assumes that the Germans deploy first (and face up) and that they can defend only one of the two zones; the Allies, in turn, can attack the defended zone or the undefended zone. These two pairs of intersecting strategies allow us to set up a two-by-two grid, the preliminaries of a game matrix. The matrix, however, is empty: to solve the problem, each space of the matrix must be filled in with a quantitative evaluation (called a "payoff") of the results of the interaction of each set of opposing strategies. In both examples, the payoffs represent the probabilities (expressed in percentage points) of an Allied victory (e.g., 25 means a 25 percent chance that the Allies will win the game); the numbers I assigned to each possibility are necessarily arbitrary but not unreasonable.

It is obvious from a glance at Diagram 12-2A that it is silly for the Germans to defend the South, since only an idiot would attack the South and get wiped out when certain victory lay in the North. Similarly, there is no point in the Allies attacking the zone the Germans are defending, since they would have *at best* only a 25 percent chance of winning; on the other hand, if they attack the undefended zone, the *worst* that can happen is a 50 percent chance of victory. Note that these facts cause a convergence of German and Allied strategies in the lower lefthand quadrant: the best Ger-

Germans Defend:

		North	South
Allies	Same	25	0
Attack:	Opposite	50	100

A

Germans Defend:

		North	South
Allies	North	25	100
Attack:	South	50	0

B

Diagram 12-2

man strategy is to defend the North, and the best Allied strategy is to invade the South (the undefended, opposite zone). Note further that this is true even if each side knows what the other side knows. Such a point in a matrix is called a "saddle point," and its payoff is the "value" of the game. In this case, since the value is 50 (50 percent), the game is "fair"; both sides' chances are even. (This is not, of course, a completely faithful reflection of the odds in a *real* game of D-Day, since, among other things, it takes no account of one of the Allies' strongest weapons, the threat of a second invasion.)

Diagram 12-2B assumes a different situation: here the Allies must secretly commit themselves to an invasion zone *before* the German units are placed on the map (or else the Germans are deployed face down, with plenty of dummy units). Although the same payoffs are used, this time there is no saddle point; if one side knows the other's intentions, or if one side insists on using one "pure" strategy all the time, the other side can take appropriate countermeasures. In such a case, when there is no single, simple solution—no saddle point—each player optimizes his prospects by adopting a "mixed strategy," a blend of some or all of his possible pure strategies according to a specific ratio derived mathematically from the payoffs involved. In a mixture of two pure strategies (as we have here), the strategy offering the larger range of outcomes (e.g., the German "South" as opposed to its "North") will be used *less* than the strategy with a smaller range of outcomes; indeed, the use of each is directly proportional to the *other* strategy's range of outcomes.* In the matrix of Diagram 12-2B, the Allies should adopt a 40-60 North-South mix and the Germans an 80-20 North-South mix. The value of *this* game is 40; i.e., it is unfair to the Allies, which should not be surprising, since hidden deployment would obviously improve the Germans' chances compared to the conditions of the game of Diagram 12-2A.

One way of interpreting this data is that, over a great many games, the Allies should invade the North 40 percent of the time and the South 60 percent. On any particular game (since the opponent may have access to the same matrix) a game theorist would suggest using a properly weighted randomizing device to make your final decision. One simple way to do this is to glance at the second hand of your watch when you are ready to decide on your course of action: assuming you are the Allied player, following the mixed strategy just mentioned, if the second hand lies within the first twenty-four seconds (i.e., the first 40 percent) of the minute, you attack the North; otherwise, you attack the South. The German player can follow a similar procedure (using forty-eight seconds for the North and twelve seconds for the South). Even if either opponent knows—or has calculated—the mixed strategy of the other, this weighted randomization prevents him from taking advantage of his knowledge.†

This is not, however, the only way of using the matrix in connection with the *real* game of D-Day. One alternative would be for

---

* This, as you may have noted, is perfectly in keeping with the conservative nature of game theory, which avoids large risks as much as possible.

† It should also dispel the silly notion that, simply because dice are not used, there is no chance involved in the Kriegspiel Battle Table.

the Germans to deploy 80 percent of their troops in the North and 20 percent in the South. Similarly, the Allies might split their forces (using two invasions) according to their 40-60 mix.

Game theory, to be sure, has its limitations: complicated matrices become very tedious (at best) to solve without a computer, and precise quantification of payoffs is not always possible. Nonetheless, the possibilities are enormous and are not even limited to competition gaming. Game theory can be a bonanza for the solitaire gamer: after deriving proper mixed strategies for any of the choices he faces (tactics, placement of units, routes, etc.)—for both sides—he can use a suitably weighted chance device to make his final selections. This keeps him from "fudging," allows him to play both sides reasonably, and still maintains an element of suspense and uncertainty so often lacking in solitaire play.

MAXIMIZING YOUR STRENGTHS AND MINIMIZING YOUR WEAKNESSES

One obvious way to improve your war-gaming abilities is to study military history and tactics. If the game is reasonably well designed, historically appropriate tactics should be effective. Furthermore, the basic principles of military strategy and tactics—Liddell-Hart's "indirect approach," the flank attack, envelopment, the pincers movement, surprise, mobility, the superiority of interior lines, etc. (all of which, perhaps, can be summarized as the attainment of a position from which you can throw your strength at an enemy weakness)—should hold true in *all* war games, regardless of setting or period.

Underlying all such military principles, but not limited to them, is what I call (for lack of an established nomenclature) "basic grand strategy." Like game theory, it can be applied not only to games—all games—but to most human activity. It is the "common sense" (what a misleading phrase!) approach behind such clichés and catch-phrases as "Make the most of what you have" and "Accentuate the positive; eliminate the negative." In every situation of potential conflict, each person/player/side/team/army/nation has a certain unique combination of attributes. The key to success is to take advantage of your strengths, whatever they are, and minimize the effect of your weaknesses; to attack—or make use of—your opponent's weak points and avoid his strengths, and to prevent him from doing the same to you. Do unto others, but do it first.

These very basic ideas apply to all levels of conflict, from winning a fist fight to winning a war game (or a war), from surviving in the wilderness to making the most of your life.

An example may be helpful. Consider the case of Archie and Bill, two men who have gotten into an argument which leads to a fight. Archie is taller, heavier, and stronger; Bill is nimbler, faster, and in better shape. It would be folly for Bill to get into a toe-to-toe slugging match (a "frontal assault," in other words), and, in fact, Bill does not want to *exchange* blows at all, since any such "exchange" works generally in favor of the stronger party (cf. "exchange" results in a war game CRT). Bill's strategy should be to avoid Archie's blows at all costs and prolong the bout as much as possible, to wear Archie down until he is too tired and too slow to fight effectively; then, and only then, can Bill afford to close with his opponent and finish him off. Tactically, he has a choice of approaches: (1) he can simply run, letting Archie wear himself down trying to catch up with him or land a blow, or (2) he can dart in, strike, and retreat, wearing Archie down with his own blows (if Bill has endurance but not speed, he should opt for the first alternative; if he has speed but not endurance, the second). A third alternative is kicking, since his legs can match the strength and reach of Archie's arms. As a strategy, this is not his best policy (unless, perhaps, he is an expert in *savate*, or Thai kick-boxing, which we have not assumed), since it does not make use of any of his unique advantages; there is nothing wrong with its use as a *tactic*, however, as long as he keeps his overall strategy in mind. Archie should be more willing to chance a frontal attack (especially if he lacks an advantage in reach), but this does not make maximum use of *all* his favorable attributes: *his* best policy is to corner Bill so that he can't run away and then keep him at bay with his longer reach. After slowing and weakening Bill with his long-range (and unreturned) punches, Archie can move in closer for stronger blows should that prove necessary.

What is important here is not that the two men's advantages "even out," but that each has particular advantages that should be utilized in such a contest. By adopting a strategy inappropriate to his special attributes, either will reduce considerably his chances for victory. (Remember the lessons of Monopoly?)

Keeping in mind the example of Archie and Bill and the principles behind their "battle plans," let's take a brief look at some war games. In some of the scenarios of Panzerblitz, for example, the Germans have a couple of superweapons, the Wespe and the Hummel, with enormous firepower and a greater range than anything else in the game. In such cases, regardless of the overall strategic objective, the Germans should get those units to a point of high ground from which they can "view" a large expanse of hexes. They should then sit there and blast away at any enemy units that show themselves. Since their defensive factors are relatively small, they should be stationed well back of the front and should be screened by advance tank and artillery units; they are too valuable to risk in any "exchanges"; so enemy tanks should not be allowed to get close enough to return their fire.

One of the virtues of Richthofen's War is that there are so many different aircraft, each with its own unique capabilities. Tactics, accordingly, should vary from plane to plane. The strong, heavily armed, maneuverable Fokker Dr-1 (the Red Baron's famous triplane) should seek to grapple with its opponent at close quarters, to "dogfight." The Spads, on the other hand, should use their speed and diving ability to make long-distance passes at opposing aircraft. Any plane gifted with the good but asymmetrical maneuver schedule E should always try to turn right (clockwise); a plane on a lesser—but *symmetrical*—maneuver schedule, if involved in a dogfight with an E plane, should always try to get the action moving to the *left*, counterclockwise, destroying the E's advantage. Similarly, in Foxbat & Phantom, fighters armed with cannon or short-range, heat-seeking missiles should try to get as close as possible to the opposing aircraft; fighters with long-range, radar-homing missiles should stay away from the enemy.

In Jutland, the German fleet is greatly outnumbered by the total British fleet but is a match for any of its three contingents, separately. Strategically, then, the Germans want to tackle the British forces one at a time; the British, in order to avoid such a "defeat in detail," want to combine forces before combat. Tactically, the situation is more complex: the Germans are outnumbered and outgunned, but they have, in general, better armor—i.e., their "protection factors" are higher. "Crossing the T"—an obvious example of a position in which comparative strength confronts comparative weakness—is a desirable tactic for either side, and one that is, therefore, difficult to accomplish. Slugging it out in parallel lines at normal range—in the advanced game a matter of filling in the hit record boxes (themselves essentially a measure of *offensive* strength) until a ship is crippled or sunk—would lead to a certain German defeat; the Germans can't afford such "exchanges." However, a British weak spot—their battlecruisers' low protection factors—allows the Germans a "shortcut." By closing to short, or "double," range, the concentrated fire of a German battle line can sink the offensively powerful but defensively weak British battlecruisers in a single turn without the necessity of filling in all those boxes. (At very short—"triple"—range, *all* ships become vulnerable to such one-turn sinkings.) Another tactic the Germans can use to good effect is a properly timed "battle turn-away": when a number of hits have been registered on German ships, the entire battle line can reverse direction, presenting to the enemy a new set of near-empty boxes—which is almost as good as a whole new fleet!

USING GAME RULES TO BEST ADVANTAGE

A final general principle: *use* the rules; don't get *abused* by them. For example, the Combat Results Table of D-Day (and the other early AH games) makes a 2:1 attack very undesirable: the odds of winning the battle are even, but the attacker has at least twice as much at stake. Under such a CRT, it is far better to mount one 1:1 and one 3:1 attack than to risk two 2:1 battles. The CRT of 1776, on the other hand, specifically encourages 1:1 attacks. In nearly all cases (including The Major Battles and Campaigns of General George S. Patton, as you may recall), it is enormously advantageous to have a defender surrounded (even if not all the attacker's units are participating in that particular attack); with some recent CRTs, it is the only way to destroy an enemy unit. Defending against this may involve a solid front or a defense in depth, depending on the other rules involved.

Other examples of two-edged rules are the peculiarities of dice combat in General George S. Patton and Risk, the "housing short-age" in Monopoly, and the maintenance/leasing dodge I suggested using in Airport. Closer to home (in several respects), I played a game of Tactics II once upon a time with my brother. We were using the atomic weapons option, so I was careful never to bunch up my units, but at one point in a battle two of my units were forced to retreat (and, according to the rules, in a direction at the discretion of the opponent). He—sneaky fellow—retreated them next to another pair of my units and then destroyed the two-by-two square, and my four units which occupied it, with an H-Bomb. Ouch!

The lesson here is not that there are loopholes in all rules, but that, in a valid sense, *all* rules are loopholes—for anyone who has the sense to use them.

Keeping in mind the principles discussed in the last few pages should not only improve your play, but also, as I suggested at the beginning of this book, increase your enjoyment of games. It might even help when you're *not* playing games.

Suggestions for Further Reading

The major war-gaming journals were listed in the last chapter; their addresses can be found under Game Publishers and Their Addresses. *Games & Puzzles* is the only general gaming magazine I know of; it is published in England by Edu-Games (U.K.) Ltd. and is available direct by writing *Games & Puzzles,* P.O. Box 4, London N6 4DF. You can also subscribe from agents in the United States, two of whom are F. O. Armbruster (Products of the Behavioral Sciences, 1140 Dell Ave., Campbell, CA 95008) and Dr. John Boardman (234 E. 19th St., Brooklyn, NY 11226), who is also the publisher of *Graustark,* the oldest bulletin of postal Diplomacy.

Sid Sackson's *A Gamut of Games* (Castle Books) is mainly a collection of original games, but it also includes a series of brief (and now often outdated) reviews of various contemporary board games. The two standard works on "classic" board games are *Games Ancient and Oriental and How to Play Them,* by Edward Falkener (Dover), and R. C. Bell's two-volume *Board and Table Games from Many Civilizations* (Oxford University Press). *Scarne's Encyclopedia of Games,* by John Scarne (Harper & Row), devotes 90 percent of its attention to card games and its usefulness is lessened by inaccurate information.

Perhaps the simplest chess book for beginners is *The Programmed Method for Learning to Play Chess,* by Dr. M. W. Sullivan (Quadrangle/The New York Times Book Co.). Other good books for the novice are Reuben Fine's *Chess the Easy Way* (Cornerstone Library/ Simon & Schuster) and the two-volume set, *Learn Chess: A New Way for All*, by C. H. O'D. Alexander and T. J. Beach (Pergamon Press), but my favorite is an amusing and entertaining book, *The Collier Quick and Easy Guide to Chess*, by Richard Roberts (Collier Books). A small step up in complexity is *Logical Chess Move by Move* by Irving Chernev (Simon & Schuster). More advanced players are on their own.

There are two good elementary go books available in English, *Go for Beginners*, by K. Iwamoto (The Ishi Press), and *How to Play Go*, by S. Takagawa (The Japan Go Association). For intermediate players, a good choice is *Go Proverbs Illustrated*, by K. Segoe (The Japan Go Association).

The best backgammon book for total newcomers is *Backgammon*, by Prince Alexis Obolensky and Ted James (Macmillan). *The Backgammon Book*, by Oswald Jacoby and John R. Crawford (The Viking Press), can be used by beginners but is generally aimed at a more advanced audience. The last word on the subject, however, is now *Modern Backgammon Complete*, by Charles Goren (Doubleday & Co.).

For newcomers to other games, *Let's Play Checkers*, by Kenneth M. Grover and Tom Wiswell (Tartan Books/The David McKay Co.), *Let's Play Mah Jongg*, the handbook of the National Mah Jongg League, Inc., and *Dominoes*, by Dominic C. Armanino (Tartan Books/The David McKay Co.), are recommended for their respective subjects.

The standard beginning bridge books are Charles Goren's *Bridge for Beginners* and *Point Count Bidding* (both from Simon & Schuster). If for some reason these will not do, try Alfred Sheinwold's *First Book of Bridge* (Barnes & Noble).

For other card games, there are the various "Hoyles," *Scarne on Cards*, by John Scarne (Crown), and John R. Crawford's somewhat dated but interesting *How to Be a Consistent Winner in the Most Popular Card Games* (Dolphin Books/Doubleday).

For the inveterate gambler, there's *The Complete Guide to Winning Poker*, by Albert H. Morehead (Simon & Schuster), and *Poker, A Guaranteed Income for Life*, by Frank Wallace (I & O Publishing Co., P.O. Box 644, Wilmington, Delaware 19899). The most famous book on winning at blackjack is Edward O. Thorp's *Beat the Dealer*, now available in a second, revised edition from Random House. A more recent book along the same line is *Playing Blackjack as a Business*, by Lawrence Revere (Lyle Stuart).

For gamblers and card players, the reference book to end all reference books is *The Theory of Gambling and Statistical Logic*, by Richard A. Epstein (Academic Press), which, using very advanced math, goes into the problems of probability underlying all games of chance. On a far more understandable level, don't forget *The Compleat Strategyst*, discussed in the last chapter.

Most, though not all, of these books are in paperback.

Game Publishers and Their Addresses

American Publishing Corp., 144 Moody St., Waltham, Mass. 02154
Avalon Hill Company, 4517 Harford Rd., Baltimore, Md. 21214
Donald E. Benge, 1122 West Burbank Blvd., Burbank, Calif. 91506
Cadaco, 310 W. Polk St., Chicago, Ill. 60607
Dynamic Design, 1433 N. Central Park, Anaheim, Calif. 92802 (now a division of Reiss Associates)
Gameophiles Unlimited, Inc., P.O. Box 34, Berkeley Heights, N.J. 07922
Games Research, 48 Wareham St., Boston, Mass. 02118
Gamut of Games, 1133 Broadway, New York, N.Y. 10010 (now a division of Reiss Associates)
Golden's, Costa Mesa, Calif., 92627
Grid Games, Box 2263, Huntington Beach, Calif. 92647
Hexagonal Chess Publications, 39A Glasford St., London SW179HL, England
House of Games, Box 316, Don Mills, Ontario, Canada
Hypergames Co., P.O. Box 3026, Richmond, Va. 23235
Lakeside Industries, 4400 W. 78th St., Minneapolis, Minn. 55435
E. S. Lowe Co., 200 5th Ave., New York, N.Y. 10010
The Middle Earth Co., P.O. Box 294, Portage, Mich. 49081
Milton Bradley Co., Springfield, Mass. 01101
Parker Brothers, P.O. Box 900, Salem, Mass. 01970

Reiss Associates, 230 5th Ave., New York, N.Y. 10001
RGI/Athol, 200 5th Ave., New York, N.Y. 10010
Selchow & Righter, 2215 Union Blvd., Bay Shore, N.Y. 11706
Simulations Design Corporation, Box 19096, San Diego, Calif. 92119
Simulations Publications, Inc., 44 E. 23rd St., New York, N.Y. 10010
Skor-Mor Corp., 6390 Cindy Lane, Carpenteria, Calif. 93013
Spartan International, Box 1017, Bellflower, Calif. 90706
Sports Illustrated Games, Box 619, Radio City Station, New York, N.Y. 10020
Statis-Pro Games, Box 484, Waterloo, Iowa 50704
Strato-Various Products, P.O. Box 67, Utica, Mich. 48087
Third Millennia, Inc., 465-N Woodland Hills, Philadelphia, Miss. 39350
3M, 3M Center, St. Paul, Minn. 55101
Whitman Games, Western Publishing Co., Inc., Racine, Wisc. 53404
Lou Zocchi, 1513 Newton, Biloxi, Miss. 39530.

The first place to look is a good game store, but if you cannot locate the game you want, write directly to the publisher. Although changes of address, omissions, or slight inaccuracies are perhaps inevitable, they are unintentional, and the author wishes to apologize in advance to anyone who may be misled or inconvenienced thereby.

Index